UNEXPLAINED
MYSTERI
WORLD WAR II

A FIREFLY BOOK

Published by Firefly Books Ltd. 2014

First printing

Publisher Cataloging-in-Publication Data (U.S.)

A CIP record for this title is available from the Library of Congress

Library and Archives Canada Cataloguing in Publication

A CIP record for this title is available from Library and Archives Canada

Published in the United States by
Firefly Books (U.S.) Inc.
P.O. Box 1338, Ellicott Station
Buffalo, New York 14205

Published in Canada by
Firefly Books Ltd.
50 Staples Avenue, Unit 1
Richmond Hill, Ontario L4B 0A7

Printed in China by 1010 International Ltd

Conceived, designed, and produced by
Quantum Publishing Limited
6 Blundell Street, London , N7 9BH

Publisher Sarah Bloxham; **Quantum Editorial** Sam Kennedy and Hazel Eriksson; **Designer** Natalie Clay; **Production Manager** Rohana Yusof

UNEXPLAINED MYSTERIES OF WORLD WAR II

Discover the conspiracies, cover-ups and coincidences that won and lost the war

Jeremy Harwood

FIREFLY BOOKS

Contents

Introduction

Some mysteries are big, some small. Some affect the lives of millions, others only the people immediately involved with them. World War II is replete with mysteries of both kinds. Although the number diminished as time went by, there are enough that remain unexplained and unresolved to make investigating them interesting and well worthwhile.

An example or two of the bigger mysteries is sufficient to provide a taste of what follows in the main part of this book. One of the greatest riddles of the war's opening phase, for instance, is why, when Hitler launched his Blitzkrieg in the West in May 1940, the French armies facing the Wehrmacht collapsed so spectacularly, enabling the Germans to win a crushing victory and force the capitulation of France in record time?

INCOMPETENCE AT THE TOP

For years, the received wisdom was that the Wehrmacht's military superiority was such that its success in the West was inevitable. This, in fact, was not the case. On the ground — if not in the skies, where the Luftwaffe undoubtedly enjoyed aerial superiority — the balance of forces was roughly equal. Indeed, the Allies between them possessed more and, in some cases, better modern tanks than did Hitler's vaunted panzer divisions.

What the French generals disastrously lacked, as events immediately showed, was the ability to react quickly and decisively when the Wehrmacht finally struck. Field Marshal Gerd von Rundstedt, in command of Army Group A, which was charged with making the crucial breakthrough in the Ardennes, certainly lived in fear of a speedy, bold French reaction. According to General Gunther von Blumentritt, his Chief of Operations, he expected "a great, surprise counter-offensive by strong French forces from the Verdun and Chalons-sur-Marne area, northward toward Sedan and Mezieres."

No such attack ever materialized. Within 10 days of the start of the offensive, the Germans had advanced 150 miles (240 km) and reached the Channel coast. The Allied armies had been cut in two. On June 14, the same day that the Maginot Line was penetrated south of Saarbrucken, the Germans entered Paris. Three days later, Marshal Petain's new French government sued for peace.

Even Hitler was surprised by the speed and extent of the success, which may explain

why he ordered his panzers to halt rather than pursue the retreating British into Dunkirk. General Franz Halder, the Army Chief of Staff, noted in his diary: "Frightened by his own success, he is afraid to take any chances and so would rather pull the plug on us." Many still believe that this was the Führer's first and most significant military mistake. This is not the case. Hitler did not act unprompted. Despite what they said and wrote after the war, Rundstedt and other leading generals argued for the pause first. They then got Hitler to agree to it. By the time he rescinded the order, it was too late to stop the evacuation. More than 300,000 British and French troops got away to fight another day.

A "SPECIAL RELATIONSHIP"

Dunkirk certainly was not a victory. As Churchill, Britain's newly appointed successor to Neville Chamberlain as Prime Minister, told the House of Commons, "wars are not won by evacuations." In any event, Churchill's hold on power was shaky. Regarded as reckless, untrustworthy, and opportunistic by many of his fellow Conservatives, his opportunity had arisen as a result of the fiasco of the Norwegian campaign for which he, in fact, was chiefly responsible. When it became clear to even Chamberlain that he must go, George VI, most of the press, the Conservatives, big business, the top civil servants, and the Labour leaders initially would have preferred Lord Halifax, the Foreign Secretary, as Prime Minister.

Across the Atlantic in Washington, Churchill was also regarded as a suspect character. Harold Ickes, the Secretary of the Interior, recorded Roosevelt's verdict when he heard of the appointment, "I suppose he is the best man England has even if he is drunk half of his time." As well as suspecting him of being an unreliable alcoholic, the President also harbored a personal distaste for the man. He told Joseph Kennedy, the American Ambassador to Britain, "I have always disliked him since the time I went to Britain in 1918." Roosevelt was recalling his one and only face-to-face meeting with Churchill when, as Undersecretary for the Navy and before he was crippled, he had given a speech in London at Gray's Inn. Churchill had been in the audience. He behaved, Roosevelt later remarked, "like a stinker ... lording it over all of us."

Only one thing united the two men — their hatred of every aspect of Nazism. They both understood that Hitler epitomized a new and terrible force with which any sort of peaceful coexistence would prove impossible. Roosevelt, however, was a long way from actively resisting Hitler, as Churchill was soon to discover. When he told his son Randolph that his intention was to "drag the United States in," Roosevelt was equally determined to avoid such an entanglement.

Even when he finally agreed to a desperate British request to supply them with 50 old destroyers, the President went to great pains to assure Massachusetts Senator David I. Walsh, a leading Democratic isolationist, that he was "absolutely certain that this particular deal will not get us into war and, incidentally, that we are not going to war anyway unless Germany wishes to attack us."

What Churchill failed to understand was that nothing Roosevelt said necessarily could be taken at face value. He was an impossible man to pin down. Eleanor Roosevelt herself recognized this fact. Later, she would warn the premier: "When Franklin says 'yes, yes, yes,' it doesn't mean he's agreeing, it means that he's listening." Even when the Lend-Lease Bill was finally passed by the U.S. Senate by 60 votes to 31 on March 8, 1941, it did not mean that the British had been given the blank check they believed they had been granted. In Berlin, Joseph Goebbels noted: "Roosevelt wants to encourage England to a prolonged resistance, so that afterward it will be easier for him to inherit everything that's left. Now in London they'll once again forget all the defeats and setbacks and cheer on Washington. But how long will it last?"

THE ENIGMA OF STALIN

Churchill, Hitler, and Roosevelt were three of the warlords. Stalin was the fourth. In many ways, he was the most enigmatic of the four.

This book focuses on what is probably one of the greatest unexplained mysteries of the entire war — why, despite all the warnings he received, the Soviet dictator was taken totally unawares when Hitler struck at Russia in June 1941.

It was certainly not the case that Stalin blindly trusted Hitler to abide by the terms of the Nazi-Soviet Non-Aggression Pact, which, to the world's astonishment, the two dictators had hastily concluded in August 1939. A British Foreign Office spokesman summed up the revolutionary about-face in the pithy phrase "all the isms are wasms." By November 1940, however, it was clear to Stalin that the two sides were drifting apart. "Hitler is playing a double game," he pronounced to Vyacheslav Molotov, the Soviet Foreign Minister, after the latter's fruitless visit to the Führer.

Stalin, however, believed that time was on his side. In early December he told his generals: "We know that Hitler is intoxicated by his victories and believes that the Red Army will need at least four years to prepare for war. Obviously, four years would be more than enough for us. But we must be ready much earlier. We will try to delay the war for another two years."

For once, Stalin miscalculated. Hitler was busy planning with his generals for the attack. Reports started to flood into the Kremlin about the German buildup on the Soviet western frontier. Stalin refused to be alarmed. He told Marshal Zhukov, the Soviet Army's newly appointed Chief of Staff, to prepare to speed up Russian mobilization if and when it was authorized, but, at the same time, to avoid "wild unrealistic plans for which Russia lacked the means." As for the German troop concentrations in Poland, he assured his worried generals, the troops were there simply for training exercises.

The warnings mounted. Advised by his Bletchley Park cryptologists that the attack was imminent, Churchill wrote personally to Stalin to warn him of the impending assault. Stalin dismissed the warning as a "provocation." If the Soviets acted on it, he reasoned, "Hitler would have a direct and fair reason to launch a preventive crusade against the Soviet Union." On May 12 he similarly failed to react to Marshal Semyon Timoshenko's report of the increasing number of Luftwaffe reconnaissance flights over Russian territory. "I'm not sure Hitler knows about these flights," he replied. In Berlin, it was generally believed that the Soviet leader was determined to avoid war at all costs. Stalin "stares like a rabbit with a snake," Goebbels noted in his diary.

Stalin simply scoffed at all the predictions he was receiving that weren't from his own intelligence service as to what the date of the attack might be. On June 5, he told the Central Committee of the Communist Party:

"At first, our intelligence gave 14, 15, 20 May as possible dates of the attack. Now they claim it's going to be either 15 or 22 June. Apparently, these dates could also be wrong. Let's instead cherish the hope that 1941 will remain peaceful." On June 12, 10 days before Operation Barbarossa was finally launched, he assured his generals: "I am certain that Hitler will not risk creating a second front by attacking the Soviet Union. Hitler is not such an idiot."

We can only guess at what exactly Stalin felt when he received the news of the German attack. Certainly, as the tales of disaster poured in, we know that he fell into a deep depression. On July 10, by which time the Germans had penetrated more than 300 miles (480 km) into Russian territory, he stirred himself to issue a peremptory order to his commanders on the northwestern front. "Officers who do not carry out orders, abandoning their positions like traitors and leaving the defensive ridge without orders have not yet been punished," he declared. "It is time to put a stop to this shameful state of affairs."

Soon, several high-ranking Soviet commanders were standing in the dock before Vasiliy Ulrikh, the corpulent, vicious President of the Military Collegium of the Supreme Court of the USSR., accused of "betraying the interests of the Motherland, violating the oath of office, and damaging the combat power of the Red Army." They were Stalin's scapegoats. Among them was General Dimitry Korobkov, the luckless commander of the troops in the west whose forces had buckled at Minsk in the face of the Nazi onslaught. He, together with seven other senior army and air force generals, was shot.

GLOBAL WAR

Thousands of miles away, a new theater of war was about to open. Some months previously, the U.S. had imposed an embargo on exports of oil to Japan. The Japanese response was immediate. They began preparing for war.

Where the Japanese might strike was a mystery. Perhaps they might pull back from the brink at the last minute after all. Certainly, Roosevelt thought this was at least a possibility. "I wish I knew whether Japan was playing poker or not," he confided to Secretary of the Interior Harold Ickes. One thing seemed clear. The consensus was that the Japanese might attack the Philippines, or possibly British possessions in the Far East. No one dreamed that such an attack would be directed against the U.S. itself. After a cabinet meeting on November 25, Secretary of War Henry Stimson noted: "The question was how we should maneuver them (the Japanese) into the position of firing the first shot without allowing too much danger to ourselves."

Roosevelt left Washington for a short Thanksgiving break. On his return, he was handed four intercepts of decoded messages sent from Tokyo to the Japanese embassy in Berlin. One of them was from General Hideki Tojo, the Japanese Prime Minister, to the ambassador in person. "Say very secretly to them (the Germans)," Tojo instructed, "there is extreme danger that war may suddenly break out between the Anglo-Saxon nations and Japan through some clash of arms. This may come sooner than anyone dreams."

The President and Cordell Hull, the Secretary of State, conferred. "We both agreed," Hull later recollected, "that from all the indications a Japanese attack was in the imminent offing." Roosevelt decided to send a last-minute message personally to the Japanese Emperor. It was to be a plea to preserve peace.

Before the message could be sent, however, events intervened. On the evening of December 6, Roosevelt received another decrypt. This time, it was part of a long message sent by Tokyo to the Japanese Ambassador in Washington. Roosevelt read it and then handed it to Harry Hopkins, one of his closest associates. "This means war," the President told him. Hopkins replied that it was "too bad we could not strike the first blow." Roosevelt apparently nodded. "We can't do that," he said. "We are a democracy and a peaceful people."

The next day, at 10:00 a.m., Roosevelt received the last part of the decoded message. It read simply: "The earnest hope of the Japanese government to adjust Japanese-American relations and to preserve and promote the peace of the Pacific through cooperation with the American government has been lost." At 1:40 p.m., while he and Hopkins were eating lunch together, the telephone in the Oval Office rang. It was Secretary of the Navy Frank Knox. He reported that Pearl Harbor had signaled it was being bombed by the Japanese. In the words of the signal, "this is not a drill."

Why Pearl Harbor was not at least on alert to the possibility of such an attack has never been totally explained. The evening before, having read the first part of the Japanese message, Roosevelt had tried to contact Admiral Harold Stark, the head of the U.S. Navy, but was told he had gone to the theater and was unavailable. He got the same response when he called General George Marshall, the Chief of Staff, the next morning. Marshall had gone for his customary Sunday morning horseback ride.

Some attempt was made to warn Pearl Harbor directly. Radio communications, however, were apparently out of order. Instead, a Western Union telegram was despatched. It did not reach its destination until after the attack.

Not all of this book is concerned with great events, like the ones cited here. The events leading up to Pearl Harbor, indeed, are well documented; it is certainly incorrect to argue, as some have tried to do, that Roosevelt deliberately failed to put the naval base there on high alert and provoked the Japanese into launching their attack. What this book does show, however, is that there is much about World War II that still remains unexplained, and that various incidents that took place during it still demand historical probing. It is a certainty there are still secrets to be revealed.

Bomb in a Beer Cellar

On November 8, 1939, Adolf Hitler narrowly escaped death when a massive bomb planted in a Munich beer cellar exploded only minutes after the Führer had left the building. Who was ultimately responsible for the bombing remains a mystery. Was it the work of a lone conspirator? As the Gestapo steadfastly maintained, was the British Secret Service behind the plot? Or was it a put-up job, stage-managed by the Nazis themselves?

It was one of the few events Hitler never missed. Every year since his coming to power in 1933, the Führer had visited Munich on November 8, to mark the anniversary of the 1923 Beer Hall Putsch by delivering a rousing speech to a handpicked audience of Gauleiters and other Nazi veterans in the Buergerbraukeller, where the attempted Putsch had begun. This year, however, the arrangements differed slightly from normal.

Hitler usually began to speak around 8:30 p.m., finishing at precisely 10:00 p.m. This year, he started and ended slightly earlier at 8:10 p.m. and 9:07 p.m. respectively. Usually, too, it was his habit to spend half an hour or so chatting with the "Old Fighters" from the time of the "struggle for power" once he had finished speaking, but this time he left immediately after he had concluded. The reason for this departure from custom remains unclear. Some say that Hitler was anxious not to run the risk of being caught in a British air raid. Others argue that bad weather forced the change of plan. Hitler's initial intention had been to fly back to Berlin for an important meeting at the Reich Chancellery the next morning, but Munich's airport was fog-bound and his aircraft was grounded. He decided to take the train instead. This snap decision almost certainly saved his life.

Above: *Hitler greets Paul von Hindenburg, President of Germany until his death in 1934. The aged Field Marshal was the last barrier between the Führer and supreme power.*

Opposite: *Hitler is photographed with Brownshirts and Nazi supporters in the Munich beer cellar where he launched his failed putsch against the Bavarian government in 1923.*

THE BOMB EXPLODES

In the beer cellar the "Old Fighters" milled around, many disappointed that the Führer had left so abruptly. Most of them slowly started to drift away, leaving the hundred or so staff to clear up after them. At 9:20 p.m., less than half an hour after Hitler's departure, a massive explosion ripped through the hall. The gallery and roof fell in and the blast blew out the windows and doors. An eyewitness gave an account of what had happened in a radio broadcast two days later.

"About a hundred 'Old Fighters' were in the hall and I myself was about a yard from the door. Suddenly there was a flash overhead and a sudden pressure forced me out of the door. Almost immediately afterward came a thunderous sound and then everything was over before we could think what had happened. The air was full of dust, we could neither see nor breathe. We held our handkerchiefs over our mouths and got into fresh air. When the dust settled, we went back and found that the ceiling

Right: *Hitler captured in a characteristic pose, saluting his followers at a rally held shortly after his assumption of power in 1933.*

Below: *Troops and police comb the wreckage of the beer cellar for survivors after the deadly bomb blast. Had Hitler not left earlier than anticipated, he almost certainly would have perished in the explosion.*

had fallen in. There were about 50 'Old Fighters' in the hall uninjured and we set about rescue work. It was dangerous because at any minute more of the ceiling might have fallen in. We worked for some time getting out the injured and the dead."

In all, three of the bomb's victims were killed outright, five died of their injuries later and 62 more were wounded, some seriously. Among the latter was Fritz Braun, a 60-year-old schoolteacher who was the father of Eva Braun, Hitler's mistress. Many of the people who managed to struggle out of the wreckage — choking, coughing, bleeding and covered in dust — assumed that they had been the victims of a British air raid. Only gradually did they realize that the explosion had been caused by a bomb deliberately concealed in one of the beer cellar's central pillars.

Hitler got the news of the explosion when the Berlin express stopped briefly at Nuremberg. At first, he thought it must be a joke, but his entourage immediately disillusioned him. It swiftly became clear that the Führer had escaped death by a whisker, saved by providence, as he said to his companions, so that he could carry on with his divinely appointed mission.

From his viewpoint, Hitler told Heinrich Himmler, the Reichsführer SS who was traveling with him on the train, the immediate priority was not just to catch whoever had planted the bomb, but also to establish whether the bomber had been acting alone or was part of a deeper conspiracy. The Führer himself had no doubt that the latter was the case. He was sure that the British Secret Service had masterminded the assassination attempt. Himmler agreed with his master. He also told him that he would take immediate action to bring the likely culprits to account.

THE VENLO INCIDENT

For some months, Dr. Franz Fischer, a German spy posing as a political refugee in neutral Holland, had been in contact with Captain Sigismund Payne Best and Major Richard Stevens, two leading British intelligence agents there. Fischer purported to have links to a dissident group of high-ranking officers, who were plotting Hitler's overthrow. Walther Schellenberg, an ambitious young SS Sturmbannführer who was rising swiftly to the top in SS counterintelligence, had crossed the border himself to meet with Best and Stevens and convinced them of his bona fides as an army captain representing an influential German general who was leading the opposition within the Wehrmacht to the Nazi regime. In his memoirs, Schellenberg recorded how he was about to meet the British again — this time

complete with a fake "general" — when the assassination attempt forced a dramatic change of plan.

"I had taken a sleeping pill to ensure myself against another sleepless night and had sunk into a deep sleep when the insistent buzzing of the telephone awoke me," Schellenberg wrote. "It was the direct line to Berlin. Drugged with sleep, I groped for the receiver and reluctantly grunted 'Hello.' At the other end, I heard a deep, rather excited voice: 'What did you say?' 'Nothing so far,' I replied. 'Whom am I speaking to?' The reply came sharply, 'This is the Reichsführer SS Heinrich Himmler. Are you there at last?'"

"My consternation struggling with my sleepiness," Schellenberg recalled, "I replied with my habitual, 'Yes sir.' 'Listen carefully,' Himmler continued: 'Do you know what has happened?' 'No sir,' I said, 'I know nothing.' 'Well, this evening, just after the Führer's speech in the beer cellar, an attempt was made to assassinate him! A bomb went off. Luckily, he'd left the cellar a few minutes before. Several old Party comrades have been killed and the damage is pretty considerable. There's no doubt that the British Secret Service is behind it all. The Führer and I were already on his

train to Berlin when we got the news. He now says — and this is an order — when you meet the British agents for your conference tomorrow, you are to arrest them immediately and bring them to Germany. This may mean a violation of the Dutch frontier, but the Führer says that's of no consequence. The SS detachment that's been assigned to protect you … is to help you to carry out your mission. Do you understand everything?' 'Yes, Reichsführer, but … ' There's no "but," Himmler said sharply. 'There's only the Führer's order — which you will carry out. Do you now understand?' I could only reply, 'Yes, sir.' I realized it would be quite senseless to try to argue at this point."

KIDNAPPED AT GUNPOINT

Schellenberg obeyed. In a book published in 1950, Best described what happened as he and his companions waited for the Germans outside a cafe just across the frontier at Venlo.

"Somehow or other, it seemed to me that things looked different from what they had on the previous days," Payne Best wrote. "Then I noticed that the German barrier across the road which had always been closed was now lifted; there seemed to be nothing

LVCE

Above: *Hitler and Mussolini, the leader of Fascist Italy, review a Munich parade during the Duce's 1937 state visit to the Reich. The two dictators had met first three years earlier in Venice.*

between us and the enemy. My feeling of impending danger was very strong. Yet the scene was peaceful enough. No one was in sight except a German customs officer in uniform lounging along the road toward us and a little girl who was playing at ball with a big black dog in the middle of the road before the cafe."

"I must have rather checked my speed, for Klop (the Dutch General Staff officer accompanying the British agents) called out, 'Go ahead, everything is quite all right.' I felt rather a fool to be so nervous. I let the car drift slowly along to the front of the cafe on my left and then reversed into the car park on the side of the building farthest from the frontier. Schaemmel (Schellenberg's alias) was standing on the veranda at the corner and made a sign which I took to mean that our bird was inside. I stopped the engine and Stevens got out on the right. My car had left-hand drive."

"I had just wriggled clear of the wheel and was following him out when there was a sudden noise of shouting and shooting. I looked up, and through the windscreen saw a large open car drive up round the corner till our bumpers were touching. It seemed to be packed to overflowing with rough-looking men. Two were perched on top of the hood and were firing over our heads from sub-machine guns, others were standing up in the car and on the running boards; all shouting and waving pistols. Four men jumped off almost before their car had stopped and rushed toward us shouting: 'Hands up!'"

"I don't remember actually getting out of the car, but by the time the men reached us, I was certainly standing next to Stevens, on his left. I heard him say: 'Our number is up, Best.' The last words we were to exchange for over five years. Then we were seized. Two men pointed their guns at our heads, the other two quickly handcuffed us."

"I heard shots behind me on my right. I looked round and saw Klop. He must have crept out behind us under cover of the car door which had been left open. He was running diagonally away from us toward the road; running sideways in big bounds, firing at our captors as he ran. He looked graceful, with both arms outstretched — almost like a ballet dancer. I saw the windscreen of the German car splinter into a star, and then the four men standing in front of us started shooting and after a few

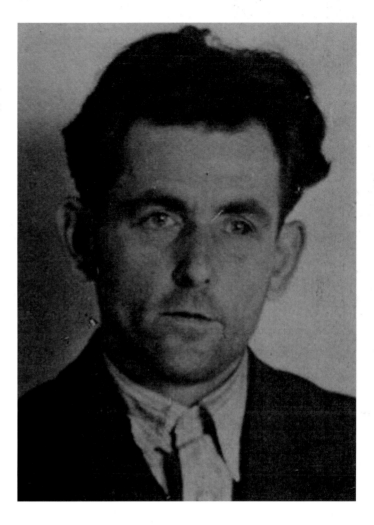

more steps Klop just seemed to crumple and collapse into a dark heap of clothes on the grass."

"'Now, march!' shouted our captors, and prodding us in the small of our backs with their guns, they hurried us, with cries of 'Hup! Hup! Hup!' along the road toward the frontier. As we passed the front of the cafe I saw my poor Jan held

Above: *Georg Elser, the carpenter behind the beer cellar bomb, photographed in Gestapo custody. Though he worked alone, Hitler and other Nazis claimed the British Secret Service was behind the plot.*

Opposite: *A packed audience in the beer cellar awaits the arrival of their Führer. Even at the height of the war, the meeting to commemorate the 1923 putsch was one of the few occasions Hitler always attended.*

by the arms by two men who were frog-marching him along. It seemed to me that his chin was reddened as from a blow. Then we were across the border. The black and white barrier closed behind us. We were in Nazi Germany."

CATCHING THE CULPRIT

Even before Himmler contacted Schellenberg, the actual perpetrator of the assassination attempt had been arrested. Georg Elser, a quietly spoken 36-year-old carpenter, was detained by a border patrol while attempting to cross the Swiss frontier illegally earlier that evening. In his knapsack, the police found a sketch of what looked like a bomb mechanism, bits of a fuse, a Communist Party membership card, and a picture postcard of the beer cellar itself. These would have been incriminating enough at the best of times; now, they were to prove fatal. While Elser was being questioned, an urgent message arrived. It warned all border posts to be on the lookout for the beer-cellar bomber.

Elser was handed over to the local Gestapo and then taken back to Munich, where he was interrogated by Heinrich Mueller, the head of the Gestapo, and then by Himmler himself. At first, none of Elser's interrogators believed

that he could have possibly acted on his own, even though he stubbornly insisted that he had acted entirely on his own initiative. He explained how, as a former member of the Communist Party's Red Front Fighter's League, he had come to loathe the Nazis and all that they stood for, and eventually decided to make his assassination attempt. He described in detail the months of patient work it had taken him to plan, build, and install the bomb. He even built another one in a workshop the Gestapo put at his disposal.

However, Mueller failed in his main aim, which was to force Elser to admit that he had been part of a wider conspiracy masterminded by Best and Stevens. "I haven't been able to get anything out of him on that point," the Gestapo chief told Schellenberg. "He either refuses to say anything or else tells stupid lies. In the end, he always goes back to his original story: he hates Hitler because one of his brothers who had been a Communist sympathizer was arrested and put into a concentration camp. He liked tinkering with the complicated mechanism of the bomb and he liked the thought of Hitler's body been torn to pieces. The explosives and the fuse were

given to him by an anonymous friend in a Munich café."

Himmler was equally unsuccessful. He admitted to Hitler that there was "no possibility of any connection between Elser and Best and Stevens. I don't deny that British Intelligence may be connected with Elser through other channels," the Reichsführer went on. "Elser admits he was connected with two unknown men, but whether he was in touch with any political group we just don't know ... They may have been Communists, agents of the British Secret Service, or members of the Black Front (a German dissident movement led by the refugee former Nazi Otto Strasser). There is only one other clue: our technical men are practically certain that the explosives and the fuses used in the bomb were made abroad."

The Führer was unconvinced. "I want you to use every possible means to induce this criminal to talk," he told Reinhardt Heydrich, the head of the Reich Main Security Office. "Use hypnosis, give him drugs — everything that modern science had developed in this direction. I've got to know who the instigators are, who stands behind this thing." Heydrich faithfully carried out his orders. Elser was injected with massive doses of

Pervitin, the latest truth drug, and hypnotized by four of the best hypnotists in Germany. He still stuck stubbornly to his original tale.

DEATH AT DACHAU

Eventually, even the Gestapo was forced to admit failure. Elser was despatched to Sachsenhausen concentration camp where he was held in solitary confinement until the last month of the war. He was then transferred to Dachau, where he was executed. Coincidentally, Best and Stevens were imprisoned in the same camp. They survived to be liberated by the Allies.

The identity of the two men who apparently aided Elser has never been discovered. After the war it was even alleged, by Georg Thomas, a former Wehrmacht general giving evidence at the Nuremberg War Crimes Trial, that the Nazis had stage-managed the bombing themselves to give the regime the excuse for a savage clamp-down on dissidents in high places who were opposed to the war. The truth, however, almost certainly will never be fully known.

Above: *U.S. troops on guard at the gates of Dachau concentration camp shortly after the German capitulation in 1945. It was here that Elser, after years of imprisonment in solitary confinement at Sachsenhausen, was finally executed in April 1945.*

The Phantom Spy of Scapa Flow

When Kapitan-Leutnant Gunther Prien, commander of the German submarine U-47, penetrated Scapa Flow, Britain's vast naval base in the Orkneys, on the night of October 14, 1939 and sank the battleship Royal Oak, *there was rejoicing in Berlin and consternation in the Admiralty. The sinking left the British with crucial questions to answer. How had a single U-boat managed to break through Scapa Flow's supposedly impregnable defenses? Was it down to British naval incompetence or had there been a spy at work?*

Above: *The remains of the Balfour battery, built at Hoxa Head during World War I, was one of 19 coastal batteries intended to cover the approaches to Scapa Flow and Kirkwall Bay, so protecting the fleet from surface attack. It never saw action.*

Left: *The* Royal Oak, *one of Britain's Resolution-class battleships, first saw action at the battle of Jutland in 1916. With a maximum speed of less than 20 knots, she was obsolete before the war broke out in 1939. When she was sunk by U-47 at anchor in Scapa Flow on October 14, 833 out of her 1,208-strong crew were killed or died of wounds.*

William Shirer, an American journalist based in Berlin, summed up the general feeling on both sides when the news of the sinking broke. "The place where the German U-boat sank the British battleship *Royal Oak* was none other than Scapa Flow, Britain's greatest naval base," he wrote in his diary. "It sounds incredible. A World War submarine commander told me last night that the Germans tried twice to get a U-boat into Scapa Flow during the last war, but both attempts failed and the submarines were lost."

Shirer went on to describe Prien's unexpected appearance at a hastily convened press conference. "Captain Prien, commander of the submarine, came tripping into our afternoon press conference at the Propaganda Ministry this afternoon, followed by his crew — boys of 18, 19 and 20," he recorded. "Prien is 30, clean-cut, cocky, a fanatical Nazi and obviously capable. Introduced by

Hitler's press chief, Dr. Dietrich, who kept cursing the English and calling Churchill a liar, Prien told us little of how he did it. He said he had no trouble getting past the boom protecting the bay. I got the impression, though he said nothing to justify it, that he must have followed a British craft, perhaps a minesweeper, into the base. British negligence," Shirer concluded, "must have been something terrific."

BRITISH BUNGLING

Shirer was closer to the truth than he knew at the time. Far from being impregnable, Scapa Flow's defenses were decrepit. The old steel underwater netting guarding its main points of entry had rotted, rusted, or broken up. Warned that these points were "not properly netted," Winston Churchill, who had returned to the Admiralty as First Lord on the outbreak of war, issued an urgent order authorizing new nets and booms to be installed and more blockships to be sunk. By the middle of October, however, nothing had been done. Work on the improved antisubmarine defenses Churchill had ordered to be constructed only began after the sinking of *Royal Oak* and then took two years to complete.

There was even more to it than this. In 1938, a maritime survey had revealed that Kirk Sound, part of Holm Sound and one of the key access points to the base, had a deep channel some 300 to 400 feet wide running clear through it. The following March, the Admiralty ordered an old merchant vessel to be sunk in it as a blockship. Just two months later, however, a further survey revealed that the channel was still navigable. Admiral Sir William French, commanding

Orkney and Shetland, confirmed this, warning that a submarine or destroyer could make it through the channel easily at slack water. At the time, the Admiralty dismissed his fears. Indeed, after the *Royal Oak* was sunk, it did its best to cover up the survey's findings and French's report.

DOENITZ PREPARES

What the Admiralty may have been counting on was German ignorance of the state of Scapa Flow's defenses and the fact that there was an open channel leading right into the heart of the base. Unfortunately for the British, the Germans were not. On October 1, Commodore Karl Doenitz, then the commander of Hitler's U-boat fleet, summoned Prien to see him on board a depot ship moored in Kiel harbor. Doenitz knew Prien as a skillful and daring submarine commander. He had decided to entrust him with the execution of Special Operation P, one of the most daring naval missions of the entire war.

Doenitz had been planning the venture for some time. He handed over all the documentation for Prien to study. Aerial reconnaissance photographs, taken by the Luftwaffe as early as September

Above: *Scapa Flow, seen from one of the Churchill Barriers, built to block the small channels to the east of the anchorage.*

Opposite: *The corvette* Camellia *was credited with the sinking of U-47 while on escort duty southeast of Iceland.*

6, showed the entire British Home Fleet at anchor with antisubmarine booms and blockships notionally blocking the bay's seven entrances. Or were they? In Kirk Sound, the three blockships the British had sunk there lay just far enough apart for a U-boat to zigzag through between them in the still water just after high tide. It would require skillful seamanship, though. A U-boat Doenitz had sent to scout the inlets had faced powerful 10-knot rip

tides. Even in daylight let alone at night, navigation would be tricky at best. Nevertheless, the Grand Admiral concluded that "a penetration at this point (Kirk Sound) on the surface at the turn of the tide would be possible without further ceremony."

Prien assessed the wealth of information Doenitz had provided at home that evening. "I worked through the whole thing like a mathematical problem," he later wrote. The next day, he reported to Doenitz again. The

Commodore was sitting at his desk. "He did not acknowledge my salute," Prien recalled. "It seemed he hadn't noticed it. He was looking at me fixedly and asked me 'Yes or no?'"

Prien answered simply "Yes, sir." Doenitz rose to shake his hand. "Very well," he said. "Get your boat ready." U-47 sailed from Kiel on October 8.

"TORPEDO LOS!"

Having successfully negotiated a northern course around the blockships that had been sunk in Kirk Sound to make the passage supposedly impassable, Prien slipped into Scapa Flow shortly after midnight on October 14. Still on the surface, he headed west across the flow toward the main fleet anchorage. Much to his surprise, he found this empty. He turned his U-boat about and made for the northeastern corner of the flow. Here, he struck lucky. He spotted two targets, one of which was *Royal Oak* lying peacefully at anchor. The other Prien thought looked like the battle cruiser *Repulse*; in fact it was a seaplane carrier.

Prien fired his first torpedo salvo at the silent battleship, scoring a single hit. His second salvo missed. He then maneuvered to fire a third. This was the fatal blow. All three torpedoes struck home. There was a tremendous explosion and the mortally wounded *Royal Oak* started to sink immediately. With the help of a Ministry of Propaganda ghost writer after the event, Prien vividly recalled what he himself saw. "A wall of fire shot up toward the sky. It was as if the sea suddenly stood up on end. Loud explosions came one after another like drumfire in a battle and coalesced into one mightily ear-splitting crash. Flames shot skyward, blue ... yellow ... red. Behind this hellish firework display, the sky disappeared entirely. Like huge birds, black shadows soared through the flames and fell hissing and splashing into the water. Fountains yards high sprang up where they had fallen, huge fragments of the mast and funnels. We must have hit the munition magazine and the deadly cargo had torn the body of its own ship apart. It was as if the gates of hell had suddenly been torn open and I was looking into the flaming furnace."

Prien decided to run for home. Back in Kirk Sound, he took the gap to the south of the blockships. With the tide now falling, U-47 had to battle against a fierce 10-knot current, but eventually she reached the comparative safety of the open sea. Prien and his crew reached Wilhelmshaven and safety on the morning of October 17. They were immediately flown to Kiel to be greeted by Doenitz, now promoted to the rank of Rear Admiral, and Grand Admiral Erich Raeder, the commander-in-chief of the Kriegsmarine. From Kiel, they were flown to Berlin to be decorated by the Führer himself.

SEARCH FOR SCAPEGOATS

No sooner had the news of the sinking been released by the Admiralty than the search for scapegoats began. Why, for instance, had the crew of *Royal Oak* apparently failed to realize that they were under enemy attack as soon as Prien's first torpedo hit their ship? It appeared that many of the crew were sure that the explosion had been an internal one — probably of inflammable materials in the paint store — and that the ship's fire crew could be trusted to deal with it. Many of the ship's portholes, which had been left open, were never closed, with the result that seawater was free to pour through them when *Royal*

Right: Karl Doenitz, head of the U-boat arm of the Kriegsmarine, personally planned the operation that led to the successful torpedoing of Royal Oak.

Oak began to list. No one ordered the watertight doors to be closed. Above all, no formal order was ever given to abandon ship. Out of *Royal Oak*'s 1,146-strong crew, 833 of them perished with her. One hundred and twenty were boy sailors aged between 14 and 18; all had been sent to the battleship as their first naval posting.

It was useless trying to blame Rear Admiral Henry Blagrove — he had gone down with his ship. Captain William Benn and the *Royal Oak*'s other officers were exonerated by a Board of Enquiry.

Benn went on to become a Rear Admiral himself. French was less fortunate. The Board of Enquiry blamed him for the poor state of Scapa Flow's defenses and, after the sinking, for the slowness to react to the presence of Prien's submarine. He was forcibly retired. MI5, the British counterintelligence service, was also blamed. The Admiralty was convinced that a German secret agent in the Orkneys must have provided the information that enabled Prien and his U-boat to reach their target. MI5 agents were rushed to

Above: *Churchill Barrier 1 was belatedly built to block Kirk Sound, which Kapitan-Leutnant Gunther Prien, commander of U-47, used to enter Scapa Flow and sail out of it to safety after torpedoing Royal Oak.*

Opposite: *Prien, like many of his fellow U-boat commanders, preferred to attack his targets on the surface, rather than submerged. Unlike this U-boat, seen here under air attack in the Atlantic, he managed to get in and out of Scapa Flow undetected.*

the islands to flush out the elusive Nazi spy. Their search failed. Major-General Vernon Kell, the head of MI5, paid the price for failure. The mysterious events surrounding the sinking of *Royal Oak* were seized upon as an excuse to get rid of him. He, too, was forced to resign.

THE SCAPA FLOW SPY

In the spring of 1942, the *Saturday Evening Post*, one of the most popular U.S. magazines of the day, published a sensational article, which supposedly shed new light on the entire Scapa Flow disaster. It claimed to have solved the hitherto unanswered question as to how Doenitz had obtained his knowledge of the state of Scapa Flow's defenses by identifying a Captain Alfred Wehring, a World War I officer in the Imperial German Navy where he had served under Admiral Wilhelm Canaris, subsequently head of the Abwehr (German Intelligence), as the Scapa Flow master-spy.

According to the *Post*, after World War I, Wehring had left the navy and settled in Switzerland, where, as instructed by German intelligence, he trained to become a jeweler and watchmaker. In 1927, armed with a Swiss passport, he moved to Britain using the name of Albert Oertel, and became a

naturalized British citizen four years later. Shortly after that, he opened a small jewelry store in Kirkwall in the Orkneys. His main business, of course, was to spy on British naval activity at nearby Scapa Flow.

It was in the late summer of 1939, said the *Post*, that Wehring brought off his greatest and most audacious coup yet. He signaled detailed information about the state of Scapa Flow's defenses to the Abwehr, including the invaluable news that its eastern approaches were not closed off by antisubmarine nets but only by hulks lying relatively far apart. It was this vital intelligence that prompted Doenitz to draw up the plans for Special Operation P and brief Prien to carry out the planned attack.

This was by no means all. Again according to the *Post* — and again as late as 1959 by *Coronet* magazine — Wehring actually boarded U-47 before she entered Scapa Flow and acted as Prien's pilot and right-hand man during the course of the actual attack. The story was repeated by Walter Schellenberg in the memoirs he dictated after the end of the war and shortly before his death. Wehring's achievement, Schellenberg said, amply demonstrated "how important intelligently planned long-range preparatory work can be — and how rewarding in the end." Schellenberg concluded: "The sinking of this battleship took less than 15 minutes, but

Above: *Gunther Prien, the commander of U-47, photographed after his triumphant return to Germany. His sinking of Royal Oak made him into a national hero.*

15 years of patient and arduous work by Alfred Wehring had been the necessary foundation for this supremely successful mission." After his enforced retirement in June 1940, Vernon Kell chimed in as well. "The Germans," he opined, "had been supplied with up-to-date information by a spy."

FACT OR FANTASY

It was an impressive tale. Unfortunately, it was almost certainly fiction. The writer of the original article, Curt Reiss, a refugee newspaperman who wrote the original *Saturday Evening Post* article, never revealed his sources. Prien perished in March 1941 when his U-boat was sunk by a British destroyer. Wilhelm Canaris, implicated in the July 1944 bomb plot against Hitler, was executed in Flossenburg concentration camp on April 9, 1945. Schellenberg's memoirs were published posthumously. Karl Doenitz rose to the rank of Grand Admiral, succeeded Raeder as commander-in-chief of the Kriegsmarine and, after Hitler's suicide, took over from him as Führer. Sentenced to 10 years' imprisonment for war crimes, Doenitz was released in 1956 and lived in retirement until his death in 1980. He made no mention

of the Scapa Flow spy in his autobiography.

Even more to the point, journalists investigating in the Orkneys after the war failed to find anyone who had even known of, much less seen, Wehring during the entire 12 years he was supposed to have lived there. One leading Kirkwall tradesmen testified: "I certify with the utmost assurance that never at any period has there been a watchmaker in Kirkwall known as Albert Oertel, or any person connected with the trade who could possibly be identified with the mystical 'Watchmaker Spy of Kirkwall.' I am convinced beyond possibility of doubt that such a person has never existed and is only a journalist's fabrication." Checks of the archives of the Imperial German Navy, the Kriegsmarine, and the Abwehr found no mention of a Captain Alfred Wehring — or, indeed, of an Albert Oertel — either.

If there was no spy living on Orkney, what was the source of the information on the basis of which Doenitz decided on the attack? The answer is that there was a real-life spy involved — a secret agent working for Commander Hermann Menzel, head of the Abwehr's naval

intelligence division. In August 1939, Menzel arranged a trip to the Orkneys for one of his most astute operatives. He was Captain Horst Kahle, the skipper of the freighter *Theseus* who doubled up as an Abwehr operative. Kahle returned with a detailed account of the state of Scapa Flow's defenses, which he had obtained through his own observations or from what he had heard being talked about in Kirkwall itself.

Added to this was the information brought back by Kapitan-Leutnant Horst Wellner, commander of U-14, who had been despatched to scout the approaches of Scapa Flow almost immediately after the outbreak of war. Wellner discovered that, though the British had blocked Hoxa and Switha Sounds effectively, Kirk Sound was comparatively clear. It was via Kirk Sound that Prien cautiously made his way into Scapa Flow to launch his deadly attack.

If It Hadn't Been Churchill

For Britain, May 8, 1940 was one of the decisive days of World War II. At the end of a two-day debate on the conduct of the war, the government majority in the House of Commons fell from 213 to 81; 33 Conservatives voted with the Opposition and 60 abstained. It was clear that Neville Chamberlain could no longer carry on as Prime Minister. The question was, who could, or should, succeed him?

When it came, Chamberlain's downfall was swift. It was also unexpected. In April 1940, he had confidently told a Conservative Party meeting: "After seven months of war, I feel 10 times more confident of victory than I did at the start." Having explained to his enthusiastic audience just why he was so sure that the Allies would defeat the Nazis, he concluded: "One thing is certain. Hitler has missed the bus."

These injudicious words were to come back to haunt the premier. Unknown to him, Hitler's Wehrmacht was poised to invade Denmark and Norway. What U.S. Senator William Borah had christened "the phony war"

Above: *Troops from the British Expeditionary Force march through Paris in September 1939.*

Left: *Neville Chamberlain, Prime Minister at the outbreak of war, was forced out of office in May 1940.*

was about to end. Chamberlain's premiership ended with it. On May 7, with the evacuation of Allied forces from Norway in full swing after a short-lived and disastrous campaign, he faced the House of Commons to debate the government's conduct of the war.

"IN THE NAME OF GOD, GO!"

The House of Commons was packed. Harold Nicolson, an ex-diplomat and now a prominent writer, broadcaster, and National Labour MP, described the scene. "The House is crowded and when Chamberlain comes in, he is greeted with shouts of 'Missed the bus!' He makes a very feeble speech and is only applauded by the yes-men. He makes some reference to the complacency of the country, at which the whole

House cheers vociferously and ironically, inducing him to make a little, rather feminine gesture of irritation."

Nicolson went on to give his view of the rest of the day's debate. "Attlee (Clement Attlee, the Leader of the Opposition) makes a feeble speech and Archie Sinclair (Sir Archibald Sinclair, leader of the Liberals) a good one. When Archie sits down, many people stand up and the Speaker calls on Page Croft. There is a loud moan from the Labour Party at this and they practically all rise in a body and leave the House. He is followed by Wedgewood, who makes a speech which contains everything he ought not to have said. He gives the impression of being a little off his head. At one moment he suggests the British Navy has gone to Alexandria since they are frightened of being bombed."

Wedgewood's speech provoked the first dramatic intervention of the two-day debate. "When Wedgewood sits down," Nicolson chronicled, "Keyes (Admiral Sir Roger Keyes) gets up and begins his speech by referring to Wedgewood's remark and calling it a 'damned insult.' The Speaker does not call him to order for his unparliamentary language and the whole House roars with laughter, especially Lloyd George who racks backward and forward in boyish delight with his mouth wide open. Keyes then returns to his manuscript and makes an absolutely devastating attack upon the naval conduct of the Narvik episode and the Naval General Staff ... It was by far the most dramatic speech I have ever heard and when Keyes sits down there is thunderous applause."

Leo Amery's speech later in the evening was even more powerful.

A former cabinet minister and now one of the most prominent Conservative backbenchers, he attacked not only the mishandling of the Norwegian campaign, but also the government's complacency as a whole. "We cannot go on as we are," he said grimly, "there must be a change." He finished as dramatically as he had begun. "This is what Cromwell said to the Long Parliament when he thought it was no longer fit to conduct the affairs of the nation," he concluded. "You have sat here too long, for any good you have been doing. Depart, I say, and let us have done with you. In the name of God, go!"

THE FATEFUL DIVISION

The battle had been joined. It was to be fought to a bitter conclusion when the debate continued the following day. Herbert Morrison, the deputy leader of the Labour opposition, began by announcing that his party would demand a vote on the motion of adjourn the House. This was tantamount to a vote of censure and Morrison's closing remarks made it clear this was exactly what he had in mind. "If these men remain in office," he asserted, "we run grave risk of losing this war."

No sooner had Morrison sat down than Chamberlain sprang to his feet to answer him. The Prime Minister was visibly incensed. "I do not seek to evade criticism," he exclaimed, "but I say this to my friends in the House — and I have friends in the House. No government can prosecute a war effectively unless it has public and parliamentary support. I accept the challenge. I welcome it indeed. At least we shall see who is with us and who is against us and I call upon my friends to support us in the lobby tonight."

The appeal backfired. Many MPs felt that the issue was one upon which the outcome of the war might depend and that it was no time for a personal appeal to friendship. Alfred Duff Cooper, who had resigned from Chamberlain's Cabinet as First Lord of the Admiralty in protest against the Munich Agreement, said as much when he spoke. He told the premier that he, for one, would be voting against the government. David Lloyd George, the veteran Liberal politician who had led Britain to victory in World War I, was even more vitriolic. He and Chamberlain had disliked each other for years and it was now Lloyd George's chance to take his revenge on the beleaguered premier.

Chamberlain, Lloyd George said, had "met this formidable foe of ours in peace and in war. He has always been worsted. He is not in a position to appeal on the grounds of friendship, he has appealed for sacrifice. The nation is prepared for every sacrifice so long as it has leadership, so long as the government show clearly what they are aiming at and so long as the nation is confident that those who are leading it are doing their best. I say solemnly that the Prime Minister should give an example of sacrifice, because there is nothing which can contribute more to victory in this war than that he should sacrifice the seals of office."

The vote, when it came, was as dramatic as anything that had gone before it. When the division was called, MPs filed out of the chamber and into the respective lobbies. Chamberlain's supporters catcalled "Quislings" and "Rats" at the Conservative rebels as they made for the "noes" lobby. The latter replied with the taunt of "yes-men." Some were highly emotional. Duff Cooper saw "a young officer in uniform, who had been for long a fervent admirer of Chamberlain,

walking through the Opposition lobby with the tears streaming down his face." He and Amery were joined by two other former ministers — Lord Winterton and Leslie Hoare-Belisha — in voting against the government.

"RULE BRITANNIA!"

Shortly after 11:00 p.m., the tellers returned to the chamber to give the Speaker the result of the vote. Captain David Margesson, the Conservative Chief Whip, stood to the right, indicating that the

government had won. The crucial question was the size of the majority. First Margesson and then the Speaker slowly read out the result: "Ayes to the right 281, noes to the left 200."

There was an audible gasp, then pandemonium broke out. The government's normal majority of well over 200 had been slashed to just 81. The Opposition chorused "Resign" while the loyal government supporters sat shocked and silent as if in a trance on their benches. Forty-

Left: *Winston Churchill, newly appointed as premier by George VI after Neville Chamberlain's fall from power in May 1940, salutes a Downing Street crowd with his celebrated "V for Victory" sign.*

one Conservative MPs had voted against their leader and another 88 had either deliberately abstained or failed to vote for some reason or another. It was clear that a fifth of the government's backbenchers were in revolt. Nicolson noted: "The figures are greeted with a terrific demonstration during which Joss Wedgewood starts singing 'Rule Britannia' (joined in uneasy chorus by Harold Macmillan from the Conservative benches), which is drowned in shouts of 'Go, go, go, go!'" Henry "Chips" Channon, a loyal Chamberlain supporter who had spent the debate sitting behind his leader, hoping to "surround him with an aura of affection," noted in his diary that the Prime Minister "appeared bowled over by the ominous figures." A sympathetic parliamentary correspondent wrote "he (Chamberlain) left the chamber with the pathetic look of a surprised and sorely stricken man."

SEARCH FOR A SUCCESSOR

Shortly after the result of the vote was announced, Margesson and his fellow Whips conferred in anxious conclave. Was it the end of the road for the Prime Minister? How solid was the backbench opposition to him continuing in office? The Whips tried to buy off some of the leading rebels, assuring them that Chamberlain would agree to sacrifice Sir Samuel Hoare and Sir John Simon, his two most unpopular ministers. Others were also plotting and scheming to try to ensure Chamberlain's survival. Prominent among them were Channon, Lord Dunglass, the Prime Minister's Parliamentary Private Secretary, and R.A. Butler, universally known as Rab, who was Undersecretary of State at the Foreign Office. Chamberlain's position was ambivalent. At first, it looked as if he was going to resign. Then on May 10, when Hitler's armies struck in the West, it seemed as though he had changed his mind. Everyone from King George VI downward waited to see what the Prime Minister would decide to do.

There were two possible successors waiting in the wings — Lord Halifax, the Foreign Secretary, and Winston Churchill, whom Chamberlain had called back from years in the political wilderness to be First Lord of the Admiralty at the beginning of the war. Halifax started off as the clear favorite. He had the backing of the king, much of his party, most of the press and Chamberlain himself. The premier summoned both men to see him. When he asked Churchill if he knew any reason why a peer should not be Prime Minister, the First Lord looked out of the window and did not reply. The ensuing silence was broken by Halifax. He said that, as a member of the House of Lords, he would be "more or less honorary Prime Minister, living in a kind of twilight just outside the things that really mattered." Churchill, Halifax went on, had "qualities preferable to his own at this particular juncture." For this reason, he would not accept the premiership.

It was decided to wait until the Labour leaders, who were consulting their party at its conference in Bournemouth, made up their minds as to whether they would serve in a new government. Late on the afternoon of May 10, Clement Attlee telephoned through their decision. He confirmed that his party was prepared to enter a coalition — but only under another Prime Minister. Within an hour, Chamberlain had resigned. On the outgoing premier's recommendation, the king sent for Churchill.

Left: *Lord Halifax, Chamberlain's Foreign Secretary, was the establishment's preferred choice to succeed him. He turned down the opportunity, saying that a member of the House of Lords would find it impossible to be Prime Minister.*

Right: *British troops prepare to embark for France. After months of phony war, the might of the Nazi Blitzkrieg soon drove them out of Belgium and back to Dunkirk.*

FROM SUFFERANCE TO ACCEPTANCE

In his postwar recollections, Churchill wrote vividly of his personal reaction to being appointed premier. He went to bed at nearly 3 a.m. the next morning, he recorded, "conscious of a profound sense of relief" he had at last the "authority to give directions over the whole scene." He continued: "I felt as if I were walking with destiny, and that all my past life had been but a preparation for this hour and for this trial."

In fact, Churchill became Prime Minister by default. He had reached the top of the greasy pole only because Halifax had declined the office. Many Conservative MPs distrusted him and resented his appointment. Even while he was still at Buckingham Palace kissing hands with the king, Channon, Dunglass, Butler, and Jock Colville, Chamberlain's junior Civil Service secretary, gathered at the Foreign Office to open a bottle of champagne and drink the health of the "King over the Water." Channon recorded in his diary how, on "perhaps the darkest day in English history ... we were all sad and angry and felt cheated and outwitted." Butler

was particularly vehement. "He believed," Channon wrote, "this sudden coup of Winston and his rabble was a serious disaster and an unnecessary one: the 'pass had been sold' by Mr. C., Lord Halifax, and Oliver Stanley (the Secretary of State for War). They had weakly surrendered to a half-breed American whose main support was that of inefficient but talkative people of a similar type."

Such feelings were by no means unique. When Churchill entered the House of Commons to speak as Prime Minister for the first time on May 13, his reception from the Conservative backbenches was no more than tepid. On the other hand, Chamberlain received a standing ovation. According to Sir Alexander Erskine-Hill, the chairman of the powerful 1922 Committee, three-quarters of Conservative MPs would have welcomed the former premier back as Prime Minister.

Churchill recognized his weakness. As soon as he returned from Buckingham Palace, he wrote to Chamberlain telling him "how grateful I am to you for promising to stand by me and to aid the country at this extremely grievous and formidable moment." He asked him to become Lord President of the Council with a seat in the War Cabinet. It was there the new premier faced his first open challenge. As the military situation in France went from bad to disastrous, Halifax — still Foreign Secretary — argued for making concessions to Mussolini to try to stop Italy from entering the war.

The unspoken thought was that, if this move was successful, it would be worth finding out via the Duce if Hitler would offer acceptable peace terms. Halifax told Churchill that, if "reasonable terms could be obtained," he "would think it right to accept an offer which would save the country from avoidable disaster." Churchill, who was determined to fight on at all costs, opposed the notion. He appealed to the ministers outside the War Cabinet for backing. They gave him their unquestioning support. So, too, did Chamberlain.

The premier, however, faced continuing difficulties in the House of Commons, The turning point came on July 4, when he told Parliament why and how, following France's surrender, he had ordered the navy to bombard the French fleet at Oran. According to an observer in the gallery, "the Chief Whip, Margesson, rose to his feet. Turning toward the Tory backbenchers, he waved his Order Papers in a gesture clearly conveying that they too should rise. At his signal, all the

Conservatives ... rose to a man and burst into enthusiastic cheering at the tops of their voices."

Churchill appeared taken aback. It was the first unanimous display of support he had received from the parliamentary Conservative party. He slumped in his seat with tears pouring down his cheeks. At last, the Conservatives were mirroring popular sentiment. By August, a Gallup poll showed that the premier's personal approval rating had reached an unprecedented 88 percent. Churchill was finally secure.

Opposite: *George VI inspects a Royal Air Force (RAF) base "somewhere in France." The Allied air forces were completely outclassed by the Luftwaffe, which quickly won total air superiority over the battlefield.*

Above: *Winston Churchill, as portrayed by Ambrose McEvoy early on in his career. After years in the political wilderness, his appointment to the War Cabinet in 1939 was unexpected.*

The "Miracle" of Dunkirk

After the surprise German breakthrough at Sedan in May 1940, the British Expeditionary Force (BEF) soon found itself fighting for its life as the French and Belgian armies collapsed around it. Its evacuation back across the English Channel from the port of Dunkirk has passed into British historical folklore as a "miracle." Was this really the case, or was the evacuation the inevitable outcome of a military catastrophe that could well have been prevented?

The news that the great German offensive in the West had finally begun was greeted by the Allied High Command with near complacency. Having issued his orders for the cream of his armies to advance into Belgium to meet the advancing German thrust head-on, General Maurice Gamelin, the Allied generalissimo, was seen by a staff captain "pacing up and down the corridor of the barracks, humming audibly with a martial air." The Secretary-General of the French War Ministry remarked: "If you had seen, as I have done this morning, the broad smile of General Gamelin when he told me the direction of the enemy attack, you would feel no uneasiness. The Germans have presented him with just the opportunity which he was awaiting."

In London, General Sir Edmund Ironside, the Chief of the Imperial General Staff, was almost as sanguine. "On the whole, the advantage is with us," he confided to his diary. *The Times* was even more confident: "This time at least there has been no strategic surprise," it declared. "It may be taken as certain that every detail has been prepared for an instant strategic reply. The Grand Alliance of our time for the destruction of the forces of treachery and oppression is being steadily marshaled."

THE TRAP IS SPRUNG

Gamelin's orders were followed to the letter, despite the misgivings of General Georges, the overall commander of the crucial northeastern section of the Allied front. The BEF, commanded by General Lord Gort, together with the French 1st and 7th armies, set off across the Franco-Belgian border. Units of the BEF and the 1st Army headed for the River Dyle, the 7th Army made for Breda, where the plan was for it to link up with the Dutch, whom Hitler had also attacked.

Left: *Admiral Sir Bertram Ramsey was reponsible for organizing and overseeing the evacuation from Dunkirk.*

Right: *Exhausted but heartened troops jammed into vessels for the voyage back across the English Channel to safety.*

The British were welcomed enthusiastically. Captain R. J. Hastings, second-in-command of D Company, the Royal Norfolk Regiment, recorded how he and his men were greeted by the Belgian civilians as they advanced. "In towns and villages, they lined our route," he wrote, "and little children ran along with the trucks, throwing flowers to the troops ... people in motor cars drove up and down the convoy, distributing cigarettes and chocolate, and whenever we stopped the women came out of houses with hot coffee ... No expressions of a nation's goodwill could have been more complete."

The whole thing went smoothly — too smoothly, according to some observers. The Luftwaffe was noticeably absent from the Belgian skies. "We all expected to be bombed on the way," Hastings noted. "Actually we saw no enemy aircraft all day." Kim Philby, working for *The Times* as a war correspondent, was apprehensive. "It went too damn well," he remarked to an American fellow-correspondent. "With all that air power, why didn't he bother us? What is he up to?"

The Allies were soon to find out. The move into Belgium could not have suited Hitler better than

Top: *An RAF signals unit heads for Dunkirk. British and French troops both bitterly complained of lack of air cover. The common cry was "Why don't our planes protect us?"*

Above: *A stray dog, picked up wandering on the Dunkirk beaches, was an unlikely evacuee. He, too, reached safety in Britain, where he was promptly popped into quarantine against rabies.*

Above: *British tanks hastily being loaded onto railway flat cars on May 25, 1940. They arrived on the battlefield too late to make a difference.*

Above: *General Maxime Weygand was hastily recalled from Syria to succeed the disgraced Gamelin as Allied generalissimo. He, too, failed to halt the German advance.*

Opposite: *Trucks form an improvised jetty into the sea at Dunkirk. When the evacuation started, many believed that only a relatively few men would be lifted from the beaches.*

The German plan worked to perfection. As they had intended, the Allies were mesmerized by the thrust in the north. Meanwhile, Army Group A — 45 divisions strong, headed by seven out of the 10 panzer divisions Hitler had available — was boring its weight unnoticed through the Ardennes. The aim was to cross the River Meuse between Dinant and Sedan. In a two-day battle, starting on May 12, the panzers forced the crossing of the river and drove relentlessly forward to open up an 50 mile (80 km) gap in the Allied line. With the Luftwaffe's dive bombers acting as their flying artillery, the panzers powered through the gap as French resistance started to collapse.

"OU EST LA MASSE DE MANOEUVRE?"

It would have taken inspired leadership to take the necessary steps to halt the Germans as they thrust forward. Neither Gamelin nor any of his subordinate generals seemed capable of getting a grip on the situation and providing it. Indeed, it was not until the evening of May 15 that the Allied generalissimo was forced to admit the extent of the crisis. He had spent the afternoon reassuring the French War Cabinet that he had

if he had dictated the orders for it himself. Far from staging a rerun of the Schlieffen Plan, with which the Germans had gone to war in 1914, what they were intending was a kind of Schlieffen-in-reverse. Just enough of the Wehrmacht had been concentrated to ensure a quick breakthrough into Belgium and Holland — a matador's red cape acting to attract the Allied

bull. The *Schwerpunkt* (main thrust) of the attack was to be farther south through the hilly and heavily forested Ardennes. Gamelin and the rest of the French high command considered the region impassable for tanks. Nevertheless, this was where the bulk of Hitler's panzer divisions, backed by the cream of the Luftwaffe's dive bombers, were concentrated.

the situation well in hand. Later, however, he telephoned Edouard Daladier, the Minister of National Defence, with very different news.

William Bullitt, the U.S. Ambassador to France, was closeted with the minister when the call came through. According to Bullitt, Daladier exclaimed as Gamelin revealed the extent of the catastrophe: "No, what you tell me is not possible! You are mistaken; it's not possible." Daladier then shouted down the phone: "We must attack soon." Gamelin replied: "Attack! With what? I have no

more reserves." He gave much the same answer to Churchill, when, in response to a desperate telephone call from the French premier Paul Reynaud, the new British Prime Minister flew to Paris the following day. After listening to Gamelin outline the military situation, Churchill immediately "asked: 'Where is the strategic reserve?' and, breaking into French, which I used indifferently in every sense, 'Ou est la masse de manoeuvre?' General Gamelin turned to me and, with a shake of his head, said; 'Aucune (there are no longer any).'"

Churchill was dumbfounded. Daladier interjected: "The mistake, the unpardonable mistake, was to send so many men into Belgium." Churchill seized on the point. Why, he asked, were the Allied armies falling back in northern Belgium, abandoning Brussels and Louvain to the enemy? Surely they should be counterattacking the northern flank of the sinister and ever-growing bulge the Germans had driven into the Allied line? Turning to Gamelin, Churchill demanded point-blank: "When and where are you going to counterattack the flanks of the bulge? From the north or from the south?" Gamelin's reply confirmed the bankruptcy of his military thinking. All he could mutter was: "Inferiority of numbers, inferiority of equipment, inferiority of method." He shrugged his shoulders hopelessly. It was the last time Churchill was to meet him. On May 19, Gamelin was sacked. General Maxime Weygand, who had been called back hastily from Syria, replaced him.

THE BEF FALLS BACK

It was true that the BEF was falling back together with its French and Belgian allies. Starved of information from the French high command, its generals, from Gort downward, failed to appreciate the true nature of the French predicament. They also complained from the highest level downward about the absence of any clear instructions from London.

Lieutenant-General Henry Pownall, Gort's Chief of Staff, wrote bitterly: "Nobody minds going down fighting, but the long and many days of indigence and recently the entire lack of higher direction ... have been terribly wearing on the nerves of all of us." When orders did arrive from Churchill for a counterattack southeastward by the whole of the BEF, Pownall was even more indignant: "Can nobody prevent him from trying to conduct operations himself as a super commander-in-chief? How does he think we are to collect eight divisions and attack as he suggests? Have we no front to hold? He can have no conception of our situation and condition ... The man's mad."

Churchill was determined that the BEF should carry out the attack. Ironside himself was despatched to Gort's headquarters to order him to "force his way through all opposition in order to join up with the French in the south." Gort received the order with obvious consternation. He and his staff had already started on working out a contingency plan for a retreat to the Channel coast and, after some thought, said he could not agree to the attack. He told Ironside that everything he had seen of the French forces and their leaders in recent days increasingly led him to doubt whether they could stage "an organized counteroffensive on a large scale." What he would agree to was to launch a limited attack southward from Arras.

Armed with Gort's reluctant agreement, Ironside set off to tackle Generals Billotte and Blanchard, commanders of the French First Army Group and the 1st Army respectively. Both seemed totally demoralized. Though Ironside finally bullied them into agreeing to strike northward, Gort, on his return, told him he was certain that "they would never attack." His foreboding was correct. The British attacked at Arras, but the French did nothing.

Weygand, in the meantime, had been planning a pincer movement of his own to sever the corridor the Germans were carving through France as the panzers headed for the Channel. Gort, however, was convinced by this time that the only hope of saving anything of the BEF was to fall back on Dunkirk. He ordered his troops to withdraw from Arras and start moving westwards back toward the port. Weygand abandoned his plan.

THE PANZERS HALT

As Gort's troops retired, Operation Dynamo, the code name for the intended evacuation, was hastily set in motion. The first troops were evacuated on May 26. "And so here we are back on the shores of France on which we landed with such high hearts over eight

months ago," Pownall lamented. "I think we were a gallant band who little deserves this ignominious end to our efforts." Ironside had already penned his own comment. "God help the BEF," he wrote in his diary. "Brought to this state by the incompetence of the French Command." In private, he reckoned that the British would be lucky to evacuate 30,000 men. Gort was as pessimistic. "I must not conceal from you," he signaled the War Office, "that a great part of the BEF and its equipment will inevitably be lost even in best circumstance." Churchill, too, prepared for the worst. On May 28, he warned the House of Commons to "prepare itself for hard and heavy tidings."

Two days later, Pownall arrived in London to brief the Cabinet's Defence Committee on Gort's plans for holding the Dunkirk

Above: *Though hundreds of small civilian crafts — the famous "little ships" — sailed for Dunkirk to rescue the BEF, the navy had the dominant role. Here, the river gunboat* Locust *is pictured sailing for the port.*

Above: *By no means did all the "little ships" make it back across the Channel safely. Here the Isle of Man ferry* Mona's Queen *is sinking off Dunkirk having been hit by a German bomb.*

perimeter. "No one in the room," wrote Ian Jacob, a member of the War Cabinet secretariat, "imagined that they could be successful if the German armored divisions, supported by the Luftwaffe, pressed their attack." Had the panzers pressed home their advantage, Dunkirk undoubtedly would have fallen and the evacuation would have been stifled at birth. They did not. It was one of the most controversial decisions the German high command made during the entire war.

After the war, the German generals roundly blamed Hitler for single-handedly insisting on halting the panzers in their tracks. In fact, it was Field Marshal Gerd von Rundstedt, commander of Army Group B, who ordered them not to cross the Aa Canal and press home their advantage. He was concerned that 50 percent of the panzers were temporarily out of action and that he needed to conserve those which were operational for the next phase of the battle against the French south of the River Somme. In addition, he considered the muddy Flanders terrain ill-suited to tank warfare. Hitler concurred with the decision. Rounding up the "remnants" of the BEF would wait. Dunkirk was to be "left to the Luftwaffe" to subdue.

This was the true "miracle" of Dunkirk. Gort gained three invaluable days to set the port's defenses in order before Hitler was persuaded to rescind his orders and allow the panzers to resume their attack. In his postwar memoirs, General Heinz Guderian, Hitler's most successful panzer commander who had led the drive from Sedan to the Channel, commented: "What the future course of the war would have been if we had succeeded at the time in taking the British Expeditionary Force prisoner at Dunkirk, it is now impossible to guess." He was being diplomatic. Had the BEF been compelled to surrender, there is little doubt that Britain would have found it militarily impossible to carry on with the war.

THE EVACUATION

Slowly but surely the evacuation got underway. The Luftwaffe did its best to put a stop to it, but its attempts were hampered by fog and poor visibility, while Fighter Command threw in every single plane it could muster to protect the bridgehead. Over the course of the action, its pilots flew a total of 2,739 sorties, sometimes flying as many as four a day. Although by the evening of May 27, only 7,669 men had been evacuated successfully, the next day's figure shot up to 17,804, and the day after that to 47,310. A peak of 68,014 was reached on May 31, the day a reluctant Gort himself sailed for home, leaving General Sir Harold Alexander in command. By the time the last ship left the port at dawn on June 4, 337,000 men, of whom 110,000 were French, had been snatched to safety.

Not everything went smoothly. Though the Royal Navy did the lion's share of the work, its task would have been impossible without the assistance of a plethora of small boats despatched across the Channel with their volunteer civilian crews to help to rescue the BEF from the beaches. Some were not impressed by the apparent chaos they found. "It seems to me incredible that the organization of the beach work should have been so bad," wrote Lieutenant Robert Hitchens of the minesweeper *Niger*. "We were told that there would be lots of boats and that the embarkation of the troops would all be organized," he wrote. "That was what all the little shore boats were being brought over from England for ... One can only come to the conclusion that the civilians and small boats packed up and went home with a few chaps instead of staying there to ferry to the big ships, which was their proper job. As for the shore organization, it simply did not exist ... a more disgraceful muddle ... I have never seen."

Be that as it may, Dunkirk was a success of sorts. However, it was not a victory by any stretch of the imagination — as Churchill told the House of Commons, "wars are not won by evacuations." It was, in fact, an unmitigated defeat. It was little wonder, therefore, that, at midnight on the day the port fell, Hitler ordered that church and civic bells be tolled for three days throughout the Reich to celebrate the end of the "greatest battle in world history."

The Windsor Kidnapping

After the Duke of Windsor — Edward VIII until his abdication from the British throne in 1936 — and his American Duchess fled from France to neutral Portugal as France fell in June 1940, Churchill was presented with a dilemma. Was the Duke a pro-Nazi or a loyal patriot? Would he even connive at his own kidnapping in return for Hitler's pledge to restore him to the throne? It is still one of World War II's greatest controversies.

Churchill, a long-time friend of the Duke of Windsor who had supported him resolutely through the crisis caused by Edward's determination to marry Wallis Simpson, a twice-divorced American, in 1936, was always convinced that the Duke "never wavered in his loyalty to the British cause." Even he could not deny, however, that before, during, and after his short reign, the Duke, at times, had displayed pronounced pro-German sympathies.

In 1936 — the year of Edward's abdication — Hitler moved into the Rhineland, which had been demilitarized ever since the signing of the Treaty of Versailles in 1919. The move provoked a European crisis and was the Führer's first and greatest gamble. Had Britain and France stood up to him, he undoubtedly would have been forced to pull back his troops and might well have fallen from power as a result. "If the French had marched into the Rhineland," he told Paul Schmidt, his personal interpreter, "we would have had to withdraw with our tails between our legs."

As it turned out, Britain and France confined themselves to muted protests. The French refused to move without British backing and the British refused to move

Left: *The Duke of Windsor is photographed in naval uniform during his days as Prince of Wales. As prince and king, he was hugely popular.*

Opposite: *The Duke of Windsor looks on as Hitler warmly greets the Duchess during the couple's ill-timed visit to Germany in October 1937. British Intelligence suspected her and the Duke of harboring Nazi sympathies.*

at all. Lord Lothian, a prominent British political figure, spoke for many of his fellow-countrymen when he declared that "the Germans are only going into their own back garden." According to Leopold von Hoesch, the German Ambassador in London, Edward himself intervened during the crisis. He telephoned Hoesch personally to offer him reassurance. "I sent for the Prime Minister (Stanley Baldwin) and gave him a piece of my mind," Hoesch claimed Edward had said to him. "I told the old so-and-so that I would abdicate if he made war. There was

a frightful scene, but you needn't worry. There won't be a war."

For her part, Wallis Simpson appears to have been even more pro-German than Edward. According to an FBI report, specially compiled during a visit by the Duke and Duchess to the U.S. on the personal orders of J. Edgar Hoover in April 1941, she had become the mistress of Joachim von Ribbentrop soon after his appointment to succeed Hoesch as German Ambassador in London. The report stated that the FBI's informant (believed to be the former Duke of

Above: *The Duke reviews an SS guard of honor during his 1937 German visit. Public opinion at home was scandalized when it was rumored that he had greeted his hosts with a Nazi salute.*

Opposite: *Stanley Baldwin, Prime Minister at the time of the Abdication, told Edward that he and his cabinet would resign if the king dared to try to marry the twice-divorced Mrs. Simpson.*

Württemberg "knew definitely that von Ribbentrop, while in England, sent the then Wallis Simpson 17 carnations every day. The 17 apparently represented the number of times they had slept together." Ribbentrop kept in close touch with her even after he had returned to Germany to become Foreign Minister. If the informant was telling the truth, it was little wonder that, embittered at her social ostracism by the British establishment after Edward's abdication, the Duchess did absolutely nothing to hold her husband back.

VISITING THE FÜHRER

In October 1937, shortly after their marriage in France, the Duke and Duchess accepted an invitation to visit Germany as Hitler's personal guests. The Duke announced that the purpose of the visit was to study the ways in which Germany had tackled its unemployment problems, but the trip was soon mired in controversy. The Duchess later wrote somewhat naively that "it never occurred to David (the family name for Edward) that this purely private trip could become a cause for public concern," but she was wrong. The Nazis did their best to turn it into a fully fledged state visit.

The couple were feted wherever they went, the Duke responding to the cheers with the raised-arm Hitler salute on several occasions. They met privately with Hitler at his Bavarian holiday retreat and dined with Rudolf Hess, then the Deputy Führer. Robert Ley, head of the Labour Front, was officially in charge of the visitors until, visibly drunk, he drove the Duke and Duchess straight through a set of locked factory gates in his Mercedes. On Hitler's orders, he was hurriedly replaced by Herman Goering for the rest of the visit.

What exactly the Duke and the Nazi leaders talked about remains unknown, but there is no doubt that Hitler and the other top Nazis were impressed by what they heard. Edward was unstinting in his praise of German industrial developments and social progress. He certainly was all for appeasing the new Germany; he also believed that the Nazi regime would be an invaluable bulwark against the possible spread of Communism, which he loathed. Propaganda Minister Joseph Goebbels summed up the Nazi view: "It's a shame he is no longer

king. With him we would have entered into an alliance."

Hitler concurred. Later, he told Albert Speer, his personal architect: "I am certain that through him permanent friendly relations could have been achieved." As for the Duchess, the Führer apparently won her heart by telling her that she "would make a good queen." She recorded her impressions of the Führer as follows: "At close

quarters, he gave one a feeling of great inner force … his eyes were truly extraordinary — intense, unblinking, magnetic, burning with the same peculiar fire I had earlier seen in the eyes of Kemal Ataturk."

In fairness, the Duke and Duchess were by no means the only high-ups from Britain to be impressed by the Nazis and their Führer. A month after their trip to Germany, David Lloyd George, the veteran Liberal politician who, as Prime Minister, had led the British to victory in World War I, also visited the Führer. After his return home, the "Welsh wizard" described what a deep impression Hitler had made on him in an article he wrote for the *Daily Express*. Having paid tribute to the Führer for "the marvelous transformation" he had brought about in "the spirit of the people," Lloyd George continued: "One man has accomplished this miracle. He is a born leader of men. He mixes a magnetic, dynamic personality with a single-minded purpose, a resolute will, and a dauntless heart. Lloyd George concluded: "He is the George Washington of Germany — the man who won for his country independence from all her oppressors." In his conversation with Hitler, Lloyd George had gone even further. When Hitler told him that during the war it had been he who had "galvanized the people of Britain into the will for victory," Lloyd George replied that he was glad to receive this compliment from "the greatest German of the age."

LOOSE CANNON

The British government heartily disapproved of the Duke's and Duchess's visit. It was equally disconcerted when, in May 1939, the Duke unilaterally decided to broadcast an appeal for "a peaceful solution to the world's problems" to the U.S. from the World War I battlefield at Verdun. The broadcast, whether deliberately or not, coincided with George VI's and Queen Elizabeth's state visit to the U.S. There was no stopping Edward, however. On August 27, as the German Wehrmacht prepared to strike at the Poles, he cabled Hitler directly "as a citizen of the world" pleading with the Führer to use his best efforts to preserve peace.

The telegram read: "Remembering your courtesy and our meeting two years ago, I address to you my entirely personal, simple though very earnest appeal for your utmost influence toward a peaceful solution of the present problem." The Führer did not reply. So matters rested until the fall of France in June 1940. The Duke and Duchess fled their adopted country — Edward had been serving as a liaison officer between the BEF and the French Army — for safety.

It was after the Duke and Duchess arrived in neutral Portugal after a tortuous journey via Biarritz and then Spain that Hitler received a report that gave him cause to think. Apparently, the Duke had openly expressed his dislike and distrust of his family because of the way they had persistently snubbed the Duchess, and criticized Churchill equally severely for his unnecessary prolongation of the war. According to the report, Edward had gone on to predict that "protracted heavy air bombardment would make Britain ready for peace."

The Führer was intrigued by the Duke's apparent loathing of Churchill and his dislike of the war. He came round to the belief, rightly or wrongly, that Edward would be more than willing to return to the throne, albeit as a puppet king, following a British surrender and the conclusion of an armistice. Ribbentrop, Foreign Minister since 1937, concurred. He cabled Eberhard von Stohrer, the German Ambassador in Madrid, telling him to assure Edward that, if he wished it, Germany was willing to smooth the path for "the Duke and Duchess to occupy the British throne."

Edward, who had now taken up residence in Lisbon, where he and the Duchess were the guests of Ricardo do Espirito Santo Silva, a banker who was

Above: *Joachim von Ribbentrop, German Ambassador in London in 1936 and later Hitler's Foreign Minister, was rumored to have been one of Mrs. Simpson's lovers.*

Left: *Walter Schellenberg, the rising star of SS Intelligence, was put in charge of the Nazi attempt to persuade the Duke to leave Portugal for pro-Nazi Spain in the summer of 1940.*

thought to be a Nazi sympathizer, received the message with some consternation. He told the Spanish grandee who was acting as Ribbentrop's intermediary, that the British constitution made it impossible for a monarch who had once abdicated to return to the throne. When the emissary then suggested that events might bring about changes even in the British constitution, the Duchess, in particular, became "very thoughtful."

OPERATION WILLI

Ribbentrop was determined not to let matters rest there. He summoned Walter Schellenberg, the rising star of SS Intelligence, into consultation. Ribbentrop started by explaining the Duke's current position — at least as

far as he understood it. "We've had word," he told the cynical Schellenberg, "that he (the Duke) has even spoken about living in Spain and that if he did go there he'd be ready to be friends with Germany again as he was before." The Foreign Minister continued: "The Führer thinks this attitude is extremely important and we thought that you with your Western outlook might be the most suitable person to make some sort of exploratory contact with the Duke — as representative, of course, of the Head of the German State."

Ribbentrop had not finished. "The Führer feels that if the atmosphere seemed propitious you might perhaps make the Duke some material offer," he went on. "Now, we should

be prepared to deposit in Switzerland for his own use a sum of 50 million Swiss francs, if he were ready to make some official gesture dissociating himself from the maneuvers of the British Royal family. The Führer, of course, would prefer him to live in Switzerland, though any other neutral country would do so long as it's not outside the economic or the political or military influence of the German Reich."

"If the British Secret Service should try to frustrate the Duke in some such arrangement," Ribbentrop went on, "then the Führer orders that you are to circumvent the British plans, even at the risk of your life and, if need be, by the use of force. Whatever happens, the Duke of Windsor must be brought safely

Left: *Mrs. Simpson fled the country to take refuge in the south of France when the abdication crisis broke. It was there that Edward married her.*

Below: *The Berghof was Hitler's Bavarian retreat on the Obersalzburg. He entertained the Duke and Duchess of Windsor with tea there.*

to the country of his choice. Hitler attaches the greatest importance to this operation and he has come to the conclusion after serious consideration that if the Duke should prove hesitant, he himself would have no objection to your helping the Duke to reach the right decision by coercion — even by threats or force if the circumstances make it advisable."

Schellenberg sat stunned. He rose and was about to leave when Ribbentrop got Hitler on the telephone. The Führer confirmed that the plan was to go ahead. He added that Schellenberg "should particularly bear in mind the importance of the Duchess's attitude and try as hard as possible to get her support. She has great influence over the Duke." After this, Schellenberg was finally able to make his getaway. He immediately began planning what he christened Operation Willi. The next day, he left for Madrid.

PLOT AND COUNTERPLOT

On his arrival, Schellenberg went straight to the German embassy to meet Stohrer. The ambassador told him that it was his contacts in the Spanish aristocracy who had alerted him to the Duke's apparent discontent. They had invited him to hunt with them on an estate near the Portuguese border and he had accepted the invitation, though no date for the hunt had yet been set. The hunt would give Schellenberg the chance to speak to the Duke personally and, if the Duke fell in with the plan, to spirit him across the border into Spain.

Schellenberg decided to play a waiting game. The more he thought about it, the more likely it seemed to him that the Duke's remarks — if, indeed, he had ever made them — were being taken far too seriously. He decided to go to Lisbon to assess the situation. Within a few days, he had reached a conclusion. The Duke no longer intended to accept the hunting invitation. Though he disliked the fact that he was being shadowed by the British Secret Service and did not like the prospect of being sent as Governor to Bermuda, which was Churchill's current intention, he equally

Above: *German troops inspect an abandoned British tank in France. The Duke abandoned his post as a liaison officer with the French Army, fleeing with the Duchess first to Spain and then to Portugal.*

Right: *Although the British prepared to fight to the last man in the event of a German invasion, the Duke let it be known that he was in favor of a negotiated peace with Germany.*

had no intention of going to live voluntarily in a neutral or hostile country. The most he had ever said, according to his Portuguese friends, was that he would rather live in any European country than go to Bermuda.

Churchill, for his part, was determined that the Duke and Duchess should leave Europe as soon as possible. An injudicious interview the Duke gave to the press, which Churchill regarded as defeatist, was probably the final straw. The Prime Minister despatched Sir Walter Monckton, previously one of the Duke's closest advisers, to Lisbon to warn Edward to prepare to leave for Bermuda immediately or face the possibility of court-martial. The Duke and Duchess reluctantly obeyed.

Schellenberg, in the meantime, was coming under increasing pressure from Berlin to end his apparent inactivity. About two weeks after his arrival in the Portuguese capital, he received a peremptory telegram from Ribbentrop. It read baldy: "[The Führer] orders that the abduction is to be organized at once." Schellenberg decided to get around the order by arranging through his contacts with Portuguese officials for extra police to be drafted in to guard the Duke and the Duchess. With the British Secret Service already on high alert, Schellenberg had the pretext he needed to abandon any kidnap attempt. The day after Edward and Wallis finally sailed, he left for Berlin.

Even Hitler accepted that Schellenberg had acted for the best. "The Führer has studied your last telegram carefully," a dispirited Ribbentrop told him, "and asks me to tell you that in spite of his disappointment at the outcome of the whole affair, he agrees with your decisions and expresses his approval of the manner in which you proceeded." As Schellenberg wrote in his postwar memoirs, "the chapter was closed."

Europe's Looted Treasures

History demonstrates that conquerors are rarely respecters of property; after the Nazis stormed through most of Western Europe, they proved to be no exception. With many of the great European cultural centers firmly in their clutches, the Nazi leaders — chief among them Hitler himself, followed by Hermann Goering — embarked on a systematic looting spree on a scale unmatched since the barbarians swarmed into the Roman Empire.

Above: *Soldiers from the Hermann Goering Division pose outside the Palazzo Venezia in Rome with a looted landscape by the 18th-century artist Giovanni Paolo Pannini. The photograph was taken in 1944 before the Germans evacuated the city.*

Nazi determination to secure the cream of European art for the Reich was clearly in evidence even before the outbreak of war in 1939. On June 26 that year, Adolf Hitler engaged the services of Hans Posse, an art historian and museum director in Dresden, and put him in charge of amassing the art collections that would be needed to fill the grandiose galleries and museums the Führer planned to have built in Berlin and Linz, his birthplace.

Posse and, from 1942, Herman Voss, Posse's successor after his death from cancer, quickly set to work. By 1945 they had gathered together more than 8,000 works of art for their Führer. The collection included 12 Rembrandts, 23 Breughels, two Vermeers, and 15 Canalettos, plus paintings by Titian, Leonardo da Vinci, Botticelli, Holbein, Cranach, Rubens, and many others. Many of them were simply expropriated from their owners, or acquired at knock-down prices that did not come anywhere near reflecting their true value.

Jewish art dealers and collectors were particularly at risk. After the French surrender in 1940, Hitler ordered all their possessions in France to be confiscated. The property of 15 major Jewish art dealers was promptly seized, together with the fabulous art collections painstakingly built up over the years by Jewish art connoisseurs — most notably the Rothschilds. Vermeer's *The Astronomer* was one of the masterpieces expropriated for Hitler himself. The Führer intended it to form a focal point of his Linz museum. In Holland, a team of Nazi art experts tracked down collections that had been taken to Holland by German-Jewish owners fleeing persecution before the war, confiscated them, and had them sent back to the Reich. A classic 1669 self-portrait of Rembrandt was just one of the masterpieces among their number.

France was by no means the first country the Nazis plundered during the course of the war. The looting started in Warsaw, where a grand total of 13,512 paintings and 1,379 sculptures were seized and confiscated after Poland's surrender in 1939. The plundered works of art included Raphael's *A Portrait of a Young Man,* which subsequently vanished from sight. Many were simply destroyed. Countless rare books and manuscripts went up in flames, for example, when the Nazis set fire to the Krasinski Library in the Polish capital.

THE AVARICIOUS REICHSMARSCHAL

Other top Nazis quickly followed the Führer's example. The most avaricious of them all was Luftwaffe commander-in-chief and economics overlord Hermann Goering. By the time the ebullient Reichsmarschal started collecting on a truly massive scale, he already owned 10 houses, castles, and hunting lodges scattered around the Reich, all provided by taxpayers and maintained at their expense. In all of them — most notably Carinhall, his vast and ever-expanding principal hunting lodge that he had named in memory of his deceased first wife — he was determined to display artworks, tapestries, paintings, sculptures, and much else besides to confirm his status as the second most important figure in the Reich.

Like the Führer, Goering employed an art agent — Walter Andreas Hofer — to track down the masterpieces he coveted. He also took the lead in building up his collection. A 1940 visit to Amsterdam triggered off an orgy of competitive acquisition between him and the other Nazi bigwigs; during a two-day visit to Paris that same year, he personally selected 27 works by Rembrandt, Van Dyke, and others for his pleasure. As a

result of the visit, he ended up with more than 600 paintings, pieces of furniture, and other items, which he had valued at low prices if he intended to display them at Carinhall or at much higher ones if his intention was to sell them. Highlights of his collection included Lucas Cranach's *Venus and Cupid* and Rembrandt's *Two Philosophers* as well as several Vermeers, although, after the war, the latter were discovered to be fakes. Goering and his supposed art experts had been taken in by Han van Meegeren, a Dutch artist and art dealer, who had skillfully forged the Vermeers himself.

It is still uncertain exactly how many looted works of art Goering acquired — the latest estimate is around 2,000, over 700 more than had been previously thought. What we do know is what happened to many of them. With the Soviet armies closing in on Berlin as the war neared its conclusion, Goering ordered Carinhall to be evacuated before being blown up by the Luftwaffe. The majority of the art collection was loaded onto a

Above: *Hermann Goering, seen here seated front row far right in the dock at the 1946 Nuremberg Trial, was the Third Reich's champion art looter. His collection included 10 Van Dycks, nine Rembrandts, and hundreds of other masterpieces.*

fleet of trucks and then private trains, transporting it deep into Bavaria and then toward the Austrian border. The trains were intercepted by American forces and diverted to Munich, where their content was inventoried prior to its eventual return to its rightful owners. As for the

Right: *The reconstructed Amber Room is seen in its full glory. Looted from St Petersburg and transported to Germany, the original is one of the most significant art treasures never to have been recovered.*

Reichsmarschal himself, he, too, fell into Allied hands. He was found guilty of crimes against humanity and sentenced to death at the 1946 Nuremberg Trials, though he managed to kill himself before having to face the hangman.

THE AMBER ROOM

By no means were all the works of art looted by Hitler, Goering, and the other Nazi leaders recovered. The whereabouts of the celebrated Amber Room, for instance, still remains something of a mystery. Dubbed "the eighth wonder of the world" after its creation, its story started in 1701, when Andreas Schulter, a German sculptor, and Gottfried Wolfram, a Danish amber artist, began work on its design and construction for Friedrich I of Prussia. Originally installed in the Charlottenburg Palace, Friedrich William I presented it as a gift to Peter the Great of Russia after the latter expressed his admiration for it during a state visit he paid to Berlin to cement a Russo-Prussian alliance.

The Amber Room was dismantled, crated up, and shipped to St. Petersburg, where it was reassembled in the Winter House. In 1755, Tsarina Elizabeth ordered it to be disassembled again and moved to the Catherine Palace in Pushkin. The Italian designer Bartolomeo Francesco Rastrelli redesigned it to fit into its new, larger home, shipping the extra amber he needed from Berlin to Russia. After this and other 18th-century renovations, the room was around 180 square feet (17 sq. m) in size, its amber panels, backed with gold leaf, glowing with six tons of amber and other semiprecious stones. Historians have estimated that the room at that time was worth $142 million in modern dollars.

Above: *General Tomoyuki Yamashita, the so-called "Tiger of Malaya" who became the Military Governor of the Philippines from October 1944 until the islands' liberation, was thought to have superintended the looting of millions of dollars worth of gold, although whether this was shipped from mainland southeast Asia to the Philippines is considered unlikely.*

LOOTED BY THE NAZIS

It was little wonder that the Amber Room, made by Germans for Germans, became one of Hitler's prime artistic targets as his armies swept into the Soviet Union after their surprise attack caught the Russians off guard in June 1941. As Nazi forces approached Pushkin, where the Amber Room was still housed, attempts were made first to dismantle it and then to hide it — the Russians resorted to pasting wallpaper over its amber panels to conceal them from sight. The attempts were in vain. The Germans quickly found the room. Within three days they had torn it down and packed the pieces up in crates, which were shipped to Konigsberg (Kaliningrad) on the Baltic coast. There, the Amber Room was installed in the castle museum.

The Amber Room stayed on display for the next two years until late 1943, when Alfred Pohde, the museum's curator, was ordered to take it apart again and crate it away for safety. In August the following year, RAF bombers blitzed the city, destroying most of its historic buildings including the castle. From that point in time onward, the Amber Room vanished from history.

It seems hard to credit that the crates containing the room could have simply disappeared without leaving any trace, and numerous efforts have been made to solve the mystery. Some say that the crates were destroyed in the bombing; others argue that they are still concealed somewhere in or around Konigsberg. Another theory holds that, in 1945, as the Russians closed in on the city, they were loaded onto a refugee ship, which a Soviet submarine promptly torpedoed, sending it to the bottom of the Baltic.

The search went on and on. Stasi intelligence agents in East Germany spent millions of marks in a fruitless quest that lasted for decades. Then, in 1998, two rival research teams — one in Germany and the other in Lithuania — claimed to have located the missing crates. The Germans said they had been buried in a silver mine south of Berlin, while the Lithuanians claimed that they were concealed at the bottom of a murky lagoon, close to the town of Neringa. Both teams failed to locate the treasure. The same thing happened in 2008, when treasure-hunters were sure they had located the Amber Room's hiding place in a man-made underground cavern near a village on the German border with the Czech Republic. Three years later, yet another group of researchers claimed that the room's amber panels were hidden

Above: *Joseph Goebbels, the Nazi Minister of Propaganda, visits the Exhibition of Degenerate Art held in Munich in 1937. It was designed to showcase the "deviant and decadent" art that the Nazis dismissed as the work of "Jews and Bolsheviks" — all of whom were out to destroy European culture.*

Opposite: *Hitler, Gerdy Troost, widow of architect Paul Troost, Adolf Ziegler, and Joseph Goebbels at the opening of the House of German Art in Munich in May 1937. The works of art on display were chosen to celebrate "two thousand years of German culture."*

somewhere in an underground bunker they had discovered in the woods outside Auerswalde, a small town near Chemnitz. Further investigation failed to find any trace of the lost room.

LOST OR DESTROYED?

The Nazis did not simply loot art on an unprecedented scale, they also destroyed it. In 1937 they turned out en masse for the opening of the so-called Exhibition of Degenerate Art in Munich. The aim of the exhibition was simple: to hold up

contemporary art to ridicule.

It was Hitler's chance to take his revenge on the artistic establishment of the day, which, years before, while he was a penniless art student in Vienna, had dismissed his painstakingly realistic paintings of buildings and landscapes as the work of a talentless amateur. That summer, he pledged that "works of art which cannot be understood in themselves but need some pretentious instruction book to justify their existence will never again find their way to the German people."

Works by 112 artists were featured in the exhibition. They included paintings by some of the greatest international names in abstract and expressionist art — Marc Chagall, Paul Klee, Oskar Kokoschka, Gustav Klimt, Pablo Picasso, and Henri Matisse among them — as well as celebrated German modernists, such as Max Beckmann, Otto Dix, Georg Grosz, Ernst Ludwig Kirchner, and Emil Nolde. The overall purpose of the exhibition, the catalog explained, was "to reveal the philosophical, political, racial, and moral goals behind this movement, and the driving forces of corruption which follow them."

Entartete Kunst (degenerate art), the Nazis roundly declared, was deviant and decadent. Its practitioners were all part of a conspiracy, the aim of which was to destroy European culture. They were "Jews and Bolsheviks" to a man. The way the exhibits were displayed visually reinforced the contempt the Nazis had for them and the artists who had created them. Pictures were deliberately hung askew. There was graffiti on the walls, which insulted both the works on display and their creators. The aim was to make it all seem outlandish and downright ridiculous into the bargain.

The paintings were distributed between various rooms according to category. The derogatory labels spoke for themselves. There was art that was blasphemous, art by Jewish or Communist artists, art that criticized German soldiers, and art that offended the purity of German womanhood. One room, devoted entirely to abstract art, was labeled simply "the insanity room." The catalog had this to say about it

and its contents: "In the paintings and drawings of this chamber of horrors, there is no telling what was in the sick brains of those who wielded the brush or the pencil."

THE MUNICH DISCOVERY

The message was clear — or so it seemed. All degenerate art should be got rid of. Much was thought to have been physically destroyed. In 2012, however, an accidental discovery in a Munich apartment turned the accepted view of the twisted relationship between the Nazis and modern art almost completely on its head.

Ever since the 1937 exhibition, it had been generally assumed that all the so-called degenerate art the Nazis could lay their hands on had either been destroyed or sold abroad to raise hard currency for the regime. Now, while raiding the home of Cornelius Gurlitt, an 80-year-old recluse, customs officials, who were looking for evidence of money-laundering, instead unearthed a hoard of more than 1,500 long-lost modern masterpieces. These included paintings by Cézanne, Picasso, Matisse, Munch, Renoir, Klee, Nolde, Marc, Dix, and Kokoschka. The discovery was kept secret for some months; it was not until late 2013 that news of it was made public.

Gurlitt turned out to be the son of Hildebrand Gurlitt, a Hamburg art dealer who, despite being half-Jewish, had been recruited by the Nazis as a useful expert when it came to organizing their mass confiscations of degenerate art. Rather than destroying or selling it, Gurlitt secretly hoarded much of it, carefully hiding it away in the chaos that overtook the Third Reich as it headed inexorably toward final surrender. Although the Americans discovered some of it shortly after the capitulation, he was able to convince them that he had acquired the paintings and drawings legitimately and they eventually handed them back over to him. The rest of his collection, he said, had been destroyed in the firestorm that followed the RAF bombing of Dresden in February 1945, just over two months before the end of the war.

The unanswered question is whether there were any more hoarders like Gurlitt and, if there were, what lost masterpieces might they have quietly appropriated for themselves? What, for instance, really happened to Klimt's three *University Murals* and *Schubert at the Piano?* The former, created by Klimt to decorate the Great Hall of University of Vienna, have long

been regarded as among the most radical and controversial of his artistic works. Together with *Schubert at the Piano* and nine other Klimts, they were supposed to have been destroyed in 1945, when, on May 7 — the day that Germany unconditionally surrendered to the Allies — a group of SS troopers blew up Schloss Immendorf, a castle in lower Austria where they had been stored since 1943, to prevent the castle falling into Russian hands.

Another masterpiece whose fate is considered uncertain is Van Gogh's *Painter on His Way to Work* (otherwise known as *Painter on the Road to Tarascon)*. In the painting, Van Gogh depicted himself as a traveling painter — complete with straw hat, painting equipment, and walking stick — accompanied by his prominent shadow. Van Gogh was high on Hitler's blacklist of degenerate artists and this painting was quickly seized and taken off display. Previously thought to have been destroyed in an Allied air raid, it is now one of the 100,000 masterpieces that, according to the U.S. National Archives, are listed as missing. The jury remains out as to whether, in the light of the sensational Munich discovery, any of these, too, will be found.

Top: Portrait of Wally *by Austrian painter Egon Schiele. Wally, Schiele's favorite model became his mistress.*

Left: Pferde im Landschaft *by Franz Mark was one of the paintings rediscovered in the apartment of Cornelius Gurlitt in Munich in 2012.*

The Strange Case of Rudolf Hess

It was an extraordinary event that astounded the world. On May 10, 1941, Rudolf Hess, Hitler's deputy, parachuted into Scotland. His mission, so he told his captors, was to seek an immediate end to the war, although he admitted he had flown to Britain without the knowledge or approval of the Führer. Hitler's response was immediate. He denounced Hess as being insane, a verdict with which his British captors eventually concurred.

Exactly what prompted Hess to fly to Britain on his peace mission remains something of a mystery. Though he always denied that Hitler knew anything about his intentions in advance, some still speculate that, in fact, the Führer was aware of what Hess planned. Persuading the British to come to terms and make peace meant that Germany would not have to fight a war on two fronts when she turned east against the Soviet Union. Indeed, Hess even may have hoped that the British eventually might agree to join in the attack.

There is at least one piece of hard evidence to support this claim. In 2011, a German historian discovered a 28-page handwritten document in the Russian state archives. It was written by Karl-Heinz Pintsch, Hess's former adjutant, while he was a Soviet prisoner. It said that Hitler indeed had approved of Hess's flight as a way of kick-starting peace talks between Berlin and London. According to Pintsch, Hess was to "use all means at his disposal to achieve at least the neutralization of England." Although the Soviets may well have coerced Pintsch into making his assertions, it equally might have been the case that he believed — or knew — them to be true.

Others postulate that Hess may have been the victim of a "sting" by the British Secret Intelligence Service. According to the theory, MI6 deliberately leaked false stories that prominent personalities in Britain were plotting to topple Churchill and then open negotiations to agree

Above: *Rudolf Hess, Hitler's deputy, flew to Britain in May 1941 in a misguided attempt to persuade the British to make peace and join Germany in attacking the USSR.*

Opposite: *The wreckage of Hess's Messerschmitt Me 110 is seen under British guard. Goering had assured Hitler that Hess could never reach Scotland, but instead would crash in the North Sea.*

Above: *A Messerschmitt Me 110 in flight. Having taken off from Augsburg, Hess flew across Germany and the North Sea to reach Scotland, bailing out of his plane just outside Glasgow.*

Opposite: *Rudolf Hess is seen in the center background of this group photograph, taken in March 1941. At the time he was losing out in a battle for power with the Führer's secretary Martin Bormann.*

on a compromise peace. Hess, the theorists hold, was lured into the British trap. Another possibility is that, despite officially still being the third most important figure in the Third Reich after Hitler and Goering, Hess was now finding himself more and more sidelined and his position in the party increasingly under threat. It may

be that he thought by fulfilling his self-appointed mission he would reestablish himself as one of the Führer's closest and most-trusted confidants.

"AS THOUGH OVERCOME BY A VISION"

Like Hitler, Hess fought as an infantryman during World War I.

Unlike the Führer, though, he gained rapid promotion. After recovering from a serious wound he received while fighting in Romania, he transferred to the Imperial Air Service, completing his flying training as a pilot in time to fight in the last aerial battles over the Western Front. In common with many young Germans of his generation, the 1918 surrender left him angry, bitter, and disillusioned.

Following the armistice, Hess, now a student at the University of Munich, soon became embroiled in extreme right-wing activities.

He joined the Thule Society, a secret anti-Semitic movement dedicated to asserting Nordic racial superiority, and served in the Freikorps, a group of ex-soldiers involved in putting down Communist uprisings. In July 1920, having heard Hitler speak in a small Munich beer hall, Hess joined the embryonic Nazi Party. He was its 16th member.

Hess never forgot that first meeting with Hitler and the impact the future Führer had on him. He felt, he said, "as though overcome by a vision." Hitler, Hess believed, was the only person

who could recreate German self-belief and restore the nation's national pride. From that time on, he attached himself to Hitler body and soul, carving out a niche for himself as his most faithful adjutant.

The two men were incarcerated together in Landsburg Prison after the failure of the Beer Hall Putsch in 1923, during which time Hess helped Hitler to write *Mein Kampf*, the definitive statement of the would-be Führer's political beliefs. When Hitler finally took office as Chancellor 10 years later, he

promptly made Hess the deputy leader of the Nazi Party as a reward for his years of faithful service. The newly appointed Deputy Führer was doggedly loyal and blindly obedient. "With pride, we see that one man remains beyond all criticism and that is the Führer," he told a party rally after the Nazis finally came to power. "This is because everybody feels and knows he is always right and he will be always right. The National Socialism of all of us is anchored in uncritical loyalty, in the surrender to the Führer that does not ask for the why in individual cases, in the silent execution of his orders. We believe that the Führer is obeying a higher call to fashion German history. There can be no criticism of this belief."

Hess and Hitler, though, were very different in character. Away from the speaker's platform, Hess was shy and insecure, whereas Hitler brimmed with self-confidence. According to Wilhelm Bohle, head of the organization representing Germans abroad, he was "the biggest idealist we have had in Germany, a man of a very soft nature." One of Hess's adjutants concurred. His master, he said, possessed "almost feminine sensitivities." He shared none of Hitler's destructive ruthlessness. He was also a great admirer of the British — he spoke English fluently. Perhaps this admiration played a part in spurring him on to plan his mission to Britain. It was an unquestionably sincere, although perhaps naive, attempt to bring the war between his beloved homeland and the nation he admired so greatly to an end.

THE FLIGHT TO SCOTLAND
Hess started planning his peace mission after the fall of France in June 1940. That August, he asked Albrecht Haushofer, his principal adviser on British affairs, to start

ein ständiger Strom von Waffen und Kriegsgerät aller Art.
Die alliierte Kriegsproduktion übertrifft diejenige Deutschlands und seiner Verbündeten heute bereits um mehr als das Dreifache. Nächstes Jahr wird sie sie um mehr als das Vierfache überflügelt haben.

Daran können auch die U-Boote nichts ändern. In den drei Monaten Mai, Juni und Juli wurden über 90 deutsche U-Boote versenkt. Im August wurden mehr U-Boote als alliierte Handelsschiffe vernichtet. Auch jetzt vergeht kein Tag, an dem nicht mindestens ein deutsches U-Boot versenkt wird. Anderseits wurde in den vier Monaten von Mitte Mai bis Mitte September kein einziges alliiertes Schiff im Nordatlantik versenkt. Der Neubau alliierter Schiffe übersteigt die Verluste allein für die ersten neun Monate dieses Jahres um **mehr als sechs Millionen Tonnen.** Unter diesen Umständen werden sämtliche Schiffsverluste der Vereinten Nationen seit Kriegsbeginn bald wieder wettgemacht sein.
Die U-Boot-Waffe hat wie im letzten, so auch in diesem Weltkrieg versagt.

★   ★   ★ .

Das ist die Lage von heute. Und wenn es noch einen Deutschen gibt, der dennoch Hoffnungen auf einen Verhandlungsfrieden hegt, so braucht er sich nur zu fragen: Welchen Grund hätten die Alliierten, heute einen Verhandlungsfrieden mit derselben Clique anzustreben, der England trotz seiner damals bedrängten Lage schon im Mai 1941 die Antwort gab: Keine Verhandlungen mit Hitler oder seiner Regierung!
Hitler weiss dies genau so gut wie wir. Er weiss, dass er den Krieg unwiderruflich verloren hat. Trotzdem lässt er das deutsche Volk weiterbluten, weil er weiss, dass das Kriegsende sein eigenes Ende bedeutet. Um sein eigenes Ende hinauszuschieben, opfert er euch und Deutschland.

Ihr kämpft, um Zeit zu gewinnen: Zeit für Hitler und Zeit zur Zerstörung Deutschlands.

ZUM FALL HESS

England vom Kontinent vertrieben

Luftwaffe bedroht britische Städte mit völliger Vernichtung

Täglich neue Erfolge der U-Boote

Grossbritanniens Verbindungen mit dem überseeischen Weltreich ernstlich bedroht

10. Mai 1941 : Rudolf Hess, Stellvertreter des Führers, fliegt nach England

KÜRZLICH hat die englische Regierung ihre erste ausführliche Schilderung der Ankunft von Rudolf Hess in Grossbritannien gegeben.

Hess legte den Flug in einer Me 110 zurück und landete am Abend des 10. Mai 1941 mittels Fallschirms in Schottland. Hess, der die Uniform eines Hauptmannes der Luftwaffe trug, nannte sich Alfred Horn und verlangte, „in besonderem Auftrag" den Herzog von Hamilton zu sprechen.

Am folgenden Morgen, Sonntag den 11. Mai um zehn Uhr morgens, wurde Rudolf Hess am Orte seiner einstweiligen Internierung dem Oberstleutnant der *Royal Air Force*, Herzog von Hamilton, vorgeführt. Hess, der behauptete, den Herzog von den Olympischen Spielen her zu kennen — woran der Herzog sich allerdings nicht erinnern konnte — erklärte, sein Besuch sei seiner Sorge um das Schicksal der Menschheit entsprungen. Hitler wisse mit Bestimmtheit, er werde früher oder später siegen; Hess aber wolle unnötiges Blutvergiessen vermeiden.

Der Herzog von Hamilton erstattete Bericht über diese Unterhaltung. Darauf flog ein Beamter des Britischen

G.81

thinking of ways by which he could get into contact with those in high places in Britain who favored negotiating a compromise peace. Prominent prewar appeasers, such as the Duke of Westminster, Lord Londonderry, the Duke of Buccleuch, Lord Tavistock, who succeeded as Duke of Bedford in 1940, and Lord Redesdale, father of the notorious

Unity and Diana Mitford, were all possible targets, but in the end the choice fell on the Duke of Hamilton, a member of the Anglo-German Fellowship before the war.

Haushofer had met Hamilton at the 1936 Berlin Olympics and was aware of his liking for Germany. He also knew that Hamilton recently had been appointed Lord Steward of the

Above: *The British left it to the Germans to announce Hess's flight, but soon started making propaganda out of the affair. This leaflet was one of hundreds of thousands dropped by the RAF over Germany.*

Opposite: *This annotated aerial view shows where Hess landed after parachuting from his plane and where his Messerschmitt crashed. His only injury was a badly twisted ankle.*

king's household, a position that gave him direct access to George VI. What Haushofer seems to have been completely unaware of was that, whatever his sympathies may have been before the war, the Duke was a patriot through and through and was now serving in the RAF as a Wing Commander.

Hess asked Haushofer to write to Hamilton suggesting a meeting between the two men, either in Lisbon or in neutral Switzerland. However, the letter was intercepted by the British Security Service and the Duke never received it. All that happened was that MI5 began probing into Hamilton's loyalty. In the meantime, Hess started honing his flying skills in case he had to fly to Scotland to meet Hamilton at Dungavel House, the Duke's home

near Glasgow. He had asked his friend Willy Messerschmitt for the use of an Me 110 fighter-bomber and began making training flights in it under the supervision of Willi Stoer, one of Messerschmitt's top test pilots. As Hess's request, the Me 110 was specially adapted for long-distance flying; it was fitted with two huge 238-gallon (900 l) drop tanks and a special radio compass. He also started having weather conditions in the North Sea specially monitored.

The weather on May 10, 1941 was perfect for Hess's purpose. He arrived at the Messerschmitt airfield at Augsburg in the late afternoon and immediately began getting ready for take-off. As he prepared to climb into the cockpit of his plane, he handed four letters to Karl-Heinz Pintsch, who had

gone with him to the airfield. One was addressed to Hitler, the others to Hess's wife, Willy Messerschmitt, and Helmut Kaden, a pilot whose flying suit Hess had appropriated. Telling air traffic control his destination was Norway, he took off at 5:45 p.m. that evening.

"A MISSION OF HUMANITY"

Just after 10 p.m., a radar station on the northeast coast of England detected an unidentified aircraft approaching British airspace. As it approached the coast, it dived to pick up speed, crossed the Scottish border, and headed almost due west flying at low level — so low, in fact, that three Spitfires scrambled to intercept the plane missed their target completely.

The aircraft was Hess's Messerschmitt. Having made his landfall, Hess flew on but, despite a full moon, failed to locate his target. He flew out over the Firth of Clyde before turning back inland. By now his fuel tanks were running dry and he had no alternative other than to bail out of his aircraft or make an emergency forced landing. Hess settled for the former. He parachuted gently down onto a moonlit field barely 12 miles from the Duke's estate, overcome, as he later wrote, with "an indescribable sense of elation and triumph." His plane crashed a short distance away, breaking up into pieces upon impact.

The first person to approach the wreckage was David McLean, a local plowman who had heard the Messerschmitt flying overhead. He found Hess lying on the ground with a sprained ankle. Introducing himself as Captain Alfred Horn, Hess asked to be taken to Dungavel House, saying that he had "a secret and urgent" message for the Duke of Hamilton. Instead, McLean escorted him to his nearby cottage, where his wife offered Hess a cup of tea. The Deputy Führer politely declined the offer, saying that he would rather have a glass of water.

The police and Home Guard were soon at the scene. Hess repeated his request to be taken to the Duke, but he was hauled off to the local Home Guard headquarters and then to a military hospital in Glasgow. In the meantime, Hamilton had been contacted at RAF Turnhouse. He said he had never heard of anyone called Horn, but nevertheless would drive over to the hospital the following morning. Hess immediately revealed his true identity to the bemused Duke. He told him he had flown to Scotland on "a mission of humanity" to stop the unnecessary

slaughter that would ensue should fighting between Britain and Germany continue. Hamilton listened patiently to what Hess had to say and then left to report to his superiors. That afternoon, he flew south to personally inform Churchill of Hess's unexpected arrival.

Churchill was as taken aback as Hamilton had been, but knew exactly what to do. Any hope of peace talks was out of the question. Instead of being welcomed as a negotiator, Hess would be treated as a prisoner of

Above: *Hess reading in his cell in Spandau Prison. Mystery still surrounds his death in 1987. The official verdict was suicide, but his family claimed he was murdered.*

Opposite: *A section of the fuselage of Hess's Messerschmitt on display in a local museum.*

war. The Prime Minister ordered Ivone Kirkpatrick, a high-ranking Foreign Office official and expert on German affairs, to fly north to interrogate him. Kirkpatrick concluded that Hess's obsession with his mission was bordering on

monomania. Once he had finished his task, Hess was shifted south. After being housed in the Tower of London for a few days, he was handed over to MI6 and held in close confinement in a country house near London for the rest of the war.

WAS HESS INSANE?

Churchill ordered the news of Hess's arrival to be kept top secret. Hitler reacted differently. After he had read the letter Hess had asked Pintsch to give him, his immediate response was one of blind fury. Goering, who was hastily summoned to the Berghof, the Führer's Bavarian retreat, tried to reassure him that it was highly unlikely Hess had made a successful landfall. In all probability, the portly Reichsmarschal said, he and his plane would have crashed into the North Sea.

Hitler was taking no chances. He decided to act on a suggestion that Hess had made himself. According to Isle Hess, his letter to Hitler ended: "Should, my Führer, my mission end in failure, you can always distance yourself from me and declare me mad." That was exactly what Hitler proceeded to do. A special radio communiqué broadcast on May 10 announced that the Deputy Führer had taken off on an unauthorized flight from which he had not returned. "A letter which he left behind," the communiqué continued, "unfortunately shows traces of mental disturbance which justifies the fear that Hess was the victim of hallucinations." Though it did not say so directly, the broadcast gave the clear impression that Hess was a fantasist, who was now over the edge of lunacy.

This was the same conclusion the British medical experts monitoring Hess reached as the war progressed. At first, no one

Left: *Churchill, Roosevelt, and Stalin confer at Yalta in 1945. At the time of Hess's flight, Stalin believed that he had been negotiating directly with Churchill to persuade the latter to join Hitler in attacking the Soviet Union. In fact, Churchill never met Hess.*

Right: *Hess in the dock at Nuremberg. At first, he was considered unfit to plead, but then he told the judges he had been faking his amnesia.*

questioned his mental balance. One doctor described him as being "surprisingly ordinary ... quite sane, certainly not a drug-taker, a little concerned about his health and rather faddy about his diet." As time passed, however, Hess's behavior became more irrational. He alleged that his food was poisoned or contained drugs and then claimed to have lost his memory completely. After trying to commit suicide by throwing himself down a stairwell, a psychiatrist concluded that he had "definitely passed over the border that lies between mental instability and insanity."

FROM NUREMBERG TO SPANDAU

Hess had still one more surprise in store. Before the Nuremberg Trial opened in 1946, 10 psychiatrists concluded that, though Hess was not insane, he was not fully competent to stand trial. As the court was about to rule on the

issue, Hess asked for permission to speak. He told the judges that he had been shamming amnesia. It was only his "ability to concentrate," he said, that was "somewhat reduced." He took his place with the other defendants.

Over the next months, Hess cut an increasingly remote figure in the dock, at times scarcely seeming to be following the proceedings at all. It was not until the time came for him to make his final statement that he spoke again. He had been privileged, he said, "to work for many years of my life under the greatest son whom my people had brought forth in its thousand-year history. Even if I could, I would not want to erase this period of time from my existence. I am happy to know that I have done my duty to my people, my duty as a German, as a National Socialist, as a loyal follower of my

Führer. I do not regret anything." The court sentenced him to life imprisonment.

Hess spent the last 46 years of his life in Spandau Prison, Berlin, guarded by rotating contingents of troops from the four Allied powers. He was known to his guards only as Prisoner 7 — it was forbidden to speak his name. The other war criminals held in Spandau gradually became eligible for release. The last to leave were Albert Speer and Baldur von Schirach in 1966, leaving Hess as Spandau's sole remaining inmate. The Soviets steadfastly refused to consider granting him parole.

On August 17, 1987, the 93-year-old Hess supposedly committed suicide by hanging himself from a window latch in a summerhouse in the prison garden. Even this last act was controversial. Many, including Hess's son, believed that Hess was not physically strong enough to have killed himself. Instead, they claim that he was secretly murdered to stop him from revealing any embarrassing wartime secrets. The trigger for the killing, it was alleged, was the announcement that the Russians were finally ready to consent to Hess's release.

Forewarned But Not Forearmed

When Nazi Foreign Minister Joachim von Ribbentrop flew to Moscow in late August 1939 to conclude a Non-Aggression Pact with Joseph Stalin, the world was taken completely by surprise. However, when Hitler's armies stormed into the Soviet Union on June 22, 1941, the only man surprised was apparently Stalin himself. Why did the Soviet dictator ignore the numerous warnings he had been given of an imminent German attack?

Hitler's lightning decision to come to terms with Stalin came down to one word. It was expediency. In less than two weeks time, he planned to invade Poland and, with both Britain and France guaranteeing Polish independence, he needed to ensure that the Soviet Union would not side with the West should it come to war.

For weeks the British and French themselves had been negotiating half-heartedly with Moscow, but to little or no avail. The talks were bungled from start to finish, perhaps not that surprisingly since Neville Chamberlain, the British premier, never really wanted to embark on them in the first place. Hitler had no such inhibitions. Though Nazi Germany and Soviet Russia had been at loggerheads for years, he realized that reaching an agreement with Stalin was a tactical necessity even if the Nazi and Communist political ideologies were diametrically opposed. There was no questioning the fact that, should Stalin decide to side with Poland and the West, he could put substantial military forces into the field.

The public terms of the pact Ribbentrop and Vyacheslav Molotov, the Soviet Foreign Minister, agreed were innocuous

Above: *Russian prisoners being herded into captivity in 1941. Hitler's attack on the Soviet Union took Stalin completely by surprise.*

Opposite: *Molotov and Ribbentrop meet in Berlin in October 1940. The year before the two men had negotiated the Nazi-Soviet Non-Aggression Pact.*

enough on the surface. The two countries pledged themselves not to go to war with each other or support any country at war with the other for a period of not less than 10 years. They also agreed to increase their mutual trade. The sting was in the secret clauses. These gave each country "spheres of influence" — in other words, future control — over distinct areas of Eastern Europe. Stalin demanded — and was granted — control of all the territories that had been ruled by Tsarist Russia and lost in World War I. As for Poland, the country was to be partitioned, the Germans occupying the territories to the west of the River

Vistula and the Russians those to the east of the river.

Ribbentrop and Molotov signed the pact on September 24. Six days later, the Germans swept into Poland from the west, their Blitzkrieg immediately shifting into top gear. On September 17 more than 600,000 Soviet troops invaded Poland from the east and headed rapidly for the agreed-on demarcation line. Within days, the Red Army had occupied its half of the country.

At the same time, Stalin moved into the Baltic states of Lithuania, Estonia, and Latvia, his intention being to shift the Soviet frontier westward and create a buffer

Left: *A German Panzer IV rolls forward into the attack.*

Top Right: *A Soviet playing-card shows an idealized cavalryman triumphing over a battered Hitler.*

Bottom Right: *The German advance slowed to a halt as "General Winter" came to the Russians' aid.*

zone to shield himself against any possible future Nazi attack. He also tried to bully Finland into conceding a swathe of its territory so that he could create a protective salient around Leningrad (now St. Petersburg), but the Finns refused point-blank. In late November, Stalin ordered the Red Army to attack, expecting a swift and easy victory. The so-called "winter war" that followed was a disaster. It dragged on for months and cost the Russians thousands of their best troops. Though the Finns were finally overwhelmed by sheer weight of numbers, the apparent inadequacy of Soviet military leadership was exposed for the world to see.

THE PACT'S IMPACT

Relationships with the Western powers took a dramatic turn for the worse following the pact's conclusion. In France, the government ordered the dissolution of the French Communist Party on September 27; 35 Communist Party deputies were thrown into prison and Maurice Thorez, the party's lead who had deserted from the army to escape arrest and fled to neutral Belgium, was deprived of his citizenship. From his exile, Thorez, in accordance with Stalin's dictates, defiantly proclaimed his party's new policy — all-out resistance to the continuance of the "imperialist war."

Undercover Communist agitators stirred up dissent in the French Army at the front, while saboteurs set to work to undermine armaments manufacture at home. The sorely needed Renault B1 heavy tank was a favorite target. A report itemized the damage saboteurs inflicted on its production: "nuts, bolts, various bits of old iron put in the gearboxes and transmissions ... filings and emery-dust in the crank-cases, saw-stroked producing incipient ruptures of the oil and petrol ducts, intended to make them fall to pieces after several hours' running."

More positive action directly against the Soviet Union was also mooted. At the highest levels of

government in both Britain and
France, it was agreed to allow
military supplies to be shipped
to Finland. Only that country's
eventual surrender prevented
the dispatch of an actual Allied
expeditionary force to aid the
Finns. The Allies also planned to
bomb Baku, Batum, and Grozny in
an attempt to halt the shipment
of Soviet oil to the Third Reich.
Luckily, Operation Pike, as it was
code named, was stillborn.

Hitler, in contrast, was getting
on well with his new ally. As
early as the end of September
1939, Stalin had pledged to
Ribbentrop that the Soviet Union
would not stand by and see
Germany defeated. Though the
Russian dictator later denied ever
making such a promise, recently
declassified Russian archives reveal
exactly what he said. "If, against
all expectation, Germany finds
itself in a difficult situation," Stalin
declared, "then she can be sure
that the Soviet people will come
to Germany's aid and will not
allow Germany to be strangled.
The Soviet Union wants to see a
strong Germany and we will not
allow Germany to be thrown to
the ground."

Whether Stalin meant what
he had said is open to question.
Certainly at the time Hitler seems

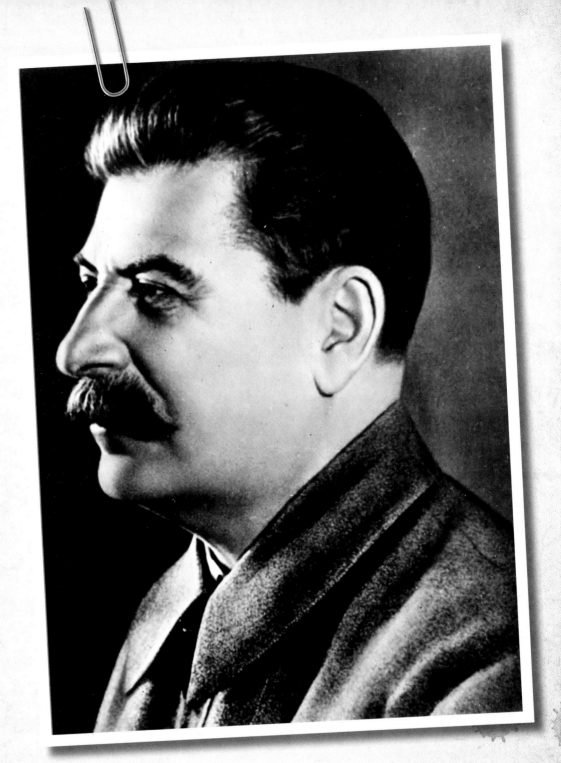

Above: *Stalin believed that Hitler would not be foolish enough to attack Russia before defeating Britain.*

to have believed him. On October 1 Propaganda Minister Joseph Goebbels wrote in his diary: "Conference with the Führer in private. He is convinced of Russia's loyalty."

THE TURNING-POINT

Events soon pressured Stalin into playing a dangerous double-game. The triumphant Blitzkrieg Hitler launched against France in May 1940 was the catalyst. Although he congratulated the Führer publicly on the Wehrmacht's "splendid success," Stalin was completely taken aback by the rapidity and the scale of the Nazi victory. What he had been counting on was a long, mutually destructive war, which would leave both sides so weakened that, regardless of which of them won it, they would not be in a position to threaten the Soviet Union. The young Nikita Khrushchev, then one of Stalin's closest acolytes, recalled his master "racing around, cursing like a cab driver. He cursed the French. He cursed the English. How could they allow Hitler to defeat them, to crush them?"

Though Stalin, believing Britain to be beaten, rejected British attempts at a rapprochement, Hitler now became convinced that he could not trust the Russians

after all. He was infuriated by the Soviet decision to unilaterally annex the Romanian province of Bukovina, a region that had not been assigned to Russia by the terms of the Non-Aggression Pact. Britain's stubborn refusal to consider entering peace negotiations convinced the ever-suspicious Führer that Churchill and Stalin were up to something behind his back. On July 31 he told his generals that he had decided to attack the Soviet Union if the British continued to refuse to come to terms with him. "Russia is the factor on which Britain is relying the most," he concluded. "Something must have happened in London. The British were completely down, but now they have perked up again. With Russia smashed, Britain's last hope would be shattered. The sooner Russia is crushed the better. If we start in May 1941, we would have five months to finish the job."

APPEASING THE FÜHRER

Stalin, for his part, knew that he had to avoid war for as long as he could. As the "winter war" against the Finns had demonstrated, the Red Army was in no fit state to face the Wehrmacht. Early that December, after Molotov had paid an inconclusive visit to Berlin, the

Soviet dictator told his generals: "We know that Hitler is intoxicated with his victories and believed that the Red Army will need at least four years to prepare for war. Obviously, four years would be more than enough for us. But we must be ready much earlier. We will try to delay the war for another two years."

To buy the time his country needed, Stalin decided to appease the Führer. On January 10, 1941, the Soviet Union ratified a new trade agreement with Germany that doubled the amount of grain being shipped from the Ukraine to the Third Reich. More trade concessions followed. The Soviet Union was now supplying nearly three-quarters of the phosphates Germany needed, more than two-thirds of its imported asbestos, a little less of its imported nickel, and, even more crucially, more than a third of its imported crude oil. Nothing, however, could deter Hitler from preparing to attack. "The Russians are inferior," he assured Field Marshal Walter von Brauchitsch and General Franz Halder, the commander-in-chief of the army and the chief of the army general staff. "Their army is leaderless." Crushing the Soviet Union, he continued, would be "child's play"

Above: *Junkers JU 87 Stuka dive bombers fly into the attack. The Luftwaffe caught most of the Soviet air force in western Russia on the ground and destroyed it.*

Opposite: *This Soviet propaganda poster carries the blunt message "Death to the German occupiers."*

compared to what it had taken to invade and defeat France.

As the winter snows in Poland melted and the ground started to thaw, a massive buildup of men and equipment began in the east. Eventually, more than three million German soldiers with another half a million troops from Romania, Finland, and other allied countries, would be poised to strike at the Soviet Union along a front stretching more than a thousand miles from the Finnish border and the Baltic to the Black Sea hinterland far to the south. They would be equipped with 3,600 tanks, 600,000 motor vehicles, and 700,000 artillery pieces. More than half the Luftwaffe would provide air support.

Many in the Soviet high command were worried that such a buildup signaled a German attack was imminent, but Stalin dismissed all such fears. Although he told a group of graduates from the Red Army Academy that "war with Germany is inevitable," he was convinced that Hitler was simply playing hard-ball with him to try to secure even more economic concessions. He failed to grasp that the Führer, rather than waiting until he had defeated or secured peace with Britain, had decided to strike in the east first. "We must be under no illusions," Stalin warned the members of

Above: *Soviet T-34 tanks pour off the production lines. Their debut took the Germans by surprise; antitank shells simply bounced off their thick frontal armor.*

the Politburo, "Fascist Germany is clearly preparing for an attack on the Soviet Union." Then he uttered a fatal caveat. "Why should Hitler want to make an agreement with England," he asked? "Because," he continued, "he wants to avoid a war on two fronts."

Even when General Georgi Zhukov, his newly appointed Chief of Staff, and General Semyon Timoshenko urged that "considering the complicated military-political situation, it was

necessary to take urgent measures in time to remedy shortcomings in the Western Front," Stalin refused to listen. Instead he warned the worried generals against the implementation of "wild unrealistic plans for which Russia lacks the means." His information, he told them, was that the German troops massing in Poland were there simply for training exercises.

CHURCHILL'S WARNING

If Stalin ignored the advice of his own senior generals, he was hardly likely to respond to a warning from Churchill. Nevertheless, despite all the rebuffs Britain had

received from Moscow so far, Churchill decided to try again. In April 1941, he wrote to the Soviet leader to tell him that "a trusted agent" — in fact, the source was decoded Enigma messages — had forewarned the British about an imminent German attack on the Soviet Union.

Stalin dismissed the approach out of hand. Then, the following month, news of Rudolf Hess's self-appointed peace mission to Britain reached Moscow. According to Sergio Beria, the son of Stalin's feared intelligence chief, Kim Philby, the Soviet spy at the heart of the British Secret

Intelligence Service, was passing the latest information through to his Russian controllers even before Churchill received it himself. On its receipt, Stalin jumped to a conclusion that was to have disastrous consequences.

Stalin had suspected Churchill's motives from the start. Now it all seemed crystal-clear. Churchill's message and the intelligence reports he was receiving were all part of a sinister conspiracy, designed to trick him into launching a preemptive attack on the Third Reich. He told the Central Party Committee: "On the one hand, Churchill sends us a personal message in which he warns us about Hitler's aggressive intentions. On the other hand, the British meet with Hess, who is undoubtedly Hitler's confidant, and conduct negotiations with Germany through him."

According to Stalin, there was only one possible conclusion. "Apparently, when Churchill sent us his personal warning, he believed that we would 'activate' our military mechanism. Then Hitler would have a direct and fair reason to launch a preemptive crusade against the Soviet Union." Stalin continued: "We must not supply Hitler with reasons to attack us ... Let's not complicate our relations with him."

COUNTDOWN TO WAR

For the next weeks, Stalin stubbornly stuck to this conclusion, dismissing warning after warning of imminent German attack. He ordered that nothing should be done that would provoke a Nazi response. "We must carefully fulfill our obligations under the Soviet-German treaty," he reiterated repeatedly, "so that Germany will be unable to find any violations of the treaty on our part." Colonel Hans Krebs, the German Military Attaché in Moscow, reported to Hitler that "Russia will do anything to avoid war."

On June 12, Stalin told his generals: "I am certain that Hitler will not create a second front by attacking the Soviet Union. Hitler is not such an idiot." Two days later, Tass, the official Soviet news agency, issued a statement hot from the Kremlin. "In the opinion of Soviet circles," it began, "rumors of Germany's intention to break the pact and open an attack on the U.SSR. are devoid of all foundations. The U.SSR., consistent with its policy of peace, has observed and intends to observe the provisions of the Soviet-German Non-Aggression Pact and therefore rumors that the U.SSR. is preparing for war with Germany are lies and provocations."

Angrily, Stalin now turned on his generals, who were urging him to authorize at least partial mobilization. "Have you come to scare us with war, or do you want a war because you're not sufficiently decorated or your rank isn't high enough?" he bellowed at Zhukov and the other members of the Soviet General Staff. "You have to realize that Germany will never fight Russia on her own. You must understand this." He stormed out of the meeting, only to return a minute or so later. "If you're going to provoke the Germans on the frontier by moving troops there without our permission, then heads will roll," he said.

On the evening of June 21, Stalin left the Kremlin to spend the weekend at his country *dacha*, west of the capital. After a grueling Politburo meeting, he retired to bed and within minutes he was asleep. Just two hours later, at 3:30 a.m., the telephone rang insistently. "Who's calling?" the NKVD security officer on duty asked. "Zhukov, Chief of Staff," was the reply. "Please connect me to Comrade Stalin. It's urgent." On the same date that Napoleon had invaded Russia, Hitler had followed in his footsteps. What the Russian eventually christened the "Great Patriotic War" had begun.

Pacific Mysteries

When U.S. Lightning P-38 fighters shot down the airplane carrying Admiral Isoruku Yamamoto, supreme commander of the Japanese fleet, on April 18, 1943, they killed the man who had made history as the architect of Japan's surprise air strike on the U.S. Pacific Fleet at Pearl Harbor. But was the planning of the attack all his own work, or did he utilize ideas put forward by unsung American and British naval experts years before the outbreak of war?

Yamamoto was a military genius. He was also less insular and far more open-minded than the bulk of the Japanese officer class. In 1919 he went to the U.S. to study at Harvard University; seven years later, he returned to the U.S. for a two-year stint as the Japanese naval attaché in Washington. Consequently, he spoke and read English fluently. During that time, he naturally took advantage of the chance to study books and papers on naval strategy written by Western experts.

One such paper was an extraordinary document entitled *Sea-Power in the Pacific*, written by Hector Bywater, a British author who specialized in naval affairs. A crucial part of it dealt with the pattern a future war in the Pacific might follow. It was first published in London in 1925 and subsequently appeared in translation in several languages, including Japanese. Shortly after its first appearance, Bywater expanded the paper — or at least

the part of it dealing directly with a future Pacific war between the U.S. and Japan — into a full-length novel, which he titled *The Great Pacific War*. Both texts rapidly became recommended reading in the naval staff colleges of all the major powers.

Bywater had a fascinating career. Welsh by birth, he moved as a teenager with his family to the U.S. from Britain in 1901. After becoming a newspaper reporter, he was appointed a correspondent by the *New York Herald*, which sent him back to Europe after he had made a name for himself through his coverage of the Russo-Japanese War. There, he combined journalism with spying for the British Admiralty, reporting on the progress of the German naval building program. He returned to the U.S. in 1915, where he helped to thwart German sabotage efforts on the New York waterfront.

It was after the Washington Naval Conference of 1921 — where he scooped the world by revealing the eventual terms agreed on by the great powers before they were officially released — that Bywater started writing about the possibility of a naval war in the Pacific between Japan and the U.S. *Sea-Power in the Pacific*

and *The Great Pacific War* followed. Bywater became something of a celebrity as a result, though his fame was relatively short-lived. During that time, it is possible he even met Yamamoto himself.

PREDICTING THE FUTURE

Later events proved many of Bywater's prophesies to be extraordinarily accurate — though he did not predict that his Pacific war would begin with a surprise Japanese assault on Pearl Harbor. Instead, his war started with a major battle between the Japanese and American fleets off the Philippines. However, he did predict that carrier-born aircraft would play a major part in such a battle. This, in itself, was not that extraordinary, because by the mid-1920s, the British, American, and Japanese navies all possessed embryonic carrier forces. An effective demonstration of what aircraft could do to warships had already been conducted in summer 1921, when a combined force of U.S. Navy and Army Air Service bombers attacked several German naval vessels that had been handed over to the U.S. after the end of World War I. They included the battleship *Ostfriesland*.

The sinking of the *Ostfriesland* was the climax of a series of bombing tests carried out by the aircraft commanded by Lieutenant-General William "Billy" Mitchell, the most prominent — and controversial — advocate of air power in the U.S. during the 1920s. He led the operation personally in his De Havilland DH-4. As well as the *Ostfriesland*, the bombers attacked a German U-boat, the old U.S. battleship *Iowa*, which had been converted into a radio-controlled fleet target ship, a destroyer, and a light cruiser. It was the *Ostfriesland*, however, that was the icing on the cake. The tests proved, Mitchell reported, "that seacraft of all kinds, up to and including the most modern battleships, can be destroyed easily by bombs dropped from aircraft and further that the most effective means of destruction are bombs."

Whether Bywater was aware of Mitchell's experiment is unclear. What was really remarkable was the accuracy of his account of subsequent Japanese attacks on Guam and the Philippines. Guam, he wrote, would be subjected to an intensive aerial and naval bombardment, after which Japanese forces would land in a pincer movement on the east and west sides of the island. American forces would be unable to counter the attack and would soon be compelled to surrender.

This was almost exactly what happened when the Japanese struck in the Pacific in December 1941. The similarity between Bywater's account of their invasion of the Philippines and what actually happened is also astonishing. He predicted that the assault would begin with massive air attacks mounted by aircraft launched from a carrier task force cruising to the west of the islands, which it did. This would be followed by a three-pronged invasion, with Japanese forces landing at Lingayen Gulf and Lamon Bay on Luzon and at Sindangan Bay on Mindanao.

The Luzon landings took place exactly as Bywater had predicted, the Japanese advancing inland to attack Manila from two sides. Only the Sindangan Bay prediction was wide of the mark; instead of landing there, on the western side of Mindanao, the Japanese went ashore at Davao Gulf at the southeastern tip of the island.

This was by no means all that Bywater predicted. He foresaw how the Americans would eventually reconquer the Pacific with the aid of powerful naval forces moving relentlessly toward the Japanese Home Islands in a series of carefully planned island-hopping operations. He also envisaged how the Japanese, faced with defeat, would throw every single available resource into the battle — including suicide planes.

The decisive naval engagement that would finally shatter Japan's dreams of Pacific victory, Bywater wrote, would take place where the war had begun — off the Philippines. Strangely, he failed to appreciate the role that air power would play in the battle. When it actually happened in late 1944, the opposing forces traded blows by means of their carrier air groups. The surface fleets seldom came within sight of one another.

LEARNING FROM TARANTO

All in all, it seems that the predictions made by Bywater and the strategy adopted by Yamamoto in the opening stages of his Pacific campaign are too closely parallel to be a coincidence. Bywater also predicted that torpedo bombers would be the main type of aircraft employed in naval warfare — and in this, too, he was absolutely correct.

If Yamamoto, who had been in favor of developing naval aviation for years previously,

Above: *Admiral Isoruku Yamamoto was the architect of the Pearl Harbor attack. Personally, he had been opposed to war with the U.S.*

Above: *A Japanese Mitsubishi "Betty" bomber, painted with green crosses as a sign of surrender, flies towards an Allied airfield in 1945. Yamamoto was shot down and killed when flying in such a plane; the Americans had found out his intended route by cracking the Japanese naval code.*

Opposite: *The former German battleship* Ostfriesland *being bombed from the air by General William "Billy" Mitchell's bombers in 1921. Mitchell was determined to prove that capital ships were vulnerable to aerial attack.*

needed any further confirmation of his theories, the British supplied it. In November 1940, a little over a year before the Japanese attack on Pearl Harbor, torpedo- and bomb-carrying Swordfish on the Royal Navy struck at the Italian fleet in harbor at Taranto. In a brilliantly executed night attack, the Swordfish crippled three of Italy's most modern battleships and two heavy cruisers. It took six months to make two of the battleships and one of the cruisers seaworthy; *Conte di Cavour* and the other cruiser had to be scrapped.

The attack was the brainchild of Admiral Sir Andrew Cunningham, the commander-in-chief of the Mediterranean Fleet. As the Italians refused to sail out to meet him and fight a surface action, he decided that his best course of action was to launch an aerial attack. The plan was a bold one. The Swordfish torpedo-bombers Cunningham was relying on to carry out the attack were ungainly, slow and cumbersome — a sitting target for modern fighters and easy prey for efficiently operated antiaircraft guns. Cunningham could muster a maximum of 21 Swordfish to make the attack.

On November 11, *Illustrious*, Cunningham's sole carrier — *Eagle* had been damaged in action and was undergoing repairs — launched two waves of Swordfish, flying about an hour apart. Two planes in each wave flew high and dropped flares to distract the Italian defenses. The others skimmed almost at sea level across the harbor to launch their torpedoes at the anchored Italian ships. *Conte di Cavour* was hit toward her bow and her forecastle erupted in flames. She sank at her moorings. *Littorio* was torpedoed twice. The second wave hit the *Caio Duilio* and damaged *Littorio* again. The attack cost Cunningham two Swordfish. More than half the Italian battlefleet was put out of action.

DISPUTES IN TOKYO

The lessons of Taranto were not lost on Yamamoto. As far as he was concerned, Cunningham's triumph finally settled the argument as to whether or not capital ships were vulnerable to aerial attack. Nor were the ones he derived from the widely publicized U.S. naval maneuvers held off Hawaii in 1932, when the Americans themselves demonstrated how it would be possible for a carrier force to approach Pearl Harbor undetected and launch a devastating surprise attack on the base at dawn.

Right: Arizona's *forward magazine explodes after the battleship was hit four times by Japanese bombers during the Pearl Harbor attack.*

Opposite: *Battleship Row before the Japanese attack. Of the seven U.S. battleships anchored there,* Arizona, California, Oklahoma *and* West Virginia *were sunk.* Nevada *was badly damaged.*

Yamamoto, too, probably looked back to 1927, when, as a young captain, he had taken part in war games held at the Japanese Naval War College, which included an examination of a possible Pearl Harbor carrier strike.

In December 1940, Yamamoto began preparatory planning for the attack. His hardest task, it seems, was to persuade the Japanese Naval General Staff that the operation was viable. Its chief concern was that such an attack was simply too risky to mount. It was not until the following August that it was agreed the war games scheduled to begin on September 11 should include an examination of the Pearl Harbor plan. On September 24, Yamamoto was told that it had been rejected. Even his fellow admirals in the Combined Fleet doubted its feasibility. All bar one of them also opposed the attack.

Yamamoto was not to be deterred. He told the doubting admirals bluntly that he was

the commander-in-chief and, for as long as he was in charge, planning for the attack would go ahead. Telling Koshiro Oikawa, who was Navy Minister from September 1940 to October 1941, that "we should do our very best to decide the fate of the war on the very first day," he gave him an ultimatum. Unless the plan to blitz Pearl Harbor was approved, he and the entire staff of the Combined Fleet would resign. The Naval General Staff gave in. Leading figures within it from Admiral Nagano Osami, the Chief of Staff, downward had already reached the conclusion that war with the U.S. was rapidly becoming inevitable. Yamamoto was officially authorized to go ahead with his preparations.

WHAT REALLY TOOK PLACE?

The carrier task force sailed from Japanese home waters on November 26. Yamamoto had put Vice-Admiral Chuichi Nagumo in command. It consisted of Japan's six crack fleet carriers, escorted by two battleships, two heavy cruisers, a light cruiser, nine destroyers, and three forward reconnaissance submarines. Seven oil tankers accompanied the task force, since mid-ocean refueling would be necessary to give the task force the range to sail to Hawaii and back again.

Each carrier could deploy around 70 aircraft — a mix of Nakajima high-level and torpedo bombers, Aichi dive bombers, and Mitsubishi Zero fighters. Deliberately choosing to take the longer northern route to Hawaii to lessen the possibility of being spotted by U.S. reconnaissance patrols, the blacked-out fleet maintained strict radio silence as it plowed its way across the stormy ocean. It was only when it reached its launch position approximately 200 miles (320 km) north of Hawaii that it received a terse signal from Tokyo. It read simply "Climb Mount Fujiyama." It was the signal to launch the attack.

The first wave of Japanese aircraft started to take off from their carriers at around 6:00 a.m. on December 7. The second wave followed 70 minutes later. Flying time to their target was approximately 1 hour, 50 minutes, the pilots tuning into Honolulu radio to get a fix on their positions. The first attack began at precisely 7:49 a.m. Four minutes later, as the bombs and torpedoes started to rain down, Lieutenant-Commander

Mitsuo Fuchida, the attack's commander, signaled Tora, Tora, Tora (Tiger, Tiger, Tiger) to the waiting carriers. It was confirmation that complete tactical surprise had been achieved.

By 10:00 a.m., all the Japanese planes had completed their mission. Fuchida's was the last aircraft to leave the scene. He had remained on station to observe both waves' attacks and assess the extent of the damage

they caused. It was certainly impressive. Of the eight great capital ships lying peacefully at anchor in Battleship Row when the Japanese struck, *Arizona*, *California*, and *West Virginia* were sunk. *Oklahoma* capsized. *Maryland*, *Nevada*, *Tennessee*, and *Pennsylvania* were heavily damaged, as were three cruisers and three destroyers. Some ships had to be totally rebuilt before they could put to sea again. The Japanese hammered the U.S. air bases as well. Ninety-two Navy planes and 71 Army Air Corps aircraft were destroyed on the ground and 31 and 128 damaged.

ABANDONING THE PLAN

So far, everything had gone according to Yamamoto's plan — indeed, the attack had succeeded beyond his wildest expectations. Now, however, things started to go wrong. Fuchida and Commander Minoru Genda, the man who had been responsible for the detailed planning of the aerial assault, urged Nagumo to launch a third strike just as Yamamoto had originally intended. The cautious Nagumo, supported by Rear-Admiral Ruyunosuke Kusaka, his Chief of Staff who had been opposed to the operation in the first place, decided against proceeding with it.

Above: *U.S. troops island-hopped across the Pacific as part of the master plan to take the war to Japan.*

Genda pleaded with the two admirals in vain. He pointed out that, despite the Japanese success, major targets — most notably the harbor's vast oil bunkers — remained intact. At least, he argued, the Japanese carriers should hold their position until the U.S. Pacific Fleet's two aircraft carriers, which had been at sea delivering fighter reinforcements to Wake Island and now were heading back toward Pearl Harbor, had been located and attacked. However, Nagumo would not change his mind. He had no idea where the American carriers were and feared they might locate him and strike first. He ordered the task force to turn for home.

ADVANCED KNOWLEDGE

By deciding to rest on his laurels rather than hunt the U.S. carriers down, Nagumo committed a major strategic blunder. Its consequences, though, were not immediately apparent. As their Pacific offensive proceeded southward, going from strength to strength, what became clear was that the Japanese possessed an almost uncanny knowledge of the whereabouts of American naval forces and air bases.

How the Japanese had obtained this information remained a mystery until after the war. It was then discovered that a special naval air force unit, initially based on Formosa, had been making clandestine reconnaissance flights over U.S. bases ever since April 1941. Among the places its planes photographed were Legaspi, on the southeast tip of Luzon in the Philippines, Jolo Island, Mindanao, Rabaul, and Guam. Then, after one of their aircraft had been detected by the Americans — though they had no idea it was a reconnaissance flight — the Japanese brought the missions to an end. They had all the aerial intelligence they needed to proceed with planning their actual attack.

Above: *A Japanese propaganda poster celebrates the Pearl Harbor Attack. Note the flags of Japan's two Axis allies in the background next to the billowing Rising Sun.*

The "Battle" of Los Angeles

Just over two months after Pearl Harbor, Los Angeles and much of southern California was thrown into a state of panic. At precisely 2:00 a.m. on the morning of February 25, 1942, the city's air-raid sirens began to wail, searchlights flickered across the sky and the antiaircraft batteries of the 37th Coastal Artillery Brigade opened fire. Thousands of citizens took to the streets, believing that their city faced a surprise Japanese air attack.

It was early in the morning of February 25 when diners at the fashionable Trocadero Club in Hollywood were startled and shocked into silence. Suddenly, the lights winked out and air-raid sirens started to wail throughout greater Los Angeles. As searchlights scanned the skies, the antiaircraft guns protecting the city's vital aircraft factories and shipyards went into action. Was Los Angeles coming under enemy air attack? Or had the Japanese landed on California's long stretches of hospitable beaches?

Author Ralph Blum, who was 9 years old at the time, had no doubts. "I thought the Japanese were bombing Beverley Hills," he later recollected. "There were sirens, searchlights, and antiaircraft guns blazing away into the skies over Los Angeles. My father had been a balloon observation man in World War I and he knew big guns when he heard them. He ordered my mother to take my baby sisters to the underground projection room — our house was heavily supplied with Hollywood paraphernalia — while he and I went out onto the upstairs balcony." Blum and his father both looked upward in amazement as subsequent events unfolded. "What a scene!" he wrote. "It was after three in the morning. Searchlights probed the western sky. Tracers streamed upward. The racket was terrific."

Peter Jenkins, a staff editor on the *Los Angeles Herald-Examiner*, was another eyewitness, as was Long Beach Police Chief J.H. McClelland. "I could clearly see the V formation of about 25 silvery planes overhead moving slowly across the sky toward Long Beach," Jenkins reported. McClelland "watched what was described as the second wave of planes from atop the seven-storey Long Beach City Hall. I did not see any planes, but the younger men with me said that they could. An experienced Navy observer with powerful Carl Zeiss binoculars said he counted nine planes in the cone of the searchlights. He said they were sliver in color."

McClelland continued: "The group passed along from one battery of searchlights to another and, under the fire of the antiaircraft guns, flew from the direction of Redona Beach and Inglewood on the land side of Fort MacArthur and continued toward Santa Ana and Huntingdon Beach. The antiaircraft fire was so heavy," he concluded, "we could not hear the motors of the planes." According to the *Glendale News Press*, some observers claimed to have counted as many as 200 planes over the area.

THE MORNING AFTER

The "battle" lasted for little more than 20 minutes. At 2:21 a.m., Lieutenant-General John L. DeWitt ordered his antiaircraft gunners to stop firing. As soon as dawn broke, hundreds and thousands of inquisitive Californians took to the streets to see if anything untoward had occurred. "When daylight and the all-clear signal came," the *Glendale News Press* reported, "Long Beach took on the appearance of a huge Easter-egg hunt. Kiddies and even grown-ups scrambled through the streets and vacant lots, picking up and proudly comparing chunks of shrapnel fragments as if they were the most prized items they owned."

Californian commuters, for their part, were confronted by giant traffic snarl-ups caused as a result of the blackout. Thousands of them were an hour or more late for work. Most of them were

Left: *A storm of antiaircraft fire lights up the sky above Los Angeles, when, early in the morning on February 25 1942, the city was believed to be threatened by a Japanese bombing attack.*

unconcerned. It had all been "a great show" and "well worth losing a few hours' sleep."

There were a handful of casualties. A State Guardsman died of an apparent heart attack while driving an ammunition truck, as did an air-raid warden. A woman was killed when a car and a truck collided in Arcadia and a Long Beach police sergeant died in a traffic crash on his way to an air-raid post. There were other incidents as well. Three Japanese-Americans — two men and a woman — were arrested in Venice on suspicion of signaling out to sea with a flashlight near the beach's pier. John Y. Harado, a 25-year-old Japanese-American vegetable man, was detained and charged with violating the blackout. Apparently, Harada was stopped while driving a load of cauliflowers to market and arrested when he refused to dim the lights of his truck.

OFFSHORE BOMBARDMENT

Almost immediately after the all-clear sounded, the controversy started about whether Los Angeles had been the victim of a Japanese aerial attack, or, indeed, whether there had been any aircraft anywhere near the city at the time at all. Speaking from the calm of Washington D.C., Frank Knox, the Secretary of the Navy, was quick to pooh-pooh the entire affair. "There were no planes over Los Angeles last night," he asserted confidently at a press conference. "None have been found and a very wide reconnaissance has been carried on." He stated categorically: "It was just a false alarm."

"Reports of enemy air activity in the Pacific coastal region," Knox concluded, "might be due largely to 'jittery nerves.'" The *Los Angeles Times* was quick to respond. It noted that the army's Western Defence Command was still insisting that the sudden blackout and antiaircraft action definitely followed the sighting of unidentified aircraft over the city, although it was admitted that no bombs had been dropped and no bombers shot down. The newspaper asked rhetorically: "Whose nerves, Mr. Knox? The public's or the army's?"

It was not surprising that tension on the west coast was running high. On February 23, two days before the alleged air raid on Los Angeles took place, the Japanese submarine I-17, captained by Commander Nishimo Kozu, surfaced half an hour after sunset about a half a

Above: *A Japanese I-class submarine noses its way out to sea. It was a submarine of this class that briefly bombarded the Ellwood oil fields on the Californian coast north of Santa Barbara.*

Opposite: *A Los Angeles searchlight battery combs the skies in a fruitless search for Japanese bombers. Why so many people believed that the city was under attack is a complete mystery.*

mile offshore near the town of Goleta, 12 miles (19 km) north of Santa Barbara. Five minutes after surfacing, its deck gun began firing at the Ellwood oil fields, close to the town. The submarine's gun crew fired between 16 and 26 shells in total before discontinuing their bombardment. Kozu then submerged and made for the open sea.

Three shells hit the Bankline oil refinery, which was the apparent target of the attack. An oil well around half a mile inland, together with rigging and pumping components, was also reported as being hit, though the oil storage tanks next to and close

by the well escaped unscathed. Two more shells dropped onto two nearby ranches. One exploded, but the second did not. It simply dug a 5-foot (1.5 m) deep crater in the ground. The other shells fell short and dropped harmlessly into the Pacific.

SUBMARINES AND SEAPLANES

It was the first time the American mainland had been directly attacked by enemy armed forces since the War of 1812. That June and September, the Japanese struck again.

On June 21, the Japanese long-range submarine I-25, having cleverly dodged an American

Above: *Secretary of the Navy Frank Knox dismissed the entire Japanese air attack on Los Angeles as nothing more than a false alarm.*

Right: *A submarine-borne Yokosuka E14Y seaplane became the only Japanese aircraft to comb the U.S. mainland successfully. It dropped several incendiary bombs on an Oregon forest in September 1942.*

minefield by following in the tracks of a fleet of fishing boats near the mouth of the Columbia River in Oregon, surfaced to fire a total of 17 shells at Battery Russell, part of Fort Stevens, from around 10 miles (6 km) offshore. The shells did little or no damage — the only thing hit was the backstop of the fort's baseball diamond, while some power and telephone lines were slightly damaged by shell fragments. Perhaps, it was not that surprising that the attack was unsuccessful. Commander Mejii Tagami, the I-25's captain, later recalled that "in shooting at the land, I did not use any gun-sight at all — I just shot." Tagami thought he was shelling a U.S. submarine base; the battery's gunners were ordered not to try to return the I-25's fire since this would give away their position.

I-25 returned to the attack just under three months later. On September 9 it catapulted the tiny fold-up Mitsubishi seaplane with which it was equipped into the air off Oregon's coast. Nobuo Fujita, the plane's pilot, was under orders to drop his bomb-load

— this consisted of a couple of incendiary bombs — on the thick forests and woods around Mount Emily. The idea was to trigger a massive forest fire.

It was a dank, foggy day and Fujita's plane went undetected. Fortunately, the fog lifted and the smoke from the fire was spotted by a Forest Ranger before it could take hold. Once it had been extinguished, the fire-fighting party found a crater in its center. They also recovered fragments of metal casings and thermite pellets scattered around the scene. The casings had Japanese markings on them. The next day, Fujita tried again, but with the same lack of success.

PROJECT FU-GO

Like their German allies, Japan's leaders prepared to produce new reprisal weapons as the tide of war turned inexorably against them.

Unlike the German V1 and V2, the weapon they hit on was not technologically advanced or costly. Instead, the Japanese developed a weapon that was relatively inexpensive and simple to build.

Project Fu-Go, as it was named, was the brainchild of Major-General Sueyoshi Kusaha, head of the Japanese 9th Army's Number Nine Research Laboratory. The plan was to launch thousands of unmanned fire balloons against the American mainland, taking advantage of the high-altitude jet stream to carry them across the Pacific, over the Californian coast, and deep into the American heartlands. They were capable of carrying two incendiaries and one high-explosive bomb.

The balloons were assembled by hand before being partially inflated with hydrogen, usually by schoolgirls working after their classes. Some 33 feet (10 m) in

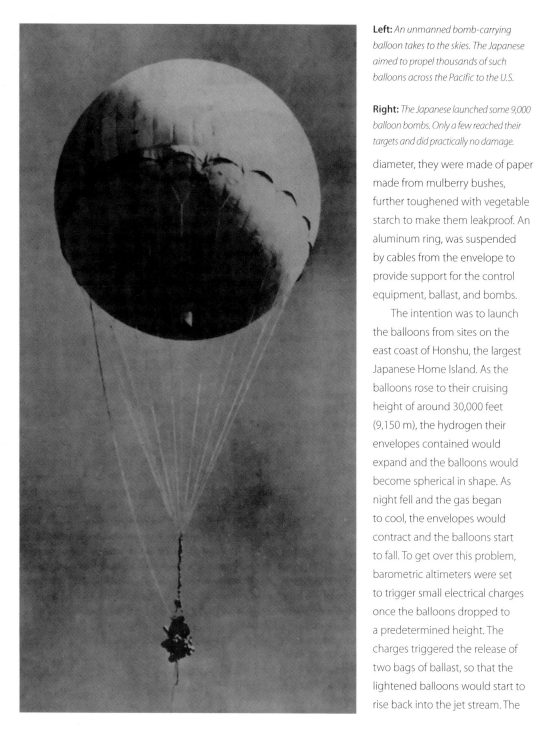

Left: *An unmanned bomb-carrying balloon takes to the skies. The Japanese aimed to propel thousands of such balloons across the Pacific to the U.S.*

Right: *The Japanese launched some 9,000 balloon bombs. Only a few reached their targets and did practically no damage.*

diameter, they were made of paper made from mulberry bushes, further toughened with vegetable starch to make them leakproof. An aluminum ring, was suspended by cables from the envelope to provide support for the control equipment, ballast, and bombs.

The intention was to launch the balloons from sites on the east coast of Honshu, the largest Japanese Home Island. As the balloons rose to their cruising height of around 30,000 feet (9,150 m), the hydrogen their envelopes contained would expand and the balloons would become spherical in shape. As night fell and the gas began to cool, the envelopes would contract and the balloons start to fall. To get over this problem, barometric altimeters were set to trigger small electrical charges once the balloons dropped to a predetermined height. The charges triggered the release of two bags of ballast, so that the lightened balloons would start to rise back into the jet stream. The

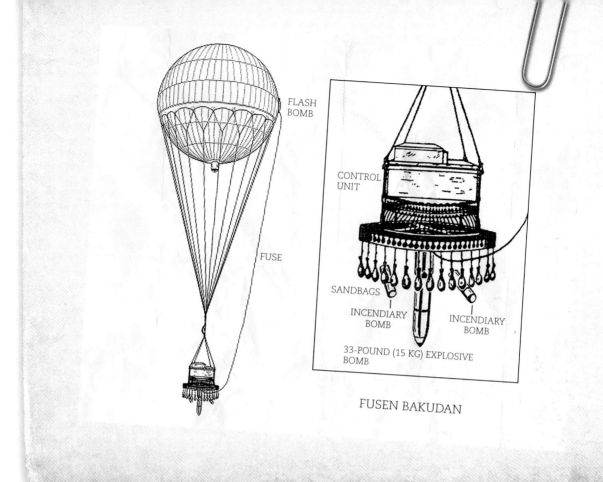

FLASH
BOMB

FUSE

CONTROL
UNIT

SANDBAGS

INCENDIARY
BOMB

INCENDIARY
BOMB

33-POUND (15 KG) EXPLOSIVE
BOMB

FUSEN BAKUDAN

cycle was repeated throughout the balloons' long journey. If they shot up to an excessive altitude, the altimeters released a spring-loaded valve to vent a puff of hydrogen.

The Japanese estimated that it would take their balloons approximately three days to drift across the Pacific and reach their target areas. If all went according to plan, blow-out plugs would fire and the balloon's bombs would be over enemy territory. Flash bombs attached to the balloons would then incinerate them, so adding to the mystery of where the incendiaries had come from and how they got to their destinations in the first place.

FU-GO IS ACTIVATED

The first balloons took to the skies on November 3, 1944, the Japanese Emperor's birthday. By the end of the month, 700 had been launched with another 1,200 following in December. In January 1945, the figure went up to 2,000 and then to 2,500 in February and March. In early April, however, the total dropped to just 400. Later that month, the campaign was abandoned. The Japanese were disappointed by the small amount of damage their balloons had done. They never managed to start the giant conflagrations that had been confidently expected. The hydrogen the balloons needed in order to fly was running short as well, thanks to the great

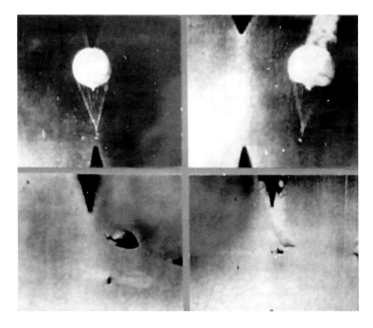

U.S. fire-bombing campaign General Curtis LeMay had launched against Japan's most important industrial centers.

Quite a few of the balloons came down over the Pacific and never got near their intended targets. U.S. records, however, indicate that some got as far as Alaska in the north, California's border with Mexico in the south, and as far east as the Great Lakes. The authorities hushed the attacks up as much as possible. Their greatest fear was the type of weapon the balloons might be carrying. In the second week of December 1944, after fragments of balloons had been found near the towns of Thermopolis in Wyoming and Kalispell in Montana, Colonel Murray Sanders, a top bacteriologist from Fort Patrick in Maryland, was hastily called into consultation.

Sanders' task was to examine the accumulated debris the Americans had amassed — more was found in Alaska and Saskatchewan — for any evidence that the Japanese were employing biological warfare. "The balloons were brought in," he later recalled, "and we all stood around them in a circle. We examined them and then we went away to make our individual reports. Mine scared them (the authorities) stiff. I told them that, if we found Japanese B-encephalitis on any of the balloons, we were in real trouble. Our population had no defense against B-encephalitis ... four out of five people who contracted it would have died, in my view."

The bacteriologist perturbed the authorities even more with his next speculation. "Anthrax is a tough bug," he opined. "The Japanese had used it in China. They could have splattered the west and southwest of Canada and the U.S. with it. They could have contaminated the pastures and forests and killed all the cows, sheep, horses, pigs, and deer — plus a considerable number of human beings."

"The hysteria," Sanders concluded, "would have been terrible. One of the strengths of biological warfare as a weapon is that you can't see it, but it kills."

OPERATION STORM

In fact, the Japanese did not deploy biological weapons

against the U.S., though they certainly had the means to do so. It is likely that they feared the retaliation that would ensue. Fu-Go was a flop. So, too, was their plan to bomb New York and Washington D.C. with Aichi NGA1 seaplanes, launched from top-secret giant I-400 submarines. These underwater juggernauts were by far the largest submarines produced by either side during the war. Each carried three Aichis, folded up to fit into their 115-foot (35 m) watertight deck hangars. All three aircraft could be assembled, armed, and catapulted into the skies in 45 minutes. The submarines themselves could travel one-and-a-half times around the world without refueling.

The Japanese left it too late. Only three I-400s were ever completed and none of them saw action before the war ended with Japan's unconditional surrender. The plans to bomb New York and Washington had long been abandoned, as was a daring scheme to destroy the locks of the Panama Canal. This operation was canceled in June 1945, when the I-400s were diverted to attack the 15 U.S. aircraft carriers massed at Ulithi atoll, preparing to launch their planes against the Japanese Home Islands. Japan surrendered before the I-400s could attack. One of them was sunk on its way to its battle-station; U.S. submariners captured the other two.

Who Torched the *Normandie*?

The crack trans-Atlantic liner Normandie *was the pride of France until she was laid up in New York harbor at the start of World War II. Two years later, while being converted into a giant troopship for the U.S. government, she caught fire and capsized at her moorings. The great ship was a total loss. Had the mysterious fire that brought about her destruction started accidentally? Or had Nazi saboteurs been to blame?*

Above: Normandie *on fire alongside Pier 88 and starting to list to port. She eventually capsized.*

As 1941 drew toward a tumultuous close, *Normandie* was berthed at Pier 88 in the Hudson River, just a stone's throw from bustling 42nd Street. She had been mothballed there ever since shortly after the outbreak of war, when she had steamed into the harbor seeking sanctuary. The U.S. government interned her.

Much had happened since then. France had been knocked out of the war by Hitler's Wehrmacht. The RAF had won the Battle of Britain and the Blitz was in full swing. As far as the *Normandie* was concerned, her future was uncertain. It was costing the French Line berthing charges of $1,000 a day to keep her in port. Consequently, most of the seamen who sailed her had been paid off. Only a skeleton crew commanded by Captain Herve Lehude remained on board. In May 1941, they were joined by around 150 U.S. Coastguards, who had been ordered by the Treasury Department to secure the ship and Pier 88 to "insure *Normandie's* safety and guard against sabotage."

So matters stood on December 7 when the Japanese attack on Pear Harbor precipitated the U.S. into World War II. Four days later, Hitler announced to a cheering Reichstag that he "had

arranged to have the American charge d'affaires handed his passports." Ever since the 1920s, it had been the Führer's belief that at some point his country would have to fight the U.S. That moment had now arrived. Benito Mussolini, Italy's bombastic Duce and Germany's long-time ally, followed Hitler's example. The whole world was now at war.

FROM NORMANDIE TO LAFAYETTE

Tension between the U.S. and the Third Reich had been intensifying for months, even though the U.S. had been still officially neutral. New York City and New Jersey were honeycombed with nests of Nazi spies and sympathizers, many holding down laboring jobs along the Manhattan, New Jersey, and Brooklyn waterfronts. Some were more upmarket — Lily Stein, a model who claimed to be an Austrian refugee, ran a smart dress store in fashionable Manhattan. The store was a post-box for the German intelligence service, the Abwehr.

Waldemar Othmer was a typical Nazi agent. He had emigrated from Germany to the U.S. in 1919 and in 1935 took out naturalization papers. He married a New York girl and settled down

to raise a family. No one dreamt that this likeable, affable character was in reality a sleeper agent for the Abwehr. Even his membership of the German-American Bund did not arouse suspicion. He became the leader of its Trenton, New Jersey, branch while at the same time working in the Brooklyn Navy Yard. He moved from there to Camp Pendleton in Norfolk, Virginia. It was not until 1944 that his spying was finally detected.

In any event, the Abwehr and its commander, the wily Admiral Wilhelm Canaris, had long been keeping a beady eye on *Normandie*. Only a fortnight after the fall of France, Canaris had ordered his spy network in the U.S. to "observe" the ship. The German High Command's fear was that, if the Third Reich and the Americans went to war, the ship would be commandeered and converted into a giant troop transport to ferry U.S. forces to Europe. It was estimated that *Normandie* would be easily capable of carrying 10,000 or more U.S. soldiers in a single Atlantic crossing.

This was exactly what happened. On December 12, 1941, five days after Pearl Harbor and the day after Hitler had declared war on the U.S., the Coast Guard took over the entire ship. Lehude

and his skeleton crew were ushered ashore. *Normandie* was to be stripped of all her luxurious trappings to be converted into a troopship, just as the Nazis had feared. Even her name was changed. She was now to be rechristened *Lafayette*, in honor of the 18th-century French nobleman who had fought on the American side in the War of Independence against Britain.

MUDDLE AND CONFUSION

Because there was no dry dock in New York harbor big enough to accommodate *Normandie*, it was decided she should be converted to her new role at her mooring alongside Pier 88. Soon, hundreds of civilian contractors were swarming all over the great ship. They were up against a tight deadline. The U.S. Navy, who, after some debate with the U.S. Army as to which of them would eventually operate the ship, insisted that she should be ready to sail by February 14. Her initial port of call was to be Boston, where she would take on board her first cargo of troops for transportation across the Atlantic — probably to Northern Ireland, where the U.S. Army was planning to set up its first European bases and training camps.

The work ran late. When Captain Robert S. Coman, the vessel's designated commander, arrived in New York, it was clear that it would not be finished by January 31 as had originally been planned. Coman had another problem to worry about into the bargain. He had been assigned just 458 men as his crew — "less than half the number," he complained, "required for the efficient operation of the vessel at sea." He and Captain Clayton M. Simmers, the 3rd Naval District

Above: Normandie *at sea. The crack trans-Atlantic liner was one of the most luxurious vessels of her day.*

Right: *Admiral Wilhelm Canaris, head of the Abwehr, was in charge of German intelligence efforts in the U.S.*

Material Officer who had already advised the Bureau of Ships that the conversion could not be completed in time to meet the Navy's deadline, both urged Washington to postpone the sailing date. At first, the Navy Department agreed. Then it changed its mind. *Normandie*, it insisted, must sail on schedule.

On *Normandie*, gangs of workmen plowed on in a desperate race to beat the ominously ticking clock. The extra pressure caused by the Navy Department's refusal to countenance a further extension of the deadline it had imposed only served to deepen the chaos and confusion that already existed on board. Frank Knox, the Secretary of the Navy, later admitted: "The enormity of the expansion of ship construction and conversion resulted in the placing of an extremely heavy burden upon the shoulders of those engaged in readying ships for military service. As a result, corners had to be cut and responsibility delegated to personnel less experienced and capable than would be the case in normal times." Coman and Simmers continued to complain. On the afternoon of February 8 both men were summoned to a top-level meeting to decide once and for all when exactly *Normandie* would be fit to sail.

The meeting never took place. At 2:30 p.m., fire broke out on board *Normandie*. Charles T. Collins, a 19-year-old workman, recalled what happed. "I was working on a chain gang," he recorded. "We had chains around some pillars and eased them down when they were cut through. Two men were operating an acetylene torch. About 30 or 40 men were working in the room and there were bales and bales of mattresses. A spark hit one of the bales, and the fire began. We yelled for the fire watch and Leroy Rose, who was in our chain, and I tried to beat out the fire with our hands. Rose's clothes caught fire and I carried him out. The smoke and heat were terrific."

FROM BLAZE TO CONFLAGRATION

Collins was wrong in two particulars. It was a pile of kapok life jackets that had been stored temporarily in the main salon that the sparks — not a single spark — from the torch welder Clement Derrick was operating set ablaze. Though prompt action might have extinguished the fire quickly, this was singularly lacking. There was no fire watch on duty and no one could locate the fire alarms, which in any case were disconnected. Though someone managed to turn on a fire hose, it ran dry almost at once.

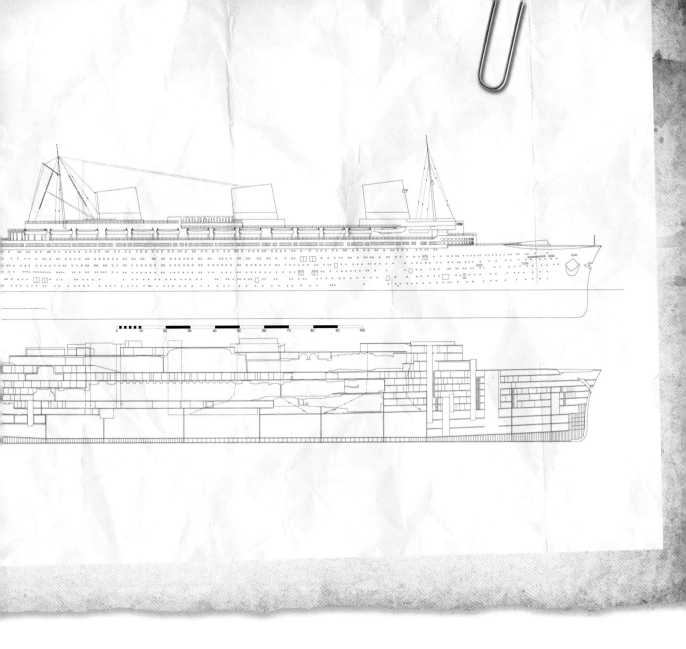

Vain attempts continued to beat the fire out, using coats, pieces of carpet, and anything else that came to hand. The efforts were in vain. The blaze, variously described as a "racing fire," a "surging fire on the surface of the bales," and a "grass fire," grew and spread inexorably, fanned by a strong northwesterly wind blowing over the ship's port quarter, which swept the fire forward. Eventually, it engulfed the three upper decks of the vessel.

Above: *The side elevation of Normandie. Had the New York Fire Department had access to such plans, it might have been able to save the ship.*

It took 12 minutes for the New York City Fire Brigade to be summoned and a further 15 for the first fire trucks to reach Pier 88. The firemen had to force their way through panicking crowds of workmen, Coast Guards, and navy sailors before they could get into action. Eventually thousands of gallons of water were being pumped over, onto, and into *Normandie* from the fire trucks on the pier and the fire boats clustered along the liner's port side — all part of the desperate effort to get the conflagration under control and save the stricken ship.

Dark black plumes of smoke spread across the Manhattan skyline as thousands of New Yorkers took to the streets to try to find out what was going on. Up to 30,000 of them massed in 12th Avenue to watch the spectacle. Hundreds more people gathered along the waterfront, while skyscraper windows all over Manhattan were thrown open as people attempted to catch a glimpse of the action.

Fiorello La Guardia, the Mayor of New York, was quickly on the scene. He had been in the middle of a radio address, assuring New Yorkers that he had no intention of raising the nickel subway fare, when news of the disaster reached him. He cut short his speech, quit the studio and raced to Pier 88. Later, having been assured that the fire was finally "under control" and "mopping-up" operations were proceeding, he and Rear-Admiral Adolphus Andrews, in command of the 3rd Naval District, decided to try and board *Normandie*. As they approached a gangplank, the sorely wounded liner suddenly lurched several feet to port. It was the beginning of the end.

NORMANDIE CAPSIZES

It was not the fire that now presented the greatest threat to *Normandie*. It was the 6,000 gallons (23,000 l) of water that the fire-fighters had pumped into her in their desperate efforts to save her. The water flowed inexorably downward into the ship's lower decks; as it did so, *Normandie* listed more and more to port. Around midnight, all attempts to right her having failed, Andrews ordered the liner to be abandoned. At 2:45a.m. she finally capsized, coming to rest on her port side at an angle

of around 80 degrees. Her stern slid under Pier 88, while her bows skewered toward Pier 90.

The one man who might have been able to save *Normandie* stood helplessly on the pier side as the list became more and more pronounced. He was Vladimir Yourkevitch, who had actually designed her. Rushing to Pier 88 when he heard of the disaster, he wanted to volunteer to go on board, make this way through the maze of corridors and passageways down into the bowels of the ship and open the sea-cocks to counter-flood her. If he had succeeded, *Normandie* would have settled on an even keel in the Hudson mud, rather than keeling over completely. Yourkevitch, however, was stopped from approaching the vessel at a police line set up to keep rubberneckers away from the pier. The police did not realize who he was and, thanks to his thick French accent, did not understand what he was desperately trying to tell them. All he could do was watch as the ship listed more and more until the inevitable happened.

ACCIDENT OR ARSON?

Immediately after *Normandie* capsized, rumors began to spread concerning what had triggered the disaster. Had the

Above: Normandie *arrives in New York harbor to be taken in tow by the waiting tugs. The Statue of Liberty can be seen in the background.*

Right: Normandie *anchored at the New York quayside. She held the record for being the biggest ship in the world for five years.*

fire been a tragic accident or had it been started deliberately by Nazi or even Vichy French saboteurs? Why had it proved so difficult to get the fire under control? Had someone slit the fire hoses? How did the fire manage to spread so fast? The nation demanded answers.

Spies were certainly active along the waterfront. Only a month before in a Brooklyn courtroom, 30 German agents had been found guilty of espionage and sentenced to serve a total of more than 300 years in prison. The spy ring had been uncovered by William Sebold, a 42-year-old German-American who was working as a counterespionage agent for the FBI. J. Edgar Hoover's men had set him up in a 42nd Street office, where they could observe his meetings with the unsuspecting spies through a two-way mirror and bug their conversations. Was this just the tip of the iceberg? How many more Nazi agents and Axis sympathizers might be at work?

Demands for a full-scale inquiry escalated rapidly. An editorial in the New York Times thundered: "The investigation should be relentless. It is not alone a ship that has been damaged. Men may have to die on the other side of some ocean because help did not get to them in time." Even President Roosevelt himself got in on the act. Immediately after the fire, his first thought was to ask Secretary of the Navy Knox if enemy agents or pro-Nazi Fifth Columnists had been allowed to work on the ship.

THE MAFIA CONNECTION

Nazi saboteurs were the obvious candidate to blame. Much later, however, there was talk of Mafia involvement. The finger was pointed at Charles "Lucky" Luciano, the uncrowned king of the New York underworld, who, so it was alleged, had ordered his henchmen to sabotage Normandie as part of a scheme to secure his release from jail.

Luciano had been held in prison in upstate New York since 1936, having been sentenced to a term of between 30 to 50 years for trafficking in prostitution. Now, he hatched a plot with fellow crime bosses Frank Costello, Mayer Lansky, and Moe Polakoff to blackmail the U.S. government into granting him parole. Alberto Anastasia and his brother "Tough" Tony — the latter was a prominent figure in the International Longshoremen's Association — were also involved.

According to Luciano's memoirs, published 16 years after his death in 1962, the plan was as follows. Torching Normandie would force U.S. Naval Intelligence to turn to Luciano to help to protect the New York docks against further acts of sabotage. It would be easy enough for Luciano to enforce his dictates as he and his fellow racketeers controlled most of the waterfront.

Whether the allegation was true or not, no one still can say. Certainly, there were meetings between mob bosses and representatives from U.S. Naval Intelligence after the Normandie fire. It was also the case that, after the war, Luciano was released prematurely and deported to Italy. He never made it back to the U.S.

The official verdict, however, ruled out all talk of sabotage. A Congressional investigation concluded that the disaster was the result of "carelessness in how the burning operations were carried out," compounded by an "absence of proper coordination between the various units on board, divided authority, and lack of a unified command" and "undue haste, indecision, and lack of careful planning in connection with the conversion." In short, it had been a bungle. Normandie paid the price.

"Project Amerika"

To avenge the Allied bombing of the Third Reich, Hitler wanted nothing more than to blitz the U.S.'s greatest homeland city to destruction. He failed, but how near did the Nazis come to fulfilling the Führer's dream of reducing New York to ruins? How far did they get toward developing a super-bomber with the range to get to New York and back? Or did they plan to unleash a devastating missile attack?

Above: *A Blohm & Voss BV 222 "Wiking" flying boat seen in flight. Only 14 of these massive aircraft were built; they had a range of some 3,790 miles (6,100 km) and could be refuelled at sea by tanker U-boats.*

Surprisingly enough for a man whom *Time* magazine chose to feature on its cover as its Man of the Year as late as 1938, Adolf Hitler always detested the U.S. and everything it stood for. It was understandable, therefore, that, as the tide of war swung increasingly against the Third Reich, the Führer's lust for revenge focused more and more obsessively on the U.S. as his favorite potential target for aerial revenge attacks.

"I never saw him so completely beside himself as toward the end of the war, when, in his delirium, he envisaged to himself the destruction of New York in firestorms," Albert Speer wrote in his *Spandau Diaries*. "He described how the skyscrapers would be transformed into gigantic burning torches; how they would collapse onto one another and how the glow of the burning city would brighten the night sky." It was part of Speer's job, as Minister for Armaments, to try to turn his Führer's fantasies into grim reality.

PLANNING TO STRIKE

Until 1972, little was known about specific German long-range bombing plans. Indeed, many military historians and researchers doubted whether any such plans had ever been devised. Those who thought otherwise assumed that the plans had been lost or destroyed as the war came to its end. Then German military historian Olaf Groehler made a momentous discovery while researching in the military archives in Potsdam in what was then East Germany. It was a copy of the actual plan the Luftwaffe had drawn up for a major transoceanic aerial bombing offensive.

Luftwaffe experts completed work on the plan on April 27, 1942. They handed it over to Reichsmarschal Hermann Goering on May 12. The final version they submitted was 33 pages long. Attached to it was a map of the world with various potential targets and flight patterns indicated on it. There were also notes of which types of long-range aircraft could be used to carry out the attacks.

The man responsible for putting the plan together was Dietrich Schwenke, a highly respected Luftwaffe colonel reporting directly to Field Marshal Erhard Milch, Goering's sometime deputy and the Luftwaffe's air armaments chief. As far as the eastern seaboard of the U.S. was concerned, Schwenke and his team reported as follows. "On the coast of the U.S.," he wrote, "there are aluminum works, aircraft-engine works, propeller works, and arms factories. These can be attacked only by Messerschmitt 264s with DB613 motors carrying 5.5 tons of bombs and starting from Brest. If the Azores could be used as a transit airfield, it would be possible to reach these targets with He 177s (refueled) with 2 tons, BV 222s (refueled) with 4.5 tons, Ju 290s with 5 tons, and Me 264s with 6.5 tons."

Persuading neutral Portugal to allow the Azores to be used as a forward air base had already been discussed. A naval briefing document dated November 14, 1940 stated that Hitler was planning to "attack America in case of war" from the islands. On March 24, 1941, the Führer confirmed this was his intention. He confided to one of his adjutants that aerial attacks on the U.S. east coast were necessary "to teach the Jews a lesson."

Among the specific targets Schwenke itemized were the Pratt & Whitney aeroengine plant at East Hertford, Connecticut, the Sperry Gyroscope factory in Brooklyn, and the Curtiss-Wright works at Caldwell, New Jersey. However, he added a caveat. "The Panama Canal cannot be attacked with the planes mentioned unless there can be a refueling at sea

(BV 222)." Colonel Victor von Lossberg, a Luftwaffe bomber expert, had come to the same conclusion. In early August, he proposed that a BV 222 should fly across the Atlantic, rendezvous with a U-boat stationed around 800 miles (1,280 km) from New York, refuel and top up its bomb-load to eight tons, and then fly on to bomb its target. The operation would be repeated the following night after which the BV 222 would fly back to Europe.

Lossberg volunteered to pilot the plane himself. He proposed bombing New York primarily with incendiaries — he calculated that a BV 222 could drop about 4,000 of them on the city each time it attacked. The bombing would target what Lossberg termed "the Jewish quarter" or the dockyards. He had high hopes that such an attack would reduce New Yorkers to a state of panic. "The 22-kilo magnesium bomb," he told Milch, "has an explosive segment which detonates after four to ten minutes ... if they (the bombs) could be laid in a swathe across New York and the bombs kept exploding round the ears of the fire-fighters like hand grenades, it would have a terrific effect." The Kriegsmarine and Blohm & Voss, the BV 222's manufacturer, both supported the plan. However, General Hans Jeschonnek, the Luftwaffe's Chief of Staff, turned it down as impractical.

THE "AMERIKA BOMBER"

Jeschonnek may well have been right in this instance. Employing a flying boat to bomb New York was probably too risky. In order to strike effectively at such a target, the Germans needed more than plans. They needed suitable planes. What the Luftwaffe lacked was a long-range bomber capable of reaching the North American continent from Europe in one

Left: *Heinkel's He 177 was the only German heavy bomber to enter service. Its coupled engines frequently caught fire in flight and the whole aircraft was unreliable. Hitler inelegantly described it as "junk."*

Above: *Eugen Sanger planned to build a rocket-powered orbital aircraft that could easily reach and bomb New York. The project, which was years ahead of its time, was cancelled in 1941. The so-called Silverbird never got off the ground.*

nonstop hop, dropping its bombs and then flying back again safely.

With the exception of the Heinkel He 177 and the BV 222, the aircraft Schwenke had listed only existed on the drawing board or, at best, were nearing the prototype stage. The BV 222, however, had been deemed unsuitable by the Luftwaffe high command. As for the He 177, it was unreliable and plagued by structural flaws in its airframe and other major mechanical problems. In flight, its wings tended to buckle under stress, while its engines, coupled together in tandem, were all too prone to catch fire in midair. An exasperated Hitler later described the plane as a "rattletrap" and dismissed it scornfully as "obviously the worst junk ever to have been manufactured."

Even before the war, Goering had recognized that the absence of such a bomber meant that there was a gaping hole in the Luftwaffe's armament. He told a gathering of Germany's leading aircraft manufacturers:

"I completely lack the bombers capable of round-trip flights to New York with a five-ton bomb-load. I would be extremely happy to possess such a bomber which would finally muzzle some of the arrogance coming from over there."

Willy Messerschmitt was the first to take up Goering's challenge. In 1937 he had started work on designing the long-range Messerschmitt Me 261 at Hitler's personal behest. Popularly known as the "Adolfine," the plane was intended to carry the Olympic flame from Berlin to Tokyo to inaugurate the 1940 Olympic Games. According to high-level rumor, Hitler intended to be a passenger on the flight himself.

It was obviously logical for Messerschmitt to develop a long-range bomber in parallel with the "Adolfine." Initial work on what he christened Project 1061 started in late 1937, though, thanks to more pressing demands on the Messerschmitt design department's time, it did not really get underway until mid-1940. Despite Messerschmitt's personal assurances to the Führer that the project was on time — he told Hitler that "the aircraft can be used for special purposes even before testing is completed" — he was promising the impossible. He even showed Hitler what the Führer took to be a finished plane — in fact, it was simply a mock-up.

The first prototype of what was now designated the Messerschmitt Me 264 did not fly until December 1942, a full year behind schedule. The intention had been to allow Messerschmitt to build an initial 28 and try them out in action against New York and other U.S. targets. The long delays led to the plan being aborted. Messerschmitt was permitted to

build just three prototypes. They were all destroyed in an Allied air raid in July 1944.

THE LUFTWAFFE OVER NEW YORK

Where Messerschmitt had failed, it looked like Junkers might succeed. Their other rivals — Focke-Wulf with the Ta 400 and Heinkel with the He 277 — never got further than wind-tunnel models before the Luftwaffe ordered them to stop work. The monstrous six-engined Ju 390 took advantage of the tried-and-tested Ju 90 and Ju 290 airframes. According to Junkers' records, the prototype made its first test-flight on October 20 ,1943. Just over a month later, it was flown to Insterburg, not far from the Führer's headquarters in East Prussia, for Hitler to inspect. Junkers nicknamed it the "New York bomber," probably to distinguish it from the rival Me 264.

The Luftwaffe immediately ordered 26 of the planes, but only a second prototype was ever built. In June 1944, the contract was canceled. The prototypes, it is believed, were destroyed by the Germans in late April 1945 to stop them falling into U.S. hands

Above left: *The prototype of the Me264, Willy Messerschmitt's "Amerika bomber," first flew in December 1942. In October 1943, all work on the aircraft was stopped and Messerschmitt told to concentrate on his Me262 jet fighter-bomber.*

Above right: *The Me264 looked elegant enough on the ground, but is performance was inferior to that of its rivals. It had a slow rate of climb, was hard to maneuver and lacked in-flight stability.*

as American forces neared the Dessau factory where they had been built.

The plane was more than capable of doing its job — that is, if various claims that the first prototype actually managed to fly to New York and back are to be believed. The earliest of these claims was made in letters published in *RAF Flying Review* in 1955 and 1956. According to the second of these letters, the flight had taken place in the latter part of 1944, when the Junkers had got to within 12 miles (19 km) of the U.S. east coast just north of New York before turning back to its base in France. Though many experts dismissed the tale as unlikely, it soon passed into aviation folklore.

The second claim dates from 2011, when an article in *Veterans Today* stated that, in August 1943, a Ju 390, apparently flying from an airfield outside Bergen in Occupied Norway and refueling in midair over Iceland, had crossed the Atlantic to photograph industrial plants in Michigan and then flown over New York before heading back to land at a Luftwaffe base near Paris, having refueled again over the Azores on the way. The author of the article also claimed that the Ju 390's co-pilot was a woman — Anna

Kriesling, the so-called "White Wolf of the Luftwaffe." She got the soubriquet, the article said, because of her "frost blonde hair and icy blue eyes."

World War II aviation authorities were quick to denounce the article's claims. How, they asked, could the Junkers have flown the Atlantic two months before its first officially documented test-flight? Why was there no apparent mention of the flight in either the Junkers or Luftwaffe archives? Others said that the story was true, but the article got the date wrong. The flight, they opine, actually took place in January 1944.

No one knows the truth. If such a flight did indeed take place, it was more than likely to have been carried out by KG 200, a mysterious Luftwaffe unit whose records are still classified, lost, or destroyed.

HITLER'S STEALTH BOMBER

Paradoxically, as the military situation deteriorated and the Luftwaffe faced the imminent threat of being driven out of the skies, prominent Nazis still clung to the dream of bombing New York, even though Germany's leading aircraft manufacturers were no longer directly involved. They were

desperately churning out fighters rather than bombers, despite the fact that fuel and pilot shortages meant that the Luftwaffe could not get many of the planes they were producing so feverishly off the ground and into the air.

Accordingly, the Germans turned to aviation mavericks to devise revolutionary new aircraft for the task. Chief among them were Reimar and Walter Horton, who devised an ingenious "flying wing" jet aircraft design, variants of which could fly as day fighters or long-range bombers. The Horton Ho 229 bomber was the result.

Still in their 30s, the brothers broke completely with convention. They had had the notion for a "flying wing" aircraft years before, but it was only now that they were given the chance to put their theories to the test. Work on the construction of an unpowered prototype began in Gottingen in early 1944. The first of them flew — or, rather, glided — successfully later that year. A second powered day fighter prototype followed in early 1945.

Carrying a 4,400-pound (2,000 kg) bomb-load and flying at a maximum height of just over 49,000 feet (15,000 m) at a top speed of 620 miles per hour (1,000 km/h), the Ho 229 was

Top: *A Heinkel He 177 rear gunner in his turret. The Luftwaffe ordered hundreds of the planes — only a few ever flew.*

Above: *The revolutionary "flying wing" Horton Ho 229 first flew in early 1945, but the jet-powered prototype crashed after a few test flights.*

Right: *Werner Baumbach commanded the Luftwaffe special duties squadron KG 200. His men would probably have flown the Amerika bombers had they been built.*

designed to fly to New York and back without the need for refueling. It was to be a pure jet aircraft, powered by either BMW 003A or Junkers Jumo 004B turbojet engines. As if this was not revolutionary enough, Reimar Horton came up with the idea of coating the plane with a mixture of charcoal dust and wood glue. This, he believed, combined with the Ho 222's unusual sculpted shape, would make it practically impossible for enemy radar to detect the aircraft. In short, the Ho 229 would be the world's first stealth bomber. It was 40 years ahead of its time.

The first unpowered prototype survived the war, to be captured by the Americans along with the blueprints for all the projected variants. The powered prototype crashed trying to make an emergency landing during a test flight after one of its Junkers Jumo engines caught fire in the air. Time ran out for the bomber prototype. Though work on it started in March 1945, it was never completed.

SPACE PLANES AND MISSILES

Austrian engineer Eugen Sanger was another maverick, who came up with an even more extraordinary notion. His plan, first

Right: *Pratt & Whitney's Connecticut aircraft engine plant.*

Left: *A German poster warns of the danger of falling flak splinters.*

mooted in the mid-1930s, was to attack New York with a rocket-powered bomber that would drop a single, TV-guided 8,800-pound (4,000 kg) bomb on the city from near space.

Sanger's suborbital "Silver Bird" was to be catapulted into the air from a rocket sledge, after the latter had powered down a 2-mile (3.25km) long monorail track. At 5,500 feet (1,675 m), the plane's own rocket engine would ignite and push the "Silver Bird" upward to a height of around 90 miles (145 km) above the Earth to the edge of space. It would then literally bounce off the denser atmospheric layer below it — rather like a stone skipping across a pond — to reach its target. Having dropped its bomb, the "Silver Bird" would fly across the U.S. and on over the Pacific to land in Japanese-controlled territory.

Though, by 1941, facilities for full-scale rocket engine tests were

under construction, the German Air Ministry decided to halt development of the project later the same year. Sanger tried again in 1944 to win official support, but it was too late. The "Silver Bird" never flew.

Other ideas, such as engineer Bodo Lafferentz's idea to tow giant floating containers by U-boat to within 100 miles (160 km) of the U.S. eastern coast and fire V2 rockets from them, also failed to get off the ground. Although construction of three prototype containers started in early 1945, Soviet troops occupied the shipyard in which they were being built before they could be completed. The plan to build a multistage A10/A9 New York rocket suggested by Wernher von Braun and his fellow-rocketeers at Peenemünde also never took concrete form, although, given time, such a project might well have succeeded.

The Mystery of the Murdered Redhead

For two hectic years at the height of World War II, beautiful redheaded socialite Jane Horney was the uncrowned queen of Swedish high society. The dominant figure in Stockholm's hectic social life, she partied hard and had a host of influential friends. Was she simply an adventuress on the make? Was she an Allied agent, a Nazi spy, or working for both sides? Like her probable murder, the riddle remains unsolved.

In the European theater of war during World War II, there were two neutral capitals where the diplomatic and other representatives of the warring powers came into frequent contact with one another. One was Lisbon in Portugal. The other was Stockholm in Sweden.

For both the Allies and Nazi Germany, it was vital to keep in close daily touch with the Swedes, since Swedish industry was trading with both sides. There were many personal negotiations and much secret mail; Stockholm was awash with spies. In addition, the capital was a transit point for mail en route to prisoner-of-war camps in the Third Reich. United States Army Air Forces (USAAF)

and RAF aircrews, too, came down in Sweden — some deliberately sought sanctuary there — while others managed to find their way there after evading capture after having been shot down or having escaped from prison camps within Hitler's Germany.

Many Norwegians seeking to flee from their Nazi-occupied country used Sweden as an alternative escape route to reach Britain, rather than risking the obvious perils and dangers of a small-boat North Sea crossing. High-ranking Allied personages helped the Norwegian effort. In March 1942 President Roosevelt himself actively supported the Royal Norwegian Air Force center in London in its attempt to obtain two Lockheed

Above: *Food lines were a common feature of daily life in the Scandinavian countries during the war — even in neutral Sweden.*

Left: *Jane Horney photographed at the wheel of her car. An attractive adventuress, she may have been a spy for both sides during her short-lived career.*

Lodestar airliners to transport 50 of their fellow-Norwegians a week from Sweden to Scotland. Some of them had been waiting 18 months for the chance to fight with the Allies.

A BATTLE FOR SUPPLIES

Even more crucially, Britain was obtaining special engineering products from Sweden, such as ball-bearings, special steels for machine tools, fine springs, and

in the British Ministry of Supply advised that it was "of the greatest importance to obtain as many bearings as possible from Sweden with the minimum of delay." After the U.S. 8th Army Air Force's raid on Germany's most important ball-bearing factories at Schweinfurt, two top British government officials were flown to Sweden by Mosquito, each Mosquito specially modified to carry one passenger each in their bomb bays. The officials' task was to try and corner all Sweden's ball-bearing exports to stop the Germans getting hold of them. In this, they were partially successful. Interestingly, the German subsidiary of the giant Swedish industrial combine SKF controlled the most important of the Schweinfurt factories.

Above: *Jane Horney married Herje Granberg in 1937. He was the Berlin correspondent for a pro-Nazi Swedish newspaper at the time. The marriage ended in divorce four years later.*

Right: *So fast that they were practically immune to German attempts at interception, RAF Mosquitoes in civilian BOAC colors ferried priority passengers to and from Sweden.*

electrical resistors. The Germans were doing the same. Ball-bearings, in particular, were an indispensable part of both the Allied and Nazi war machines. In 1942 the Swedes supplied 59 percent of the Third Reich's ball-bearing requirements and 31 percent of British needs.

Ensuring a continued supply of ball-bearings was considered essential by both powers. In 1943, the Controller of Bearings

HOTBED OF INTRIGUE

In that year, Stockholm — the only city in northern Europe where the lights still blazed every night — was a hotbed of intrigue. With the war entering a crucial phase, secret plots and counterplots were being constantly hatched in the city's most exclusive night-clubs and restaurants. It was a glittering scene, where partying and pleasure went hand-in-hand with intrigue and treachery.

In the early months of 1943, a beautiful redhead in her mid-20s named Jane Horney arrived in the Swedish capital and swept like a whirlwind onto the Stockholm social scene. Her reign as the uncrowned queen of Swedish high society lasted for only two years, but during that time she broke the hearts of diplomats from half the world. And when she vanished abruptly in January 1945, she left behind a mystery that still remains unsolved today.

WHO WAS JANE HORNEY?

Jane Horney, or Ebba Charlotta Horney to give her proper full name, was a Swedish citizen, probably born in Stockholm in 1918 though some say she was actually born illegitimately in Scotland and later adopted by her Swedish foster father and Danish mother. The truth is that no one knows the exact facts about her origins. What is known is that she was always something of an adventurer. Tall, handsome, and outgoing, she liked people — especially men.

In 1939, Jane married journalist Herje Granberg, whom she had met on a trip to Greenland. Two years later, the couple moved to Berlin, where Granberg had been appointed correspondent for the pro-Nazi Swedish newspaper *Aftonbladet*. Two years later, they divorced and Jane moved back to Scandinavia — first to Copenhagen, where she had relatives, and then to Stockholm. She was attractive, young and fancy-free. In a matter of weeks, she became one of the leading

Above: *Alexandra Kollontai was Soviet Ambassadress to Sweden during the war. She was one of the few people Stalin trusted unreservedly.*

Opposite: *Before the Mosquito came on the scene, U.S. Lockheed Lodestars flew between Britain and Sweden. To avoid being shot down by the Luftwaffe, they were forced to fly only at night or in bad weather.*

lights of Stockholm's party scene — and her escorts were almost always senior diplomats or known secret service operatives from half a dozen countries.

SPY OR DOUBLE AGENT?

Whatever game Jane was playing, it was a dark, deep, and dangerous one. Before long, the British had become convinced that she was a German agent. So had the Danes, many of whom had taken refuge in Sweden when their country was overrun by the Wehrmacht in April 1940. Rumors began to circulate that she had helped the Germans to track down and arrest some of the key figures in the Danish resistance movement.

What neither the British nor the Danes realized was that the Germans suspected Jane of being a British spy — or at least that she was a double agent. Her contacts certainly included Ronald Turnbull, a serving officer in Britain's Special Operations Executive, and Otto Danielsson and Martin Lundqvist, both members of Swedish Military Intelligence. Danielsson noted that she had "no moral scruples" when it came to trading sex for secret information. Jane was also linked with the NKVD, the Soviet espionage service. It was thought that she sometimes acted as a

courier for Alexander Pavlov, the TASS news agency correspondent in Stockholm who doubled as an NKVD agent.

In all probability, the exact truth will never be established. What we do know is that Jorgen Winkel, a prominent Danish textile manufacturer and member of the Danish Resistance, became one of Jane's lovers and that, to try to get him out of prison, she embarked on an affair with Karl Heinz Hoffman, head of the Gestapo in Denmark. Her other high-level German friends included SS Obersturmbannführer Hermann Seibold, in charge of Germany's Scandinavian counterintelligence operations.

We also know that, in summer 1943, she took up with another new boyfriend. He was 54-year-old Horst Gilbert, a German living in Copenhagen where he ostensibly ran the Scandinavian Telegraph Bureau. This was simply a cover. In actuality he was an important Abwehr military intelligence officer, who, possibly under direct orders from Admiral Wilhelm Canaris, was playing a double game. Like Canaris, Gilbert was a secret anti-Nazi, who, long before the war while he was serving in Russia as an unofficial adviser to the Red Army, had become friendly with Alexandra Kollontai, now Soviet Ambassador to

Sweden. Gilbert, using Jane as a go-between, contacted Kollontai again to try to establish whether there was a chance of the Russians agreeing to open negotiations for a separate peace with Germany.

Gilbert managed to survive until October 14, 1944, when he was shot in his office in central Copenhagen by Ella von Cappeln, a one-time nun, and other members of the cell she ran in the Danish Resistance. He died of his wounds a month later. The previous fall, Jane had often gone from Stockholm to Copenhagen to visit him. The curious thing was that she had traveled not by conventional

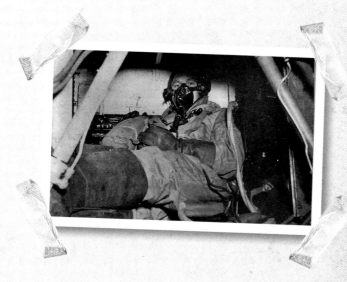

Top: *Mosquitoes in flight. From 1943 until the end of the war, they flew regularly between Leuchars air base in the north of Scotland and Stockholm.*

Above: *Mosquitoes could carry one person at a time, crammed into their bomb bays. The Danish physicist Niels Bohr was one of the first passengers.*

Opposite: *Per Albin Hansson, neutral Sweden's Prime Minister, had to tread a tricky tightrope between the demands of the Allies and those of Nazi Germany.*

means, but by a secret shuttle service set up by the Danish Resistance to ship weapons and ferry refugees across the Kattegat and Skagerrak.

PLOT AND COUNTERPLOT

Just what Jane thought she was up to trying to play one side off against the other is anybody's guess. Early in 1944, for instance, equipped with a special pass that allowed her to cross the frontiers of the occupied countries without hindrance, she went to Germany several times. Why is unclear. To complicate the story even further, she passed on information about the Nazi intelligence set-up in Scandinavia to her Swedish intelligence contacts on her return to Sweden.

In March 1944, Jane's latest boyfriend was a major in British Intelligence attached to Britain's embassy in Stockholm. No one knows whether this anonymous figure was sent to Stockholm with specific orders to become friendly with her, but he certainly did so. Jane apparently fell head over heels in love with him. For several months they were inseparable, and then the major suddenly broke off the affair. It may be that he had discovered everything there was to know about her and was ordered to terminate the liaison.

In any event, Jane was heartbroken by the break-up. She vanished from the Stockholm scene for some weeks. When she returned, she seemed to pay more attention to the Germans than ever before — whether this was because of the unhappy outcome of her love affair with the British officer will never be known for certain. In any event, the Danish Resistance was certainly becoming more and more suspicious of her. Its agents shadowed her everywhere, photographing her and the people she met. That fall, acting on information supplied by the Danes, the Swedish Secret Service arrested her and took her in for interrogation.

The Swedes questioned Jane for three weeks. Eventually, on October 13, they set her free. They told the Danes who had denounced her that she had been completely cleared of all suspicion and the Danes outwardly expressed their satisfaction with the Swedish conclusions. Secretly, however, their top agents were still convinced that Jane was a dangerous spy in the pay of the Nazis.

A COLD-BLOODED MURDER

The Danes had plotted to murder Jane before, but aborted the attempt. Now, they decided to proceed. Sven Aage Geisler and Asbjorn Lyhne, both members of the Danish Resistance, were sent to Stockholm with instructions to win Jane's confidence and then persuade her to return with them to Denmark to clear herself of the espionage allegations once and for all. Jane, taken in by Geisler's charm, eventually fell in with the plan.

For the lovely redhead who had captivated Stockholm society for so long, the clock was ticking and time was fast running out. On January 16, 1945, Geisler, Lyhne, Jane, and Bodil Frederickson, a girlfriend of hers who was also a member of the Danish Resistance, boarded the evening train to Malmo from Stockholm's Central

Station. Having arrived in Malmo, the party checked in at the Grand Hotel, where rooms had been reserved for them. They were joined there by Hjalmar Ravnbo, a young student going under the name of "Jens" who was also a member of the Danish Resistance.

Jane was completely unaware that she was in any danger. Indeed, when Geisler and Lyhne told her that they were not making the ferry-crossing to Denmark with her, she insisted on hosting a dinner party at the Savoy Hotel the following night to say goodbye to them. At 10:00 p.m., she left the hotel with Bodil Frederickson and Ravnbo to travel by taxi to Hoganas, outside Helsingborg, where she was to board the Danish ferry.

It was a stormy night, but the ferry still sailed punctually on time. Halfway through its crossing, however, it hove-to and Jane, together with two or three other men, was transferred to *Taman*, a Danish fishing boat, which pulled alongside. Several of the ferry's crew saw the transfer happen, but took no particular notice of it. Such secret exchanges were commonplace. It was only after they were later questioned by the police that they realized that something sinister had been afoot.

What happened next remains conjecture. Somewhere out in the darkness after the ferry continued on its way, Jane was cold-bloodedly murdered. The likelihood is that she was shot twice, her lifeless corpse wrapped in heavy iron chains and dumped overboard into the freezing water, sinking without a trace.

CONTINUING CONTROVERSY

Jane's disappearance, however, was only the start of a continuing mystery, rather than its conclusion. After the war, her father pressured the Swedish police to investigate her disappearance and supposed death. The investigators ran up against a wall of silence. The Swedish Secret Service closed their files on her, as did the Danes. The British claimed never to have heard of her, while former Abwehr, Gestapo, and SS officers who had known her stubbornly held their tongues.

In 1947, there was an apparent breakthrough, when Asbjorn Lyhne, who was serving a short sentence in a Swedish prison for forging documents, unexpectedly confessed to having participated in Jane's murder. Later, though, he withdrew his confession, leaving the Swedes with no alternative but to release him in the absence of any corroborative evidence. Geisler, too, was investigated but cleared.

As the years passed, the rumors escalated. Some claimed that Jane had not been killed at all. The person who had been murdered was Bodil Frederickson, who, for some unknown reason, had been persuaded to change places with her. Certainly, the two women looked remarkably alike. Staff at the Grand Hotel confirmed to the police that two striking redheads had stayed there in adjoining rooms. One of the two was later seen at Malmo station, boarding the Stockholm train. Was it Bodil or was it Jane? No one will ever know for certain.

Others argue equally confidently that, although Bodil indeed did change clothes with Jane and assume her identity for a time, this was just part of the Danish master plan to get the real Jane secretly out of Sweden. Another theory holds that Jane's death was staged so that she could be spirited to Britain to spy for MI6 against the Russians. No concrete evidence has ever been produced to prove conclusively that this was the case. Many hold the entire thing is a hoax, perpetrated by a former schoolteacher and current multimedia artiste, on the two Danish writers who put the theory into general circulation. An even more extraordinary theory claims that Jane's supposed death was engineered so that she could smuggle Princess Margrethe and another member of the Danish Royal Family to safety in Sweden.

The controversy continues. In Denmark, Jane's career was even dramatised as a TV miniseries. The jury is still out as to whether she really was a top-ranking secret agent or even a double agent. Or there might be an even more intriguing and tragic explanation — that Jane was an adventuress, a girl-about-town who lived life to the full at the expense of the secret service men who tried to use her, and who outwitted them. Put at its simplest, she was murdered because she knew too much, particularly about alleged corruption inside the Danish Resistance. If she had ever talked about what she knew, she all too easily could become a source of political embarrassment.

Right: *The voluptuous Jane Horney captured in a pensive mood. Her lovers were legion.*

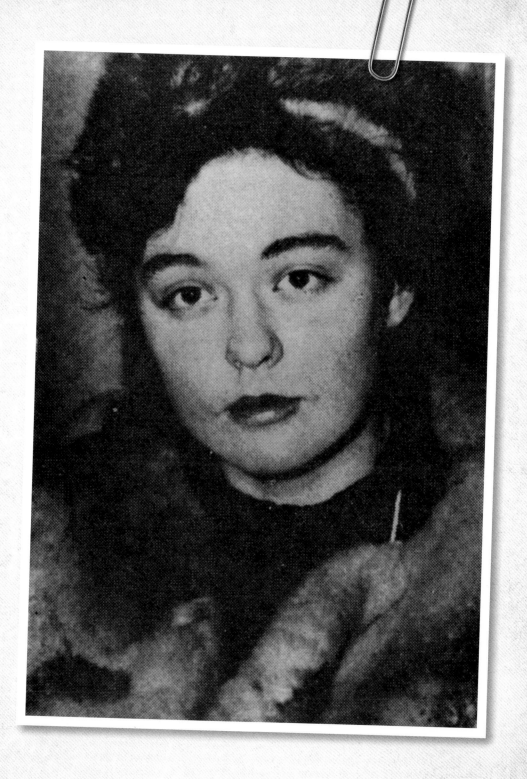

The Lost Liberator

It failed to return from a bombing raid over Italy in April 1943. Its remains were discovered virtually intact deep in the torrid wastelands of the Libyan Desert 450 miles south of Benghazi more than 16 years later. The radio still worked. The coffee in the crew's vacuum flasks was still drinkable. But what had happened to the men who flew the B-24 Liberator they had christened Lady Be Good?

Deep in the vast featureless wasteland that makes up the Libyan Desert, there lies the wreck of a wartime bomber. It is a Consolidated B-24 Liberator. On its nose it bears the number 64 and the sun-faded name *Lady Be Good*.

At 1:30 p.m. in the afternoon of April 4, 1943, *Lady Be Good* had taken off from the airfield at Soluk, on the coastal strip south of Benghazi, in company with 24 other Liberators from the USAAF 376th Bomb Group, to attack enemy airfields around Naples, some 750 miles (1,200 km) across the Mediterranean to the north. The attack had been planned to ensure that the bombers got to their targets around dusk and made their return flight at night. The darkness, it was thought, would help them to elude any pursuing Luftwaffe or Regia Aeronautica fighters. The records show that 11 of the B-24s bombed their primary target, the remainder hitting the secondary ones.

Although some of the Liberators were damaged by hostile antiaircraft fire and others suffered from engine trouble, all bar one of them made it back to Soluk safely by midnight. The exception was *Lady Be Good*. Then, shortly after midnight, the control

tower at Benina received a radio transmission from the overdue plane. First Lieutenant William J. Hutton, its pilot and commander, told the controller that he was unable to locate his home airfield because of the dense cloud that was now blanketing the entire North African coast and that his Liberator was running low on fuel. He asked for a radio fix so that he could home in on Benina and make an emergency landing there.

The Benina tower gave the fix as requested, but *Lady Be Good* never arrived. An air-sea rescue search the next day failed to find any trace of the missing bomber

Above: The crew of Lady Be Good *pose for a group photograph. They arrived in Libya just a week before their first operational flight was scheduled.*

Opposite: The nose and cockpit of Lady Be Good. *The crashed section was remarkably well-preserved — even its machine guns were still in place.*

or its crew. They were assumed to have crashed and drowned in the Mediterranean.

DISCOVERING THE WRECK
The incident in itself was not unusual. It was Hutton's and his crew's first combat mission and so they were at far greater risk

Above: *The crash site of* Lady Be Good *viewed from the air. This picture was taken shortly after the wreck's discovery by oil prospectors in 1959.*

Below: *Inside the plane, everything was surprisingly intact. Even the radio still worked, and the coffee in the crews' Thermos flasks had not evaporated.*

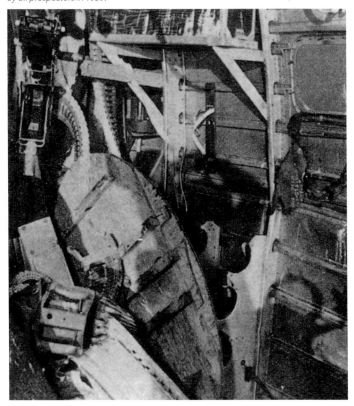

of being shot down or failing to make it home than other, more experienced aircrews. It was what happened after that return flight that made the story of *Lady Be Good* unique.

In 1959, more than 16 years later, British geologists surveying for oil deep in the Libyan Desert by air advised the U.S. Air Force's Wheelus Field airbase that they had spotted the wreckage of a large World War II aircraft some 440 miles south of Benghazi. A C-47 transport plane with a search crew on board was promptly despatched to investigate.

The C-47 touched down safely on the gravelly ground close to the wreckage and the investigators disembarked into the blistering heat. They quickly identified the crashed aircraft as a Liberator, but, as they walked toward the wreckage an amazing sight met their eyes. There was no trace of corrosion on the bomber's metalwork. The dry, furnace-like heat of the desiccated desert air had preserved it perfectly. It was almost as if the Liberator had been deposited in the desert only the day before.

INVESTIGATING THE INTERIOR

Lady Be Good lay spread-eagled on its belly, its right wing raised slightly with the left wing

Above: *B-24 Liberators returning home to their airfields in Italy after raiding enemy territory. All too many did not make it back to base unscathed.*

crumpled in the sand. The rear of the fuselage and the tail unit had broken away and was lying off to one side at an angle. One of its Pratt & Whitney R-1830 Twin Wasp radial engines had been torn away. The starboard landing gear had dropped from its well. Amazingly, its tire was still inflated.

Scattered debris lay littered around the aircraft. There were oxygen bottles, steel helmets, first-aid boxes, belts of ammunition, and items of flying clothing. Cautiously, the investigators peered inside the fuselage. There were no human remains to be seen. The interior was completely deserted. Sweltering in the blistering heat, they clambered inside to investigate further. They tested the radio and found that it was still in working order. They also discovered some vacuum flasks with coffee inside them. The coffee was still drinkable.

The Liberator's fuel tanks turned out to be practically dry. It also became clear that three of the plane's four engines must have stopped in flight because their propeller blades were feathered — that is, turned edge-on to the airflow in order to cut down drag. The fourth engine appeared to have still been in action at the time of the crash. The rear escape hatch and the bomb-bay doors of the aircraft were open and there were no parachutes or Mae West life-preservers to be found.

It was clear that the crew had bailed out of *Lady Be Good* deliberately shortly before the plane crashed. Evidently, they had not panicked when their aircraft ran into difficulties. It was well-known that Liberators were notoriously difficult to ditch or belly-land successfully. They had

Above: *Another group of B-24s in flight. More Liberators were produced than any other American aircraft in World War II. The RAF ordered them as well.*

Opposite: *The wrecked tail section of* Lady Be Good *through which the crew would have parachuted. The crash investigators' C-30 is seen in the background.*

also been dubbed "flying coffins" by some of their more disgruntled aircrews. The nickname came about because the only way in and out of the bomber was at its rear. This meant that the crew on the flight deck — pilot, co-pilot, navigator, wireless operator, flight engineer, bombardier, and nose gunner — had to scramble right back through the aircraft, battling against time and hampered by their bulky parachutes.

In this instance, *Lady Be Good* was almost certainly flying on automatic pilot as it approached its last moments. Presumably, Hutton had switched over from manual control in order to keep the aircraft flying straight, level, and steady while the crew abandoned ship. It also gave him the opportunity to get clear of the cockpit and so escape the crash.

TWO CRITICAL QUESTIONS

By now, two questions were uppermost in everyone's minds. The Liberator showed no signs of having suffered any battle damage. The crew had obviously abandoned it as it ran out of fuel. But what was it doing in the desert, hundreds of miles from where it ought to have been? And what had become of the members of its crew?

After their return to Wheelus Field, the investigators completed their report on what they had found at the crash site and forwarded it to Washington. From wartime USAAF records, details of the bomber and its crew — and of their last flight — were unearthed. Only when the investigators pieced together the story of what had happened on the night of April 4 did the truth come to light. What was revealed was a tragic chain of circumstances.

When Hutton requested the radio fix, the Benina control tower assumed that *Lady Be Good* was flying northwest of its home base and still out over the Mediterranean. What Hutton had to do was to compensate for his own speed, wind velocity, and other navigational factors and correct his course accordingly. This would have brought him safely over the Benina base. Then *Lady Be Good* could have been "talked down" through the thick cloud cover to make a safe landing on the airfield's runway. In fact, the Liberator was already a long way to the southeast of Benina and heading steadily into the wastes of the Libyan Desert.

Circumstances conspired to throw Hutton off-course. The first was a sudden change in the weather. Unknown to the Liberator's crew, the wind had veered direction to the northeast and increased in velocity as well. An aircraft's speed over the ground depends on the direction and speed of the winds it encounters. With an unexpectedly powerful tail wind behind it, Hutton's aircraft was flying much faster southward than he realized.

The second problem seems to have been the radio fix. When Hutton radioed asking for assistance from the high-frequency direction finding station at Benina, he received a directional reading of 330 degrees. What probably happened then was that the Liberator's navigator took a reciprocal reading, which seemed to indicate that the plane

Above: *A Liberator is captured banking over the Ploiesti oil refineries in Romania, having dropped its bomb load successfully. In total, 53 planes were shot down in the attack.*

was on course. Hutton therefore believed that he was still over the Mediterranean and on his way to the safety of Benina. He was not. Instead, he was mistakenly flying farther and farther south deep into the barren desert.

SEARCHING FOR THE BODIES

It took many searches to discover what had become of Hutton and his crew. The first, which lasted from May to August 1959, was unsuccessful, though the searchers did find some clues to suggest that at least some of the Liberator's crew had managed to survive.

The first clue was discovered in a shallow depression about 19 miles (30 km) from the crash site. It was a pair of flying boots arranged with their toes pointing to the north. As the searchers moved farther on, they found a succession of improvised arrowheads, consisting of parachutes weighted down with rocks. Presumably, the survivors had hoped that these markers would help an air-sea mission to locate them.

The markers stopped at the edge of a vast, shifting sand sea. Despite months of further searching, nothing more was found. Captain Myron C. Tiller decided to end the search. "The search was abandoned," he reported, "when equipment began to deteriorate and fail and the probability of the airmen being completely covered by shifting sand made the danger of further search impractical."

A REVEALING DIARY

In February 1960, British Petroleum surveyors searching for oil discovered the remains of five of the crew on a plateau inside the sand sea. What was left of their corpses was close together, surrounded by a litter of abandoned canteens, flashlights, torn pieces of parachutes, flight jackets, other items of equipment, and personal effects. Among the latter was a diary belonging

to Lieutenant Robert Toner, the Liberator's co-pilot. The hastily scribbled jottings, covering the nine days from April 4 to 12, 1943, tell the poignant story of the airmen's courageous battle for survival.

Sunday, Apr. 4, 1943

Naples — 28 places — things pretty well mixed up — got lost returning, out of gas, jumped, landed in desert at 2:00 in morning. No one badly hurt, can't find John, all others present.

Monday 5

Start walking N.W., still no John. A few rations, 1/2 canteen of water, 1 cap full per day. Sun fairly warm. Good breeze from N.W. Nite very cold. No sleep. Rested & walked.

Tuesday 6

Rested at 11:30, sun very warm. No breeze, spent P.M. in hell, no

B-24G of the 376th BG at its Italian Base (USAF via NARA)

Top: *B-24s in characteristic box formation cruise apparently unscathed through a fierce barrage of German anti-aircraft fire. It was intercepting Luftwaffe fighters that were the real killers.*

Above: *A B-24's Flight Engineer checks on the progress of the ground crew maintaining his plane. This is a B-24G variant, fitted with a ball turret and extra machine-guns in the nose.*

planes, etc. rested until 5:00 P.M. Walked & rested all nite. 15 min on, 5 off.

Wednesday, Apr. 7, 1943

Same routine, everyone getting weak, can't get very far, prayers all the time, again P.M. very warm, hell. Can't sleep. Everyone sore from ground.

Thursday 8

Hit Sand Dunes, very miserable, good wind but continuous blowing of sand, every [one] now very weak, thought Sam & Moore were all done. La Motte eyes are gone, everyone else's eyes are bad. Still going N.W.

Friday 9

Shelly, Rip, Moore separate & try to go for help, rest of us all very weak, eyes bad, not any travel, all want to die. Still very little water. Nites are about 35, good in wind, no shelter, 1 parachute left.

Saturday, Apr. 10, 1943

Still having prayer meetings for help. No sign of anything, a couple of birds; good wind from N. — Really weak now, can't walk. Pains all over, still all want to die. Nites very cold. No sleep.

Sunday 11

Still waiting for help, still praying. Eyes bad, lost all our wgt. Aching all over, could make it if we had water; just enough left to put our tongues to, have hope for help very soon, no rest, still same place.

Monday 12

No help yet, very cold nite.

The story was clear. The crew of *Lady Be Good* bailed out of their aircraft at 2:00 a.m. on April 5. Lieutenant John S. Woravika, the bombardier, was the first casualty — his parachute failed to open — though the rest of the crew were unaware of the fatality. The eight remaining survivors trekked 85 miles (140 km) north across the desert to the point at which the remains were found. Five of them — Hutton, Toner himself, Second Lieutenant D. P. Hayes, the navigator, and Sergeants Samuel Adams, one of the aircraft's gunners and Robert E. La Motte, the radio operator — were too weak to continue. Sergeants Guy E. Shelley, Vernon L. Moore, and Harold J. Ripslinger — the other gunners and the radio operator — continued to struggle on through the desert in search of help.

OPERATION CLIMAX

After the discovery of the remains of the five crewmen, the U.S. Army and U.S. Air Force launched a final, more extensive effort to find the other missing members of the crew. Operation Climax, as it was called, started with high altitude fighters flying extensive photographic reconnaissance missions over the area. The ground party flew into the desert on a C-130 cargo plane. They had helicopter back-up with them.

It was another British Petroleum surveying team, however, that made the initial discovery. On May 12, 1960, geologists came across Shelley's remains at a spot 21 miles (34 km) northwest of the place where the first five crewmembers perished. Five days later, a search helicopter carrying out an air sweep over the area spotted Ripslinger's remains on the eastern slope of a high sand dune 26 miles (42 km) north of where Shelley had been found.

The whereabouts of the last two airmen remained a mystery until August 1, when British Petroleum geologists found Woravika's body about 12 miles (19 km) northeast of where *Lady Be Good* had crashed. He was still wearing his high altitude flying suit with his parachute still attached.

Less than half a mile away to the southwest they discovered discarded parachute harnesses and more high altitude clothing. This obviously had been where the rest of the crew rallied after their bail-out. Moore's corpse has never been located.

The tragedy was all the more acute because it may well have been avoidable. It stemmed from the mistaken decision to head northward rather than southeast. Had the crew of *Lady Be Good* chosen the latter course, they would have been able to retrieve the food and water in the crashed aircraft and use its radio to signal for help. At the very least, it would have increased their chances of survival.

Good fortune, however, did not favor *Lady Be Good* and her crew on its one and only battle mission. The recovered remains were returned to the U.S. for burial. As for *Lady Be Good*, she became the victim of scavengers and souvenir hunters. What little was left of her eventually was removed from the Libyan Desert by an oil company in 1995. When last seen, she apparently was stored in the backyard of a police compound in Tobruk.

The Leslie Howard Enigma

On June 1, 1943, eight Luftwaffe Junkers 88s shot down a Douglas DC-3 airliner over the Bay of Biscay on its way from Lisbon to Britain. Everyone on board perished, including the celebrated film actor Leslie Howard and his friend and business adviser Alfred Chenhalls, who looked remarkably like Winston Churchill. Did the Germans believe that Churchill himself was on board the plane? Was Howard the target? Or was it all a tragic mistake?

Right: *The ubiquitous Junkers Ju88. This captured night-fighter variant is being evaluated by the RAF — hence the markings.*

Left: *Leslie Howard was one of Britain's best-known and most popular actors. Some say that he was also a British spy.*

The radio message that came through to the wireless room at the airfield at Whitchurch, near Bristol, at 12:54 p.m. on the afternoon of June 1, 1943 was stark in its simplicity. It read: "From G-AGBB to GKH. Am being attacked by enemy aircraft." Then, an ominous silence fell. There was no more word from the stricken plane.

The message had been transmitted from a BOAC Douglas Dakota DC-3 airliner being flown by a Dutch crew from KLM, the Netherland's national airline. There were four of them on board — pilot, co-pilot, radio operator, and flight engineer. There were also 13 passengers. In addition to Howard and Chenhalls, they

were Reuters correspondent Kenneth Stonehouse and his wife; Mrs. Rotha Hutcheon, and her young daughters, Petra, aged 11, and Carolina, her 18-month-old sister; Mrs. Cecelia Paton; Tyrrell Shervington, an oil company director; Ivan Sharp, from the United Kingdom Commercial Corporation; Wilfrid B. Israel, a prominent British-Jewish activist; Francis Cowlrick; and Gordon Thompson MacLean.

The DC-3 had taken off from Portela, the airport of Lisbon, the capital of neutral Portugal, at 9:35 a.m. Double British Summer Time on that June morning, bound for BOAC's base at Whitchurch. There was nothing particularly unusual about the flight; civilian DC-3s

flew between Britain, Portugal, and Gibraltar on an almost daily basis. The trips, though, always contained an element of risk since they involved flying across the Bay of Biscay, uncomfortably close to the Luftwaffe's airfields around Bordeaux.

For added safety, the airliners were painted pale blue overall, with red, white, and blue identification stripes on their wings. Their civilian registration markings were also painted on them in clear visible letters. Sometimes, the airliners were shadowed by German interceptors, but the latter usually broke away when the enemy pilots identified the DC-3s as unarmed civilian aircraft. June 1, however, was to prove an exception.

WHY FLIGHT 777?

Why did the journey of G-AGBB — Flight 777, the airliner bearing the name *Ibis* on its nose — end in sudden, unexpected tragedy over the Bay of Biscay? There had been no one among the passengers from whose death the enemy might have profited? Or had there been?

There had been last-minute changes to the passenger list. Originally, there had been 14 names on it, assigned seats in order of priority. At the head of the list came government officials or VIPs, whose seats were allocated by the British Embassy in Lisbon, followed by passengers who had reached the top of a usually lengthy waiting list. Out of these, women traveling with children or children traveling on their own had priority.

On this occasion, a young boy called Derek Partridge and his nanny, Dora Rowe, were bumped from the passenger list at literally the last minute. They actually had boarded the aircraft and taken their seats in its cabin when a harassed BOAC official asked them to return to the terminal. Howard and Chenhalls took their places. Another scheduled passenger, Father A. A. Holmes, a Roman Catholic priest, missed the flight after being summoned back to Lisbon by an urgent telephone call summoning him to the British Embassy.

Howard was a much-loved and admired star of stage and screen. Slight, fair-haired, and somewhat vague in manner, he was the epitome of an English gentleman, though in fact he came from a Hungarian Jewish family that had migrated to Britain in the late 19th century. At the peak of his movie success — he had starred in box office hits like *The Scarlet Pimpernel*, where he played Sir Percy Blakeney, George Bernard Shaw's *Pygmalion*, as Professor Henry Higgins, and *Gone With The Wind*, where he had been cast as Ashley Wilkes — he had bought himself out of his Hollywood contract and returned to Britain at the outbreak of war to do his bit for the war effort. He broadcast talks to the U.S. and made short propaganda films for the Ministry of Information.

The two full-length movies Howard directed and starred in after his return home particularly infuriated Joseph Goebbels and other high-ups in the Nazi leadership. These were *Pimpernel Smith* and *The First of the Few*. In *Pimpernel Smith*, Howard played an eccentric Cambridge professor, who, under the cover of leading an archeological dig in prewar Germany, conspired with his accompanying students to smuggle victims of Nazi persecution out of the Reich in the face of the Gestapo. *The First of the Few* was a biopic of the career of R. J. Mitchell, the designer of the Spitfire fighter who died of cancer at the age of only 42. It was to be Howard's last film.

THE NAZI BLACKLIST

Howard was high on the Nazi blacklist. So, too, were Wilfrid Israel and mining expert Ivan Sharp. Israel, who originally hailed from Berlin, was a leading anti-Nazi activist who helped thousands of his fellow Jews to escape the Holocaust. His family had owned Kaufhaus N. Israel, one of the largest department stores in Europe situated next to the City Hall on Berlin's Alexanderplatz, until its forced expropriation by the Nazis in 1939. Israel then went into exile, taking up residence in London, where he set up the Jewish Refugee Mission. He was the mastermind behind the so-called Kindertransport of Jewish children to Britain. Some 10,000 of them arrived there before the outbreak of war.

Above: *A British propaganda poster warns against the danger of loose talk. Howard's name, however, was prominently on his plane's passenger list, of which the Germans obtained a copy.*

At the request of the Jewish Agency, Israel flew to Portugal to help as many as possible of the Jewish refugees who were living there and in Spain to escape to Palestine. The Germans, according to some theorists, believed that he was looking in particular for scientists with special knowledge of rocketry and nuclear physics with the aim of getting them to work for the Allies. This may well have been true. Certainly, some of the people who worked on the Manhattan Project — the Allied effort to build the atomic bomb — were recruited by him.

Sharp was another passenger the Nazis had reason to wish dead. He had been tasked by the British government with the purchase of as much tungsten as he could buy, even if this meant paying vastly inflated prices. The intention was to try to starve the Nazi war machine of this indispensable mineral. Sharp's mission had been successful. He had agreed to pay £5,000 per tonne for the tungsten he had purchased — about 50 times what it is worth today. The payments were not all made in hard currency. According to Sharp's grandson, his great-aunt once "saw a small bag on the kitchen table. She felt some hard things inside it and thought that they were marbles, but, when she opened it, she saw that they were uncut diamonds. We think that he used them to pay for the tungsten."

MISTAKEN IDENTITY?

There was another possible explanation for the unprovoked attack. For years, Alfred Chenhalls had been chaffed by his friends because of his close resemblance to Winston Churchill. He had the same portly figure and pink, cherubic face. He wore black Homburg hats, just like the premier. He also smoked six-and-a-half-inch long double Corona cigars.

Like the capital itself, Lisbon's airport was a constant hotbed of intrigue. Abwehr agents were constantly on the watch, noting who might be flying to and from Britain. The British were equally active in observing who was traveling on Luft Hansa planes. Early on the morning Flight 777 was scheduled to depart, two Abwehr agents managed to sneak a look at its passenger list.

Right: In Spitfire, *as* The First of the Few *was retitled in the U.S., Leslie Howard starred as R. J. Mitchell, the designer of the Spitfire. He also directed the movie.*

Opposite: A BOAC DC-3 stands waiting on the tarmac at Gibraltar. The airline ran a regular service to neutral Lisbon to connect with the Pan American flying-boat flights to New York.

They saw the name Chenhalls on it — not so unlike Churchill to the Germans' prying eyes. They also spotted a somewhat corpulent figure preparing to board the DC-3, dressed in a belted blue Molton overcoat, wearing a black Homburg and smoking a long cigar.

To the Nazis, the well set-up cigar-puffer looked very much like the Prime Minister. Could it really be him? They knew Churchill was on his way back to Britain following the conclusion of a conference in

North Africa. Had it been decided that he should fly on Flight 777?

What the Germans overlooked was that the smiling figure on the tarmac was younger and taller than Britain's wartime leader. In any event, they and their superiors were taking no chances. An urgent message was flashed through to the German High Command.

THE FATAL FLIGHT

A few minutes after Flight 777 took to the air, eight Junkers Ju 88

Above: *KLM DC-3s, leased to BOAC, photographed at their home base near Bristol. The DC-3 Howard boarded was a KLM plane with an all-Dutch crew.*

C-6 long-range heavy fighters took off from the Luftwaffe airfield at Kerlin, to the west of Bordeaux. The planes belonged to the 5th Staffel (Squadron) of Kampfgeschwader 40, or V/KG 40 in its abbreviated form. The unit had been formed in September 1942, its primary task being to provide air cover for U-boat squadrons in the Bay of Biscay, which were coming under increasingly effective attack on their way to and from their hunting-grounds in the North Atlantic by Mosquitoes, Beaufighters, Liberators, and Sunderlands, despatched from RAF Coastal Command.

According to Luftwaffe sources, Flight 777 was not targeted intentionally. Rather, the Junkers had been despatched to locate two U-boats in the Bay of Biscay and escort them to safety. Due to bad weather, the search for the U-boats was called off and instead the Junkers initiated a general search of the area.

At 12:45 p.m. the Junkers spotted Flight 777 heading north. Approximately five minutes later, they swept in to attack the aircraft. Oberleutnant Hans Hintze, one of the pilots involved, recalled what happened. "A gray silhouette of a plane was spotted from 2,000 to 3,000 meters," he told an interviewer decades later. "No markings could be made out, but by the shape and construction of the plane it was obviously enemy."

Oberleutnant Albrecht Bellstedt, leading the attack, radioed "Indians at 11 o'clock AA," Luftwaffe shorthand for enemy aircraft ahead, slightly to the left, attack, attack. Immediately, he and the pilot of another Junkers dived to strafe the DC-3 from above and below, setting the port engine and wing on fire. At that point, Hintze, at the head of the other Junkers, caught up with the airliner. Recognizing that it was a civilian plane, he immediately ordered the attack to be aborted. It was too late. The mortally wounded DC-3 crashed into the sea where it floated for a few minutes and then sank. There were no survivors.

Hintze's version of events was corroborated by Ben Rosevink, the son of Enghertus Rosevink, the Flight Engineer of the stricken DC-3 who perished with the rest of the plane's crew and its passengers. In the 1980s, Rosevink patiently tracked down the three surviving Luftwaffe pilots who had taken part in the attack and persuaded them to talk. He interviewed all three of them independently. None were aware that the others were even still alive.

"They said the plane came straight toward them and they attacked straight away because they knew Mosquitoes were patroling the area," Rosevink reported. "They were a lot slower than Mosquitoes so it was either a case of getting in first or they got you. Once they realized it was a civilian plane, there was nothing they could do because it was already going down."

Rosevink concluded: "I sat with the commander of the group that took the planes out and he said there was no point in lying after all these years. He said if he was told to go and do it, he would say so — there was no reason not to. He said they came across it and that was that."

HOW MUCH DID CHURCHILL KNOW?

That appeared to be that, but it still left some crucial questions unanswered. Why had Luftwaffe command not warned the Junkers pilots that a civilian airliner was in the vicinity and then told them not to attack it? Churchill, for one, had no doubts about who was responsible. In *The Hinge of Fate*, the fourth volume of his war memoirs, he wrote: "As my presence in North Africa had been fully reported, the Germans were exceptionally vigilant, and this led to a tragedy which most distressed me.

"The regular commercial aircraft was about to start from the Lisbon airfield when a thickset man smoking a cigar walked up and was thought to be a passenger upon it. The German agents therefore signaled that I was on board. Although these passenger planes had plied unmolested for many months between Portugal and England, a German war plane was instantly ordered out, and the defenseless aircraft was ruthlessly shot down. Thirteen passengers perished, among them the well-known British actor Leslie Howard, whose grace and gifts are still preserved for us by the records of the many delightful films in which he took part."

"The brutality of the Germans was only matched by the stupidity of their agents," Churchill concluded. "It is difficult to understand how anyone could imagine that with all the resources of Great Britain at my disposal I should have booked a passage in an unarmed and unescorted plane from Lisbon and flown home in broad daylight. We of course made a wide loop out by night from Gibraltar into the ocean and arrived home without incident."

Churchill might have known more than he was telling. Although he was almost certainly unaware of them, there were rumors that British Intelligence had itself circulated the story that the Prime Minister might be flying back to Britain on the Lisbon plane. If true, this would have been a classic example of intelligence "disinformation." The premier almost certainly did know that Howard, with whom he was personally acquainted, was reluctant to go ahead with the Spanish part of the lecture tour, which was the ostensible reason for his trip. He had to be persuaded to do so by Antony Eden himself.

Howard, it appears, was depressed when he left Britain. Violette Cunningham, his long-time mistress, had died six months previously from meningitis. Apparently, it was Chenhalls, who himself had to fly to Lisbon on business for the British Treasury, who suggested to Howard that a trip to sunny Iberia would do him good. The actor soon seems to have shaken off his depression. Despite being warned that she was a German spy, he started a headlong affair with a certain Baroness von Podewils, who was in charge of the beauty salon at his Madrid hotel.

Through the actress Conchita Montenegro, herself one of Howard's former mistresses, he apparently made contact with General Franco himself. According to Montenegro in an interview she gave shortly before her death in 2008, Howard had been tasked with trying to persuade the Spanish dictator to remain neutral and stay out of the war. If what Montenegro said was true and Howard was doubling up as a British spy, it would certainly have given the Germans sufficient cause to remove him from the scene. Whether they finally decided that shooting down Flight 777 was the best way of achieving this remains open to question.

Right & below: *Even equipped with drop tanks, the Spitfire did not have the range to escort inward-bound DC-3s over the Bay of Biscay. Luftwaffe Junkers Ju88s regularly patrolled the area, but there was a tacit understanding between the two sides that civilian aircraft were not to be attacked. Why Howard's plane was singled out remains a mystery.*

The Man Who Never Was

In spring 1943 the Western Allies debated what their next objective would be after their victory over the Axis armies in North Africa. The problem was, as Winston Churchill famously put it, "everyone but a bloody fool would know it was Sicily." Two backroom British Intelligence officers came up with a cunning plan to deceive Hitler into believing the attack would fall elsewhere. Operation Mincemeat, as it was christened, was the result.

Above: *Together with his colleague Charles Cholmondeley, Lieutenant-Commander Montagu fooled the Germans. Into believing the Allies were not planning to invade Sicily.*

At around 9:30 a.m. on the morning of April 30, 1943, a fisherman out trawling for sardines off a beach in Spain came across a waterlogged corpse drifting in the sea. He hauled the body onto his boat, headed for the beach and brought it ashore. The dead man was dressed in uniform, was wearing a life jacket, and had a briefcase securely chained to his body. From his personal effects, he was identified by the Spanish authorities in nearby Huelva as William Martin, an acting major in the Royal Marines. The immediate supposition was that he was a British military courier who had drowned after an aircraft flying him to Gibraltar had crashed into the sea.

News of the body's discovery was reported to the British Embassy in Madrid, but not before Adolf Clauss, the local Abwehr agent, had been informed. He quickly passed on the information to his own superiors. In the meantime, because of the heat and the state of the body, which was starting to show the effects of decomposition, the Spanish organized a hasty medical examination. It was concluded that Martin had indeed drowned. Two days later, he was buried in the city cemetery. The briefcase and Martin's personal effects were sent for safe-keeping to naval headquarters in the Spanish capital. The navy passed them on to the Spanish General Staff.

The plot then thickened. The British pressed for the immediate return of the briefcase. The Spanish eventually obliged, but, in the meantime, the Abwehr had got its hands on the briefcase's contents and hastily photographed them. It also examined the personal effects. Once the photographs had been taken, the documents the briefcase contained were carefully reinserted in their original envelopes, re-sealed, and the briefcase returned to the

Spanish to hand back to the British apparently untouched.

The contents included two highly important letters — one from General Sir Archibald Nye, Deputy Chief of the Imperial General Staff to General Sir Harold Alexander, the commander-in-chief of British forces in North Africa, and another from Lord Louis Mountbatten, head of Combined Operations, to Admiral Sir Andrew Cunningham, commander-in-chief of the Mediterranean Fleet. They exposed a vital military secret. The Allies intended to strike in Greece and simultaneously capture the island of Sardinia. They had no plans to invade Sicily at all. Any attack there would be simply a decoy or feint.

"HOOK, LINE, AND SINKER"
The German Embassy in Madrid radioed the contents of the letters to Berlin and rushed the photographs to Oberkommando der Wehrmacht (OKW, "Supreme Command of the Armed Forces") headquarters, where they were examined by Admiral Wilhelm Canaris, the head of the Abwehr, Hitler's top military commanders and by the Führer himself. Initially, at least, he questioned whether Martin's corpse might be an Allied plant, but was soon convinced that he had been a

genuine courier. It followed logically that the information in the letters in the briefcase must also be correct.

Hitler acted immediately. On May 12, he reorganized German defensive priorities throughout the Mediterranean. "Measures regarding Sardinia and the Peloponnese," he ordered, "take precedence over everything else." Three panzer divisions — one from France and two from the Eastern Front — were rushed to Greece and Rommel despatched to take over command of German forces in the region. Mussolini's protests that Sicily remained the obvious Allied target were dismissed out of hand. General Alfred Jodl, the Wehrmacht's head of operations, was overheard bellowing down the telephone to the German military attaché in Rome "You can forget about Sicily. We know it is Greece." More and more troops and military equipment were hastily shifted to be ready to meet and beat the Allied invading forces when they attempted to land.

The British, for their part, were carefully examining the briefcase and its contents to see if they had been tampered with. Despite all the precautions the Abwehr had taken, they soon discovered that this, indeed, had been the case. Instead of being thrown into a state of panic, the opposite was the

Left: *The submarine Seraph transported the dead body of "The Man Who Never Was" secretly to the Spanish coast, where he and his vital briefcase were carefully dumped undetected in the water.*

case. The whole thing had been an elaborate fake. Hitler had reacted just as British Intelligence had hoped. Churchill, who had been in on the plan, was immediately signaled: "Mincemeat (the code name for the operation) swallowed hook, line, and sinker." He, too, was overjoyed. Planning for the invasion of Sicily went full steam ahead. As for the supposed Major Martin, he had never existed. He was truly "the man who never was."

MINCEMEAT'S GENESIS

Who in British Intelligence had the idea for the great deception is still uncertain. Some say that Ian Fleming, then serving in Naval Intelligence and later to win literary fame as the creator of James Bond, had the inspiration, but this seems unlikely. The real credit for what military historian Professor Michael Howard later

labeled "the most successful strategic deception in the history of warfare" was down to two men — Lieutenant-Commander Ewen Montagu, a peacetime barrister now turned Naval Intelligence officer, and Flight Lieutenant Charles Cholmondeley, a bespectacled 25-year-old RAF officer attached to MI5.

The story started in late 1942, when Cholmondeley, backed by Montagu, put up a scheme to plant a corpse carrying false documentation somewhere on neutral territory to mislead the Germans as to future Allied plans in the Mediterranean theater of war. Spain, riddled with pro-Nazi sympathizers, seemed the natural choice. The idea, indeed, might have been sparked by an incident that had taken place there some time before. That September, a few weeks before Operation Torch, the Allied

invasion of French North Africa, was launched, a British Catalina flying boat crashed into the sea off Cadiz. The body of a passenger killed in the accident and carrying a letter giving the date for the projected landings was recovered by the Spanish authorities. They passed the information on to the Germans, who for whatever reason chose to ignore it. If a fake accident could be staged, Cholmondeley and Montagu argued, the enemy this time would be far more likely to act on such information.

Cholmondeley and Montagu called the plan Operation Trojan Horse; it was rechristened Operation Mincemeat at a later date, by which time Montagu had taken over the detailed planning. At the end of March 1943, he had been given the official go-ahead and was ready to proceed. The operational order he drew up read as follows:

OPERATION MINCEMEAT

1. OBJECT

To cause a briefcase containing documents to drift ashore as near as possible to HUELVA in Spain in such circumstances that it will be thought to have been washed ashore from an aircraft which crashed at sea when the case was being taken by an officer from the UK to Allied Forces HQ in North Africa.

2. METHOD

A dead body dressed in the battle-dress uniform of a Major, Royal Marines, and wearing a "Mae West," will be taken out in a submarine, together with the briefcase and a rubber dingy.

The body will be packed fully clothed and ready (and wrapped in a blanket to prevent friction) in a tubular airtight container (which will be labeled as "Optical Instruments").

The container is just under 6 feet 6 inches long and just under two feet in diameter and has no excrescences of any kind on the sides. The end which opens has a flush-fitting lid which is held tightly in position by a number of nuts and has fitted on its exterior in clips a box-spanner with a permanent Tommy-bar which is chained to the lid.

Both ends are fitted with handles which fold down flat. It will be possible to lift the container by using both handles or even by using the handle in the lid alone, but it would be better not to take the whole weight on the handle at the other end, as the steel of which the container is made is of light gauge to keep the weight as low as possible. The approximate weight when the container is full will be 400lb.

When the container is closed the body will be packed round with a certain amount of dry ice. The container should therefore be opened on deck, as the dry ice will give off carbon dioxide.

3. POSITION

The body should be put into the water as close to the shore as prudently possible and as near to HUELVA as possible, preferably to the northwest of the river mouth.

According to the Hydrographical Department, the tides in that area run mainly up and down the coast, and every effort should therefore be made to choose a period with an onshore wind. Southwesterly winds are, in fact, the prevailing winds in that area at this time of year.

The latest information about the tidal streams in that area, as obtained from the Superintendent of Tides, is attached.

4. DELIVERY OF THE PACKAGE

The package will be brought up to the port of departure by road on whatever day is desired, preferably as close to the sailing day as possible. The briefcase will be handed over at the same time to the Captain of the submarine. The rubber dingy will also be a separate parcel.

5. DISPOSAL OF THE BODY

When the body is removed from the container all that will be necessary will be to fasten the chain attached to the briefcase through the belt of the trench coat, which will be the outer garment on the body. The chain is of the type worn under the coat, round the chest and out through the sleeve. At the end is a "dog-lead" type of clip for attaching to the handle of the briefcase and a similar clip for forming the loop round the chest. It is this loop that should be made through the belt of the trench coat as if the officer had slipped the chain off for comfort in the aircraft, but has nevertheless kept it attached to him so that the bag should not either be forgotten or slide away from him in aircraft.

The body should then be deposited in the water, as should also be the rubber dingy. As this should drift at a different speed from the body, the exact position at which it is released is unimportant, but it should be near the body, but not too near if that is possible.

6. THOSE IN THE KNOW IN GIBRALTAR

Steps have been taken to inform F.O.I.C.1 Gibraltar and his S.O. (I).2. No one else there will be in the picture.

7. SIGNALS

If the operation is successfully carried out, a signal should be made "MINCEMEAT completed." If that is made from Gibraltar the S.O. (I). should be asked to send it addressed to D.N.I.3 (PERSONAL). If it can be made earlier it should be made in accordance with order from F.O.S.4.

8. CANCELLATION

If the operation has to be canceled a signal will be made "Cancel MINCEMEAT." In that case the body and container should be sunk in deep water. As the container may have buoyancy, it may either have to be weighted or water may have to be allowed to enter. In the latter case care must be taken that the body does not escape. The briefcase should be handed to the S.O. (I) at Gibraltar, with instructions to burn the contents unopened, if there is no possibility of taking that course earlier. The rubber dingy should be handed to the S.O. (I) for disposal.

1. Flag Officer in Charge
2. Staff Officer, Intelligence
3. Director of Naval Intelligence
4. Flag Officer, Submarines (Admiral Barry)

9. ABANDONMENT

If the operation has to be abandoned, a signal should be made "MINCEMEAT abandoned" as soon as possible (see Para 7 above).

10. COVER

This is a matter for consideration. Until the operation actually takes place, it is thought that the labeling of the container "Optical Instruments" will provide sufficient cover. It is suggested that the cover after the operation has been completed should be that it is hoped to trap a very active German agent in this neighborhood, and it is hoped that sufficient evidence can be obtained by this means to get the Spaniards to eject him. The importance of dealing with this man should be impressed on the crew, together with the fact that any leakage that may *ever* take place will compromise our power to get the Spaniards to act in such cases; also that they will never learn whether we were successful in this objective, as the whole matter will have to be conducted in secrecy with the Spaniards or we won't be able to get them to act.

It is in fact most important that the Germans and Spaniards should accept these papers in accordance with Para I. If they should suspect that the papers are a "plant" it might have far-reaching consequences of great magnitude.

(Signed) *E.E.S. Montagu*
Lt.-Cdr., R.N.V.R.
31.3.43.

Top: *Abwehr intelligence officers with their Enigma machines. By this time, the British cryptologists at Bletchley Park had broken and were reading most of the Enigma codes.*

Above: *Charles Cholmondeley had the idea of planting false papers on a dead British "officer" and making it look as if he had drowned after his plane had crashed into the sea.*

WHOSE BODY?

Faking the documentation and giving the corpse an identity was easy enough. General Nye himself wrote the final draft of the key letter in the briefcase, whereas British Intelligence gathered together an imposing assortment of personal effects to bring Major William Martin — the name chosen for "the man who never was" — to life. As well as a Marine identity card, these included four other letters — one from Martin's father, two from his fiancée, and the fourth from the family solicitor — a snapshot of his fiancée (the picture was actually of a female clerk in MI5), a bill from a leading London jeweler for an engagement ring and another from his club, two theater ticket stubs, and a used bus ticket. There was even a demand from Martin's bank manager for the repayment of his overdraft.

It was left to Montagu to find a suitable body. He started by consulting Sir Bernard Spilsbury, the most celebrated forensic pathologist of the day. Spilsbury assured him that, because people perished in air crashes for many reasons, it was not essential to find a corpse that had died by drowning. Montagu then turned to William Bentley Purchase, the coroner for the St Pancras district of London, to help him in his macabre quest.

Above: *A recruiting poster for the Kriegsmarine. It was vital that the plan to invade Sicily stayed top secret until it was too late for the Germans and Italians to rush reinforcements to the scene.*

Left: *Hitler and Franco meet. Montagu chose pro-Nazi Spain as the best place to plant his dead body. He counted on the Spanish giving the Germans access to the documents in the corpse's briefcase.*

Below: *A German Panzer Mk IV prowls the streets of Athens. Operation Mincemeat worked like a charm. When the Allies landed in Sicily, they took the island's defenders totally by surprise.*

Albeit somewhat reluctantly, Purchase produced a suitable body — or so Montagu said.

For the rest of his life — he died in 1985 — Montagu kept the true identity of the corpse he obtained a secret. Speculation as to who it really was has continued to the present day. In 2003, former police officer Colin Gibbon claimed that William Martin was in fact Tom Martin, a sailor on the escort carrier *Dasher* who perished as a result of a massive internal explosion on the ship just off the coast of Scotland in March 1943. Montagu, so it was alleged, abstracted the body of

the other Martin before it could be buried in a mass grave with the other victims of the explosion. The following year, John Melville, one of Tom Martin's fellow sailors, was publicly named by a Royal Navy officer as "the man who never was."

In 2011, Professor Denis Smyth, a University of Toronto historian, came up with fresh evidence that seemed to confirm Montagu's body was indeed procured for him by the St. Pancras coroner. It was, said Smyth, definitely that of Glyndwr Michael, a 34-year-old alcoholic Welsh vagrant who committed suicide in London

in January 1943. Smyth had unearthed a hitherto overlooked secret memorandum written by Montagu in which he stated that the rat poison Michael had swallowed would be undetectable in a post-mortem and that therefore the Spanish — and the Germans — would never establish the real cause of death.

Supporters of the *Dasher* theory remain unconvinced. They argue that the body of an alcoholic could never have passed as that of a smart Royal Marine officer. Only Montagu knew the real truth — and he took it with him to his grave.

Disaster in Bombay

On April 14, 1944, the city of Bombay was rocked by two massive explosions. They were triggered by a fire, which had been raging unchecked for several hours, on a cargo ship in its bustling harbor. Next day, Japanese-controled Radio Saigon broadcast a full account of the disaster, while, in India, the censorship tried to keep the whole matter under wraps. Was the disaster caused by sabotage? Or was it an avoidable accident?

Left: *A RAF Dakota drops supplies to troops in the jungle. Air drops like this helped the besieged garrisons at Imphal and Kohima hold out against the Japanese.*

Opposite: *A Hawker Hurricane strafes Japanese troops in Burma. The one thing 14th Army could count on was air superiority.*

Early in 1944, though the tide of war had begun to turn decisively against the Japanese in the Pacific, their forces still remained in control of the whole of Burma. They were now planning a major push forward that would take them across the Burmese frontier and on into India. If they succeeded, there would be little to stop them from advancing swiftly across the fertile plains of Bengal, with the port of Calcutta as the ultimate prize.

The offensive began in March 1944, its initial targets being Imphal and Kohima, two defensive strongpoints in the foothills of Assam. The defenders were soon cut off and surrounded. The Japanese had calculated that the onset of the monsoon would effectively put an end to Allied attempts at counterattack, but General William Slim, the commander of the 14th Army, threw reinforcements into battle to relieve the hard-pressed garrisons. British and Indian troops finally broke through to Kohima on April 18. Imphal, which had come under siege on April 5, was relieved in mid-May. The Japanese fell back in confusion. Their attempt to thrust into India was over.

FIRE IN THE HARBOR

During these crucial battles, the British relied heavily on a continuing flow of supplies though the vital port of Bombay (present-day Mumbai) on the west coast of India. Military stores of all kinds would be unloaded from merchant ships there, and then shipped across India by rail or air.

On April 14, 1944, the port was jam-packed with merchant vessels of every description. Among them was the SS *Fort Stikine*, a 7,142-ton freighter. She had sailed from Birkenhead on February 24 and had steamed via Gibraltar, Port Said, the Suez Canal and Karachi to berth at her final destination two days earlier. For reasons of wartime security, she docked without flying the customary red flag to indicate there were high explosives on board. There were 1,395 tons of them, including 300 tons of TNT, together with 12 crated-up Spitfires, timber, scrap

Above left: *A shipment of railway locomotives bound for India, where they were vital for hauling supplies across the subcontinent.*

Above right: *Troops board a Dakota to reinforce the garrison at Imphal, which held out stubbornly against the Japanese until the 14th Army could relieve it.*

iron and $4,293,500 worth of gold bullion. At Karachi, she had taken on in addition 87,000 bales of cotton and a thousand drums of lubricating oil. Some of the latter appeared to be leaky, James Naismith, the ship's captain, vainly protested about being forced to carry such a mixed cargo. It contained "just about everything that will either burn or blow up," he complained. His complaints were ignored.

At about 12:30 p.m. that Friday afternoon, the stevedores who been laboring through the night to unload the ship's cargo, came back to resume work after breaking for lunch. As they boarded *Fort Stikine* again, someone — most probably Mohamed Tagi, the foreman in charge of the stevedores working in No. 2 hold — spotted smoke rising from it on the side nearest the quay and raised the alarm. As swarms of dock workers poured off the stricken vessel, Alex Gow, the ship's Chief Engineer, started its fire pump and the deck crew ran out hoses to the spot where smoke could now be clearly seen

rising from the ship's ventilators. They began to pump water into the hold, joined by the crew from the fire engine stationed on the quay alongside the ship.

Thanks to a breakdown in communication, it took another hour to alert Fire Brigade headquarters to the exact location of the outbreak. Nor were the fire-fighters warned that *Fort Stikine* had high explosives on board. Complacency may also have contributed to the scale and slowness of the reaction. Fires were not uncommon in the Bombay docks — 60 of them had broken out between 1939 and 1944. Consequently, only two more fire engines and 60 firemen were despatched to fight the blaze. No general alarm was raised and the docks were not evacuated. Instead, the stevedores were ordered back to work to continue with the unloading of the ship.

STENCH AND SMOKE

Among the cargo carried by *Fort Stikine* were considerable quantities of fish manure. For some reason, possibly because it had begun to stink appallingly as the heat of the fire grew in intensity, the stevedores were ordered to unload this part of the cargo first. For the time being, the potentially lethal high explosives were left untouched.

By this time, the fire-fighters had discovered where the fire had begun. The blaze had started among the bales of highly combustible cotton which the ship had taken on board at Karachi. Crates of shells and small-arms ammunition were stacked directly below the bales, while

masses of timber lay on top of them. The upper part of the hold also contained the rest of the high explosives. Belatedly, Fire Brigade headquarters were now advised of their presence.

Immediately, all available pumps were rushed to the scene, but, by this time, the fire was in danger of getting out of control. Captain Brinley Thomas Oberst, an army ordnance officer who had been summoned to the dockside while finishing his lunch in his Colaha apartment, went below to check on the high explosives. He returned grim-faced to report to Naismith. He told the captain that *Fort Stikine* ought to be scuttled at once.

There was an immediate problem. There was just four feet (1.2 m) of water between the keel of the berthed ship and the bed of the harbor. Even if her crew did try to scuttle her, she would not take on enough water to flood even the lower part of the affected hold. The only other option was to take her out to sea and scuttle her there. Because engineers were already at work repairing a valve on the main engine, *Fort Stikine* was immovable except by tug. It would have taken quite some time to get tugs into position to tow her out of the harbor — and time, of course, was something the fire-fighters did not have on their side.

THE FIRST EXPLOSION

There followed nearly an hour of indecision, muddle, and confusion. More and more fire engines and their crews arrived on the scene as the unequal battle continued against the heat, smoke, and flames. They were joined by Norman Combs, the head of the Bombay Fire Brigade. The rattle of exploding small-arms ammunition was heard on board and the water the firemen were standing in started to boil.

The battle to save *Fort Stikine* was lost. As Combs shouted to his firemen to "get clear," Naismith ordered his crew to abandon ship. Some of the firemen jumped onto the jetty, while others, including Combs himself, leapt overboard into the water. On *Belray*, a Norwegian freighter anchored close by *Fort Stikine*, Roy Hayward, a young Able Seaman, saw the rising flames

Left: *A Dakota drops much needed supplies of food and ammunition to the troops on the ground. The Japanese had no such aerial back-up.*

had got off her safely. He retraced his steps down the gangplank and started to walk along the quayside to where his First Mate and a marine surveyor from the Bombay office of Lloyds were standing. Then the explosives detonated. The surveyor was blown yards down the quay and rendered unconscious. When he came to, he found that every stitch of clothing had been stripped from his body to leave him totally naked. Miraculously, he was otherwise unharmed. No trace of Naismith or the First Mate was ever found.

Oberst, too, was flung up into the air by the force of the blast, landing in a pile of dunnage. As he surveyed the scene, he could see bodies lying all around him, most with their skin burnt off — 66 of them were firemen who had been killed out-right; 83 more were badly injured.

A BIGGER BLAST

Derek P. Ings, the Assistant Purser of *Chantilly*, which was moored in a nearby dock, recalled his own experiences some years later.

suddenly turn yellowish brown. Hayward had fought fires before in the London Blitz. He knew what the change in color meant. It was caused by burning explosives. He shouted a warning, although it is doubtful whether anyone heard him, and threw himself down flat on the deck.

Moments later, a pillar of fire soared upward from *Fort Stikine* and a terrific explosion echoed throughout the docks and the

city. It was precisely 4:06 p.m. The force of the blast was channeled horizontally through the ship's side, sweeping across the quay to obliterate the sheds and warehouses to landward. Jagged metal fragments scythed outward like a blast from a huge shotgun, cutting down anything and everything in their path.

Just before the explosion, Naismith had returned to his ship to check that everyone

"I remember going ashore during the afternoon for a haircut. On the return to the ship at about 4:15 p.m., I was walking along a road just inside Alexandra Dock from Green Gate when I became conscious that smoke and flames were shooting high into the sky in the distance immediately in front of me. Before I could fully realize what was happening the ground around was shaken by a tremendous explosion which made me step back a pace or two and raise my hands as though to protect myself."

"My next recollection is of the surrounding confusion as the people in the dock area took to their heels in no uncertain manner. I made my way to *Chantilly*, which was lying on the outer wall of Alexandra Dock. I expected that a nearby tanker had exploded, but, as I neared the berth, I could see that the explosion had taken place farther away than I had thought, and in fact it was in Victoria Dock."

"All the while there were minor explosions but at approximately 4:45 p.m. there was another explosion as violent, if not more so, than the first. By this time I was back on board and the whole ship shook as though hit by a torpedo. A number of windows, window frames, and door locks were shattered and shrapnel from the explosion, about three-quarters of a mile away, fell on and around the ship."

The second explosion was indeed bigger and even more destructive than the first. A huge column of flame and smoke tore through the shattered remains of *Fort Stikine* and shot up to a height of several thousand feet, flinging tons of metal — including some of the gold bullion *Fort Stikine* had been carrying — into the harbor area and the adjacent town. Flaming cotton, sulfur, and resin cascaded into warehouses and residential homes over a radius of more than half a mile, setting them aflame so that the docks were ringed by fire. Ings continued his story:

"I had to return ashore shortly afterward and, passing through the dock area, found abandoned vehicles and dhows at many points, some of the dhows in the stream with their cargoes of cotton ablaze. My journey took me through Green Gate and along Ballard Road to St George's Hospital where I intended visiting a shipmate. It was now an hour after the first explosion and all the shops, stalls, and eating places had closed. Many of the windows of offices and shops had been blown out and glass and roof tiles were strewn everywhere."

"I reached the hospital at about 5:30 p.m.; passing a dead gharry horse lying at the entrance. My friend had been put out of his bed to make room for the injured that were arriving by ambulance in a very dirty and bedraggled condition. Mattresses were being put down all over the ground floor to treat the casualties."

"On my way back to the ship I could see Royal Indian Navy sailors being sent by lorry to fight the fire at Victoria Dock, the pall of smoke from which hung like a cloud over the whole of the city. The police had now closed Red Gate and I had to walk round to Green Gate to get back into the docks. On the way and only a few yards from Mackinnons' office, I came upon a piece of twisted steel plate about 12 inches by six inches which had been blown over a mile by the explosion to land harmlessly in the road."

"As I neared the ship I saw some of the crew leaving hurriedly and found that another explosion (of 1,200 cylinders of H.P. gas) was expected at any time and we were warned to keep off the decks. The earlier explosions had flung incendiary bombs over a wide area and small fires were burning everywhere. There were now 30 burning dhows in the stream and, as they sank, their cargoes of cotton still smouldered on the surface. The ships on the harbor wall, including ourselves and Mantola, put down boats to rescue the dhow crews."

"Darkness fell and the night sky reflected the blazing parts of the city. I watched from the monkey island and could hear the hiss of the cylinders as they ignited one by one. I turned in at 11:00 p.m. to the sound of the occasional explosion of gas cylinders and with a burning dhow outside my porthole."

Left: Chantilly *was one of the other merchantmen in Bombay harbour made a casualty when* Fort Stikine *blew up.*

Left: *A fragment of Fort Stikine's propeller is still preserved where it landed after the explosion.*

Right: *General Sir William Slim (later Lord Slim) was commander of the 14th Army in Burma. Because of the lack of press coverage they received, his men referred to themselves as "the forgotten army."*

AFTERMATH

In St. George's Hospital, 200 victims of the explosions required surgery, with nearly 200 more treated for less serious injuries. No one was ever able to establish what the final death toll was, as many victims simply disappeared in the blasts. Some sources put it as high as 1,200.

For days, thousands of soldiers and sailors labored to remove explosives to safe places away from the shattered dock area. They put their own lives at serious risk, for ammunition was constantly exploding in the remains of blazing warehouses. Sixteen ships, many of them with explosives on board, had to be towed out into the open sea that night and during the following day.

The destruction inside the docks was frightful. No fewer than 27 ships had been sunk, gutted by fire or severely damaged and all the dockyard buildings had been devastated. Three swing bridges at the entrance to the docks had been partly torn from their seatings and leaned at drunken angles. It would take 10,000 British and Indian servicemen and civilians six months to clear away the wreckage and get the harbor in full working order again. In the meantime, the scale of the destruction was kept as secret as possible, thanks mainly to the strict censorship that was imposed.

What caused the fire has never been established. Many at the time suspected it was the result of deliberate sabotage. Certainly, there were a number of pro-Japanese factions active in India at the time and, with the Japanese Army knocking at India's back door, the British authorities were battling with growing civil unrest and active attempts to impede the Allied war effort. Others believed it was caused by something as simple as a carelessly discarded cigarette. The truth remains a mystery that will probably never be solved.

The Death Train

On the night of March 3, 1944, a heavily overloaded freight train stalled inside the Armi tunnel outside the hillside village of Balvano between Salerno and Potenza in southern Italy. Instead of backing the train out of the tunnel to safety, the drivers of the two steam engines hauling it unavailingly tried to force their way forward. The black clouds of smoke the effort produced were full of deadly carbon monoxide gas. The result was disaster on an epic scale.

Like dozens of other villages scattered throughout the Apennine Mountains of central and southern Italy, Balvano, which lies beside a twisting mountain road between Salerno and Potenza, is picturesque, although otherwise unremarkable. The one odd thing about it is its cemetery, which is larger than most.

Closer inspection, however, reveals a horrifying fact. The cemetery contains three mass graves, the last resting place of some 600 people. All of them died in mysterious circumstances in the same place at the same time — in the early hours of March 3, 1944.

A BLEAK WINTER

Following Italy's capitulation and their landings on the Italian mainland in September 1943, the Allies, after bitter fighting throughout the winter, had succeeded in driving Field Marshal Kesselring's German forces back to new defensive positions halfway up the peninsula. Despite all their efforts, the Allies had not yet managed to break through the so-called Gustav Line; particularly

Above: *An RAF Martin Baltimore bomber attacks enemy rail communications during the battle for Italy. Blocking rail tunnels was a primary objective.*

Opposite: *For the Germans, keeping supply trains like this one running smoothly was vital. They lacked the fuel required for automobile transport.*

bitter fighting was in progress at a place called Monte Cassino.

In the south, the Allied occupation forces were trying hard to restore order, rebuild shattered communications, and ensure a regular supply of foodstuffs and other essentials to the local

people, many of whom had been forced to live virtually at starvation level during the peculiarly severe winter. The authorities had to content with a flourishing black market centered on Naples, where men, women, and even children bargained and bartered with Allied soldiers for cigarettes, chocolate, candy, and chewing gum,. All of these could be swapped in the countryside for eggs, poultry, meat, butter and other dairy products. Consequently, every goods train that ran to and from the city was regularly crammed with hundreds of stowaway black marketers.

Getting on board the trains for free was easy at various places along the tracks. The trains, fueled by inferior wartime coal, moved at a walking pace through the mountains, especially when they hit a steep gradient. The black marketers knew exactly where to wait and then jump on board. If they were ejected by military police or Italian carabiniere at a station stop, they simply walked up the tracks and scrambled on board again once the trains were clear of the station.

PRELUDE TO DISASTER

Train No. 8017 crawled out of Salerno just after 6:00 p.m. on the evening of March 2. Running between the city and Potenza every Thursday night, it was always packed with illicit travelers — a fact that had earned it the nickname of the Black Market Express. Normally, it would have been hauled by an electric locomotive, but, as the overhead power lines of the electrification system had been damaged, a steam locomotive had to be substituted on this occasion.

The train consisted of 47 wagons, about 20 of them open box-cars or flat cars. Although as a freight train it was not supposed to carry passengers, it was common at the time for both soldiers and civilians to hitch rides on any convenient train. As it rattled into the mountains, about halfway into its journey, it had already picked up about 600 illegal passengers as well as between 100 and 200 legitimate ones. High in the mountains, about 30 miles from Potenza, its final destination, it stopped at Romagnano so that

a second locomotive could be attached to help the overloaded train cope with the even stiffer climb that lay ahead.

After some delay, the train left Romagnano, churning its way slowly up a steep gradient. After only 4 miles (6 km), however, it was forced to a halt with half its length inside a long mountain tunnel not far from the village of Balvano. The locomotive of the train ahead of it was suffering from a mechanical fault and was blocking the line.

It was nearly three-quarters of an hour before Train No. 8017 was cleared to move forward again. Most of its passengers had not noticed the delay — they were asleep. By this time it was just a few minutes before 1:00 a.m.

Balvano rail halt was half a mile beyond the tunnel. The train stopped there so that

the locomotives could take on more water and then struggled laboriously onward up the ever-steepening gradient. As it left the station, Giuseppe Salonia, the assistant station-master, telegraphed to Bella-Muro, the next station up the line, to signal that it was on the move and then watched it disappear toward the next tunnel, a narrow single-track mile-long cut through the mountains called the Galleria delle Armi. He then went indoors to the warmth of his stove and settled down to read his newspaper in peace. The next train was not scheduled for another hour.

DEATH INSIDE THE TUNNEL
The distance between Balvano and Bella-Muro was less than 5 miles

(8 km) — a run of about 20 minutes or at the speed Train No. 8017 was traveling. It never arrived. In fact, it never emerged from the far end of the Galleria della Armi.

At Bella-Muro, the station-master was curious about the non-arrival, but put it down to simple lateness. At Balvano, however, Salonia grew anxious as the time passed. He had not received the customary message from Bella-Muro to say that the train had arrived. The only thing he heard was that it was running late and that he was to hold the next train in the station until he received word that the line was cleared.

When the train arrived at about 2.40 a.m., Salonia ordered its locomotive to be detached so that he could steam up the line to see if he could find out what was going on. Almost immediately after the locomotive had started off, he spotted a man by the side of the track, shouting and swinging a red lantern wildly. As Salonia dropped down off the footplate, the man collapsed. He murmured to Salonia: "They're all dead."

Salonia was baffled. The night was still. If there had been a crash or derailment, he would certainly have heard the noise. By now, the man was crying bitterly. Salonia decided to take him back to the

Above: *General Mark Clark commanded the U.S. 5th Army in Italy. A military prima donna, he was determined his troops should be first to reach Rome.*

station and try to coax what had happened out of him.

THE BRAKEMAN'S TALE

The man turned out to be Michele Palo, the brakeman of Train No. 8017. He described how the train had suddenly shuddered to a halt after entering the curving mile-long tunnel. With the exception of his brake van and three freight cars at the rear, the entire train was stuck inside. No whistle sounded from either engine to indicate that there was anything wrong, so Palo assumed they must have stopped at a red signal. He fell into a fitful doze.

Suddenly Palo woke up and popped his head out of the window of his brake van to see if he could tell why the train

was still not on the move. He could see nothing untoward, so he jumped down onto the permanent way and started up the tunnel to investigate further. As soon as he came across some dead bodies, he turned on his heels and hurried back down the line toward Balvano.

Having listened horror-struck to Palo's grisly story, Salonia set off again on the borrowed locomotive. It was nearly 4:00 a.m. before he reached the tunnel and Train No. 8017. He climbed down from his locomotive and made his way up the track to the first carriage he could see. He slid one of its doors open and shone his lantern inside. The passengers were sprawled across their seats and on the floor. All were dead. Salonia checked the rest of the train. It was the same story. Dozens of corpses lay beside the track as well. He hastened back to Balvano to raise the alarm.

Police, railway officials, and U.S. Army troops soon arrived on the scene. They brought the locomotive into the tunnel and hooked it up to Palo's brake van. Releasing No. 8017's brakes, they towed the stricken train slowly back to the station at Balvano. It was there that the full extent of the horror was revealed.

Above: *U.S. staff officers confer at Salerno. The landings on this beach were relatively unopposed. But it was a different story elsewhere.*

Right: *U.S. troops go ashore. Operation Avalanche got off to a good start, but the Americans soon faced fierce resistance. The 16th Panzers were ordered to drive them back into the sea.*

GRISLY AFTERMATH

The entire train was choked with dead. They appeared to have died quietly, with no signs of struggle. A U.S. Army officer noted: "The faces of the victims were mostly peaceful. They showed no signs of suffering. Many of them were sitting upright or in positions they might assume when sleeping normally." There were apparently only five survivors in all. Three of them were rushed to hospital in the military vehicles that had raced to the scene of the disaster from Potenza. They had been fortunate enough to have been in the last three freight cars — the ones closest to the fresh air outside the long tunnel.

Another survivor was an olive-oil salesman, who had left the train for a few minutes to get a breath of fresh air while it was stopped at Balvano. Perhaps because of this, he was one of the few passengers who failed to drop off to sleep. After the train stopped in the tunnel, something made him start to cough violently, so he wrapped his scarf over his mouth. Then he climbed down from the train and began to pick his way unsteadily down the tunnel. He tried to climb into the train again, but collapsed by the side of the tracks. There, he was eventually discovered by two policemen, who assumed, like the rest of the victims, he was dead. He came to in the makeshift mortuary that had been set up in the station at Balvano. A second died as a result of brain damage shortly after his rescue.

WHAT CAUSED THE DISASTER?

Exactly what happened inside the tunnel will never be known, since the drivers and footplatemen of both locomotives lost their lives. The survivors — the other three disappeared after being given first aid, probably to avoid police questioning — had little or no recollection of the incident, although either one or two of them thought that the train had started to slide backward for some distance before finally coming to a halt.

The likeliest explanation of the catastrophe was that when the locomotives reached the middle of the tunnel they could no longer develop sufficient power to pull the overloaded train farther forward. Instead, they began to lose traction, causing the whole train to start to slip backward on the already icy rails. At that moment, conflicting actions by the two drivers effectively sealed the fate of the hundreds of people on board.

When railway accident investigators first climbed onto the two locomotives while they were still in the tunnel, they found an extraordinary thing. Whereas the leading locomotive's controls were set in reverse with its brakes full off, the second one had its brakes full on and its throttle set at full ahead. The two drivers, each with his own idea of how to extricate the train from its predicament and get it on the move again, had acted independently of one another and, in so doing, had succeeded only in rendering it completely immobile.

Smoke and toxic gases — mostly carbon monoxide — pouring back down through the tunnel from the locomotives' smoke stacks had done the rest. Most of the passengers must have died in their sleep, never realizing what was happening to them. The lucky ones were, like the olive-oil salesman, in the part of the train in the rearward part of the tunnel, where the air was not yet starved of oxygen. When the fumes reached them, they wakened, coughing and fighting for breath. Just five staggered out into the clean air. The rest perished alongside the train on the track. The final death toll was never precisely established, but stood between 500 and 600.

KEEPING IT QUIET

The really curious aspect of this terrible tragedy was that there does not appear to have been a searching investigation into its cause. The Americans did order a Board of Enquiry, which swiftly reached a conclusion. The five U.S. Army officers who sat on it concluded that the disaster was "an act of God." Nor were questions asked as to if anything similar had ever happened before.

In fact, it had, though neither the Italian nor the Allied authorities were aware of it. Exactly three months earlier on January 3 ,1944, between 500 and 800

people had died from asphyxiation as a result of the fire that broke out after three trains collided in the Torro tunnel near the village of Torre del Bierzo in Spain. The accident happened when the brakes of the Galicia Express from Madrid to Corunna failed. The runaway collided with the rear of a freight train that was already in the tunnel. Minutes later, an oncoming coal train plowed into the wreckage. The resulting fire took two days to extinguish.

The incident was hushed up at the time on the orders of General Franco, the Spanish dictator. Details of it began to emerge only years after the war. A similar news blackout was imposed after the Italian train disaster. Both the Italian and Allied authorities judged that allowing it to be reported fully might severely dent civilian morale. There may also have been another more sinister reason — to protect those who had authorized the purchase of cheaper low-grade coal on the railways in an effort to get around wartime shortages.

After the incident, the Italian railway authorities streamlined the procedure for the movement of trains through the mountain tunnels and established new safeguards to prevent such a disaster ever occurring again. For the bereaved families of the victims, however, it was all too little and too late.

In 1951, 300 lawsuits alleging "manslaughter through negligence" were filed against the Italian state railways by relatives of the victims. The decision to allow the use of substandard coal was cited in support of the accusation. The claimants demanded more than a billion lire in compensation. The lawyers for the railways successfully argued that the relatives were not entitled to claim compensation because none of the dead had paid for their tickets. Magnanimously, it was agreed to compensate the families of the dead train crews.

Above: *Spitfires on patrol over Sicily. Forced to fly from bases on the mainland, the Luftwaffe was conspicuously absent for much of the campaign.*

Above: *General Sir Bernard Montgomery commanded the 8th Army in Sicily and Italy until he was transferred to command the ground forces in the D-Day landings.*

The Submarine that Sank Itself

TOP SECRET ★ CLASSIFIED ★ TOP SECRET

On October 24, 1944, USS Tang *was nearing the end of her fifth wartime patrol. To date, she had sunk 31 Japanese vessels — a total of roughly 227,800 tons of enemy shipping. She had sent two more tankers to the bottom, badly damaged a troop transport, and sunk a destroyer early that morning. Now, with just two torpedoes left, she maneuvered for the kill. The first torpedo struck the wounded transport. Then something totally unexpected occurred.*

The USS *Tang* was a naval phenomenon. A Balao class fleet submarine launched in 1943, she had sunk 20 Japanese vessels on her first four Pacific war patrols. On her fifth, which began on September 24, 1944, she had already added nine more to her score. Now, as dawn broke on October 25, she began to close in on yet another Japanese convoy in the Formosa Strait, a 100-mile (160 km) wide stretch of water that separated the Island of Formosa (present-day Taiwan) from the Chinese mainland.

INTO ACTION

Commander Richard H. O'Kane, *Tang's* skipper, was confident of yet another success. In his first encounter with the enemy on the evening of October 10, he had torpedoed and sank two heavily laden freighters. The next convoy he attacked was larger — it consisted of five freighters and five escort vessels. O'Kane skillfully maneuvered *Tang* past the escorts without being detected. Then he fired nine torpedoes at point-blank range, sinking three of the five freighters.

A ferocious free-for-all followed. With freighters exploding right and left and escorts steaming flat-out in all directions attempting to locate the attacker, *Tang* dodged and weaved, trying to avoid contact with the enemy. Looming out of the smoke, a troop transport bore down on *Tang* and attempted to ram her. O'Kane managed to dodge the collision. Now, he faced the escorting Japanese destroyers. Instead of submerging, O'Kane swung his submarine around to attack his attackers. Though his torpedo tubes were not yet reloaded, O'Kane aimed *Tang's* bow straight at the nearest destroyer and charged the Japanese ship at full speed. The bluff worked. Unwilling to risk a possible torpedo hit, the destroyer swung away, and *Tang* made good her escape.

Late in the evening of October 24, *Tang* made radar contact with yet another convoy. O'Kane

shadowed it patiently through the night, before readying the submarine for a daybreak surface attack. This time, as *Tang* closed in on the Japanese, she was detected by the convoy's escorts. They immediately opened fire. The undaunted O'Kane boldly remained on the surface and calmly maneuvered into position for his attack. .

At a range of 1,000 yards (915 m), O'Kane fired six torpedoes: two at a transport, two at a second transport, and two at a tanker. All the torpedoes hit their targets.

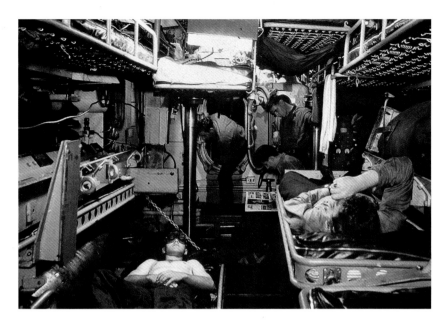

Left: *U.S. submariners relax in their crowded quarters. In an emergency, they all had to know what to do instantly.*

Top right: *A U.S. submarine commander scans the horizon through his periscope for targets.*

Bottom right: *The rogue torpedo that hit and sank* Tang *was fired from the forward torpedo room.*

As O'Kane maneuvered *Tang* to strike again, three Japanese destroyers charged at the submarine, steaming flat-out at 30 knots. Also at full speed, *Tang* countercharged her attackers. This time there was no bluff involved. The submarine's bow torpedo tubes were fully loaded. As he closed the range, O'Kane quickly fired three torpedoes to clear his way. The first torpedo struck the tanker; the second hit the transport and stopped it dead in the water; and the third struck one of the destroyers. *Tang* dashed through the resulting gap.

THE ROGUE TORPEDO

Tang had just two torpedoes left. O'Kane decided he would use them to try to finish off the transport he had crippled during his earlier attack. He brought *Tang* onto a new heading, settled down behind the torpedo sight on the bridge, and passed the deflection angle to the bow torpedo compartment below. Once he received word that the torpedo crew was ready, O'Kane gave the order to fire.

The two torpedoes streaked out of the bow tubes. The first ran straight and true toward its intended target. The other did not. Suddenly, one of the eight other men on the bridge with O'Kane, shouted in alarm and pointed out to sea. Several pairs of eyes picked out the phosphorescent wake of

a torpedo heading straight for the submarine. It was still some distance away off the port bow.

Preoccupied as he was, O'Kane still found time to wonder where the attack had come from. There were no Japanese warships within range apart from the one he had recently attacked and was now clearly out of action. Constant sonar sweeps had not detected the presence of an enemy submarine. *Tang* was fitted with the most up-to-date detection equipment. It was inconceivable that she could have been taken by surprise.

Yet the torpedo was still powering its way toward her. O'Kane was confident that it

Right: *U.S. submarine deck gunners at exercise with their weapon. Like many U-boat commanders, O'Kane favored attacking on the surface whenever possible.*

would miss. He had ordered the necessary evasive action to be taken in plenty of time. Then came the shock. The incoming torpedo was not running on a straight track. It appeared to be moving around *Tang* in a big circle — but one that was getting gradually smaller in diameter. The submarine was trapped.

In his book, *Clear the Bridge!*, which he wrote some 30 years later, O'Kane vividly described what happened next:

"'All ahead emergency! Right full rudder!' initiated a fishtail maneuver in a desperate attempt to move our ship outside of the speeding torpedo's turning circle. On our bow, and now coming abeam, the torpedo continued to

porpoise as it heeled in the turn, causing the jammed vertical rudder to become momentarily horizontal. In less than 10 seconds it had reached its maximum distance abeam, about 20 yards (18 m). It was now coming in. We had only seconds to get out of its way."

"'Left full rudder' to swing our stern clear of the warhead was our

Right: *The aft engine room of a U.S. fleet submarine. It was a fire in the nearby battery compartment that helped to cripple* Tang.

only chance. The luminous wake from our screws, the black exhaust from four overloaded diesels, each told that our engineers were doing their damnedest. The problem was akin to moving a ship longer than a football field and proceeding at harbor speed clear of a suddenly careening speedboat. It would be close."

TANG IS TORPEDOED

O'Kane continued his dramatic account:

"The torpedo hit abreast the after torpedo room, close to the maneuvering room bulkhead. The detonation was devastating, our stern going under before the topside watch could recover. One glance aft told me that there would be insufficient time to clear the bridge. My order, 'Close the hatch,' was automatic, and my heart went out to those below and to the young men topside who must now face the sea."

"Our ship sank by the stern in seconds, the way a pendulum might swing down in a viscous liquid. The seas rolled in from aft, washing us from the bridge and shears, and of small consolation

now was the detonation of the 23rd torpedo as it hit home in the transport."

"*Tang's* bow hung at a sharp angle above the surface, moving about in the current as does a buoy in a seaway. She appeared to be struggling like a great wounded animal, a leviathan, as indeed she was. I found myself orally cheering encouragement and striking out impulsively to reach her. Closing *Tang* against the current was painfully slow and interrupted momentarily by a depth-charging patrol. Now, close ahead, *Tang's* bow suddenly plunged down to Davy Jones' locker, and the lonely seas seemed to share in my total grief."

A BATTLE FOR SURVIVAL

The men in the various compartments of *Tang* were

unaware of the unfolding drama. The first they knew of it was when the submarine whipped round violently — "like a giant fish grabbed by the tail," recalled Motor Machinist Mate Second Class Jesse DaSilva — and then shook as a terrific explosion echoed through its hull from somewhere near the stern. The immediate thought of those who survived the impact was that *Tang* must have struck a mine. The men in the three stern compartments never stood a chance. Mercifully, many of them would have been rendered unconscious by concussion before the water poured in to drown them.

On the bridge, O'Kane just had time to shout an order to close the conning-tower hatch before the torpedo struck. Then the force of the explosion threw him and the eight others into the sea. Some of them were injured and unable to help themselves; no one had been wearing a life-jacket. Within seconds there were only four survivors in the water — O'Kane, Bill Leibold, the Chief Boatswain's Mate, Lieutenant Larry Savadkin, the Engineering Officer, and a radar specialist named Floyd Caverly who, seconds before the torpedo struck, had come topside to report the failure of some of his equipment.

Tang went down stern first at terrifying speed. There was another shock as her stern struck the bottom at a depth of 180 feet (55m). O'Kane's split-second action in ordering the closing of the conning-tower hatch had undoubtedly saved many lives, but the plight of the crew trapped inside the submarine was still desperate. Several were seriously injured In addition, an electrical fire had broken out in the forward battery compartment. It was quickly extinguished, but the interior of the boat continued to fill with smoke and fumes from the smoldering cables.

One of the men trapped in the boat was a seaman mechanic named Clayton Oliver. When he recovered his senses, he found himself next to the venting valve for a main ballast tank. He knew that, for the survivors to have a chance of using their Momsen Lungs — a primitive form of underwater escape apparatus — the submarine needed to be more or less on an even keel. He vented the tank and *Tang* began to settle. He and some of the other survivors then destroyed the top secret documents filed in the control room before making their way to the forward torpedo compartment and its escape chamber.

The attempt had to be delayed for four hours. Japanese destroyers had started dropping depth charges in random patterns in the vicinity of what remained of the convoy *Tang* had savaged so severely. Though none of the depth charges exploded near enough to damage the submarine further, the continual concussions were nightmarish. Some of the 30 or so survivors lapsed into unconsciousness. The rest waited patiently for the Japanese to give up their attacks. They knew that, should they proceed with their escape while the attack was still in progress, the underwater shock waves could and would kill them.

ESCAPING TO THE SURFACE

Eventually, the depth charging came to an end and the survivors, directed by Lieutenant Jim Flanagan, the *Tang's* Torpedo Officer, set about preparing to abandon the submarine. Flanagan got the first four men into the escape chamber. An inflatable rubber dinghy was passed to them before the chamber was flooded. It was drained and opened 30 minutes later. Three of the four men were still inside it, half-drowned and barely conscious. Only one had managed to get through the escape hatch, and, as Flanagan later discovered, he did not manage to make it to the surface.

Flanagan tried again. This time, five men were squeezed into the chamber and the flooding-up and draining-down process took 45 minutes to complete. When it was over, Flanagan found that only three men had managed to make their escape. The other two were still inside.

By this time, Flanagan was exhausted. Ensign Basil Pearce Jr. took over from him. Four more men entered the chamber. Although all of them cleared the escape hatch safely, only one survived to reach the surface. Pearce then persuaded Flanagan to leave with the fourth group. As he laboriously hauled himself up the cable that led from the escape chamber to the surface,

Above & left: *Lieutenant-Commander Richard O'Kane, captain of Tang, portrayed by artist Albert K. Murray and photographed, survived the sinking and subsequent Japanese imprisonment. He was awarded the Congressional Medal of Honor for the heroism he displayed on board his submarine.*

where it was attached to a float, he felt a series of concussions below. Before his departure he had noticed that the fire in the battery compartment had flared up again. It was now so fierce that the paint on the inside of the bulkhead separating the forward torpedo room from the compartment had started to bubble and blister. Worse still, the rubber gasket sealing the watertight door had begun to smolder in the intense heat. It must have given way. There was now no hope of escape for those still trapped in the wreck. They were all asphyxiated by smoke from the fire and deadly chlorine gas leaking from the battery compartment.

THE SURVIVORS

Of the 87 officers and ratings that had made up *Tang's* crew, only 15 survived. They were plucked out of the Pacific by a Japanese destroyer, one of four which were already searching for Japanese troops and naval personnel from the ships the U.S. submarine had torpedoed. The survivors were promptly set upon and beaten. O'Kane commented dryly: "When we realized that our clubbings and kickings were being administered by the burned, mutilated survivors of our own handiwork, we found we could take it with less prejudice."

For the survivors, the ordeal was just beginning. They were taken to Formosa, put on a train to the other end of the island, and thrown into a prison camp there. Two days later, they were separated and sent on two ships to Japan. After arriving at a naval training center, they were again put on a train — this time, bound for Ofuma, not far from Tokyo. It was wet and cold when they reached the town to be force-marched to their new prison camp.

"The only thing I had on was a pair of dungarees," DaSilva recalled. "I had lost one of my sandals after we were torpedoed and I kicked the other one off before I escaped, so my feet were very sore and numb from the cold." Pete Narowanski still wore the pair of Hawaiian shorts he had on when he escaped. Both men were issued with a dry shirt, pants, and a pair of tennis shoes "about three sizes too small." According to DaSilva, that was all the clothing they received for the 10 months they were prisoners.

Food was in equally short supply. "We mostly talked about food, food, food," DaSilva said, "as our rations were getting smaller." Things grew even worse when they were moved to Omori, in the vicinity of Yokohama. There, the

survivors' rations consisted of a mixture of barley and rice and a small bowl of soup three times a day. Sometimes, they were given a few small pieces of fish. They were never fed meat.

It was a starvation diet. When the prison camp was finally liberated by American troops on August 29, 1945, they found only nine of the original 15 survivors still alive. Commander O'Kane was among them. At the time he was freed, he weighed only 88 pounds (40 kg). Savadkin, Flanagan, Caverly, Leibold, DaSilva, Decker, another Torpedoman called Hayes Tucker, and Narowanski were the others.

No one was more surprised than the Navy Department that there were any survivors at all. It believed *Tang* had gone down with all hands. It also puzzled over what had caused the submarine to sink. It did not believe she had been destroyed by the Japanese, but how she had really met her end remained a mystery.

It was O'Kane who supplied the answer. *Tang* had sunk itself with its malfunctioning last torpedo. It was a tragic ending to what Vice-Admiral Charles Lockwood, commander of the submarine task force in the Pacific, called "one of the greatest submarine cruises of all time."

Above: *The 22 downed U.S. airmen* Tang *rescued from the sea on her second war patrol pose for the camera on and in front of her coning tower.*

Double Cross: The Story of the D-Day Spies

In 1944, everybody knew that D-Day, when it happened, would decide the outcome of the war. If Hitler could discover where and when the landings would take place, he might well be able to drive the Allies back into the sea. If they could fool him into believing that the landings would take place elsewhere, they would gain vital time to build up their bridgeheads before sweeping forward to victory. The scene was set for an epic battle of wits.

On June 6, 1944, 150,000 Allied troops landed on the beaches of Normandy in northern France. Operation Overlord, the official code name for the D-Day invasion, was finally underway. It had been more than a year in the planning. So, too, had a far more shadowy, but equally vital plan to fool the Germans into believing that the invasion would take place elsewhere.

The overall deception plan was called Operation Bodyguard. The name came from a chance remark made by Winston Churchill to Joseph Stalin during the Tehran Conference in November 1943, when the plans for the proposed invasion were being discussed. The British premier pronounced, "the truth is so precious that it should always be attended by a bodyguard of lies." The Soviet dictator riposted: "This is what we call military cunning." Thomas Argyll Robertson, universally known as Tar, and John Masterman, two of the leading lights of British counterintelligence, were tasked with devising a foolproof scheme for deceiving the Germans and getting it up and running in the shortest possible time. Their part of the plan was called Operation Fortitude.

Robertson was a counterintelligence professional, who had been persuaded by Vernon Kell, the Director-General of MI5, to abandon his unsatisfactory career in banking to join the Secret Service in 1933. He was now head of Section B1 (a) of MI5. Masterman was a cerebral Oxford history don, who had volunteered to join British counterintelligence when war broke out. He chaired the so-called Twenty Committee, so named because 20 in Roman numerals is a double cross. The two men were

Below: *An RAF Handley Page Halifax bomber in flight over Normandy. The Allied air forces were the ground troops' flying artillery.*

so successful that, by 1942, they had "turned" every known German spy in the UK into double agents.

WHERE AND WHEN?

The people planning Overlord were faced with an immediate problem. In the words of one of them, it was "utterly impossible to disguise the fact that the major attack would come somewhere between the Cherbourg Peninsula and Dunkirk." The most obvious place for the invasion forces to land was in the Pas de Calais in the extreme northeast of France. It was

Opposite: *British airborne troops prepare to board the transports and gliders taking them to their date with destiny in Normandy.*

the region nearest to the British coast. It possessed two large deep-water ports in Calais and Boulogne, at which reinforcements could easily be landed once both places were firmly in Allied hands. Successful landings there would also open up the shortest route to Paris and the German industrial heartland of the Ruhr. There were, however, counterbalancing disadvantages.

The Pas de Calais was where Hitler expected the Allies to strike. "It is here that the enemy must and will attack, and it is here — unless all the indications are misleading — that the decisive battle against the landing forces will be fought," he told his generals. It was also one of the most heavily fortified sections of the Führer's much vaunted Atlantic Wall. By July 1943, the Overlord planners had concluded that the coast of Normandy north of Caen was a better bet.

As to when the landings would take place, Stalin had long been agitating for them to be initiated as soon as possible. The Americans were just as enthusiastic. The British, though apparently also in favor of launching the Second Front, prevaricated. Churchill's military advisers were totally opposed to any early landing. Sir Alan Brooke, Chief of the Imperial General Staff, noted in his diary: "This universal cry to start a Second Front is going to be hard to compete with, and yet what can we do with some ten divisions against the German masses?" They then argued that there was no chance of mounting an invasion because of the shortage of landing craft.

Left: *A VI is hauled to its firing ramp. Double agents fed the Germans false information about its accuracy.*

Above: *U.S. assault troops take shelter on Omaha Beach, which was defended stubbornly by the Germans.*

Right: *A U.S. paratrooper prepares to jump into action. The airborne divisions took heavy casualties.*

Below: *One of the invasion convoys makes its slow way across the English Channel.*

The debate continued well into 1943. Eventually, after much Anglo-American discussion, D-Day was finally scheduled for May 1 1944 (it was put back to early June because of persistent storms in the English Channel).

FOOLING THE GERMANS

Robertson, Masterman, and the intelligence operatives with whom they worked were not concerned with high-level policy making and the intricacies of grand strategy.

Their task was straightforward. Once Normandy finally had been confirmed as the Allied landing site, they were to "persuade the enemy to dispose his forces in areas where they can cause the least interference with Operations Overlord and Anvil (the invasion of Southern France)" and "to deceive the enemy as to the strength, timing, and objective of Overlord and Anvil."

Through a long period of careful nurturing, Robertson

and Masterman had built up a team of double agents they believed they could trust. Even more crucially, the Abwehr, the German intelligence service, believed wholeheartedly in the information these agents were feeding back to it. The key figures — in alphabetical order, they were code named Bronx, Brutus, Garbo, Treasure, and Tricycle — were the motliest collection of individuals that even the Secret Service had ever recruited.

Bronx (real name Elvira de la Fuente Chaudoir) was an attractive 29-year-old Peruvian bisexual, who was cutting something of a swathe through wartime London's high society when she was recruited into British Intelligence by Lieutenant-Colonel Claude Dansey, the assistant chief of MI6. He sent her to Vichy France with instructions to contact German Intelligence and offer to spy for them after her return to Britain. Through a Nazi collaborator, she got an introduction to Helmut Bleil, a freelance spy who reported, so he claimed, personally to Hermann Goering. Bleil sent her back to Britain, where she became one of Robertson's star recruits.

If Bronx was a talented amateur, Brutus (real name Roman Czerniawski) was the consummate professional. He lived and breathed spying. Though a qualified pilot, the Polish Air Force had deemed him unfit to fly because he was so small. He was shifted to Polish Air Intelligence in which he was serving when the war broke out. After the fall of Poland, he fled to France. When the French, too, capitulated, he went underground, only to emerge as the brains behind the Interallie. This soon became the most important spy network in Nazi-occupied France.

Then disaster struck. Czerniawski and Mathilde Carre, his fellow-agent and mistress, were betrayed to the Germans and arrested by the Gestapo.

Carre was the first to crack. She betrayed the entire network to the Germans and then volunteered to become a double agent for them. Czerniawski, too, came to terms with the Abwehr. The decision to fake his escape and allow him to get back to Britain to spy for Germany was authorized by Admiral Wilhelm Canaris, the head of the Abwehr, himself. The Pole, however, had no intention of fulfilling his bargain. Six weeks after his return, he offered to turn triple agent. MI5 and the Free Poles both had their doubts about his sincerity. MI5's Christopher Harmer spent weeks interrogating him before deciding he could be trusted. "With his imagination and with his very original mind," Harmer reported, "we might possibly confuse and deceive

Opposite: *U.S. troops wade ashore on Omaha Beach. Even though Hitler had been fooled into holding back his panzer reserves, the landing almost turned into an Allied catastrophe.*

Above: *Some of the many U.S. casualties on Omaha are helped onto the beach. Their troop transport had been sunk before they could disembark from it.*

Above: *Landing craft approach the Normandy shore as smoke emanates from German defensive positions.*

Opposite: *U.S. soldiers examine a knocked-out German self-propelled gun. A dead crewman lies slumped over the barrel.*

the Germans to a remarkable extent." Brutus joined the Double Cross team and began sending false radio messages back to his German controllers. The Germans swallowed whatever he told them hook, line, and sinker. No one in the Abwehr ever suspected that he had been "turned" again.

THE CHICKEN FARMER WHO HATED CHICKENS

Garbo (Juan Pujol) was even more imaginative. A 29-year-old Catalan, he had failed at practically every occupation he had tried, ending up as a poultry farmer outside Barcelona, although he detested chickens. The business went bust. When war broke out, he decided he wanted to spy for Britain. In January 1941, he went to the British Embassy in Madrid to volunteer his services, but was turned down. He then approached the Germans. His reasoning was that, if he became a German agent, he could show the British just how valuable he could be to them. He did not have to be "turned." He was a natural double agent.

Karl Erich Kuhlenthal, Pujol's Abwehr controller in Madrid, dutifully supplied him with invisible ink and a substantial cash advance, and christened him Agent Arabel. He told him to go to Lisbon and make his way from there to Britain. Pujol obeyed the first instruction, but ignored the second. Though, on July 19, 1941, he cabled Kuhlenthal to confirm his safe arrival in Britain, he never left Lisbon. For the next nine months, relying on newsreels, secondhand books, and the Lisbon public library, he made up what he thought his German paymasters would most like to hear.

Soon, the amount of spurious information Pujol was giving the gullible Kuhlenthal, who then forwarded it on to Berlin, was such that he was fooling the British as well as the Germans. They suspected that the latter had managed to get a spy into Britain who was not under MI5's control. Closer examination of the decoded signals, however, revealed that Arabel not only suffered from verbal incontinence but that much of the information being supplied was laughably wrong — a fact that seemed to escape the notice of the Abwehr completely.

MI6 was the first intelligence agency to identify Arabel as Pujol. When MI5 was finally made aware who Arabel was, its comment was short and to the point. It was, they noted, "a miracle that he had survived so long." Pujol was smuggled out of Lisbon to Gibraltar and then flown to Britain. He arrived there on April 22, 1942. Over the next three years he and Tomas "Tommy" Harris, his MI5 controller,

bombarded the Germans with hundreds of thousands of words contained in 315 letters in secret ink and more than 1,200 wireless messages. Garbo even invented an entire team of subagents reporting to him.

A WOMAN AND HER DOG

Treasure (Lily Sergeyev), a 29-year-old Parisian of White Russian descent, was recruited by Major Emile Klieman in Paris to join the Abwehr in October 1941. Once he had recruited her, however, Klieman seemed not to know what to do with her. It took him well over a year to decide to employ her in the field. Then, she faced months of waiting in Madrid before, in October 1943, she flew to Britain from Gibraltar. She had already told the British she would spy for them, so they were ready and waiting for her when she finally arrived.

There was a fly in the ointment. Treasure owned a dog called Babs, a white cross between a poodle and a terrier to which she was totally devoted. Forced to leave Babs behind, she was convinced that she had MI5's promise to smuggle the animal into Britain for her in defiance of the strict British quarantine laws. The next she heard, however, was that Babs was dead, accidentally run over by a passing car. Sergeyev

refused to believe the story. She was certain that MI5 had had her dog deliberately killed to rid themselves of a nuisance. On the surface, she seemed to come to terms with her loss. Inwardly, she was plotting her revenge.

It was May 1944 — just before D-Day — that Treasure got her opportunity. Some months before, MI5 had sent her back to Lisbon to contact Klieman to demand that she should be supplied with a radio transmitter. Unbeknownst to the British, Treasure had agreed with him that she should transmit a special radio signal — inserting an extra double dash into a routine message — to indicate

she was operating under British control. She now told MI5 what she had done. What she would not reveal was the nature of the signal or whether she had already transmitted it. Robertson's view was that she was blackmailing the whole Double Cross operation for the sake of a dead dog.

In fact, Treasure never sent the signal, but, three days after D-Day, Robertson had his revenge. He sacked her. She was sent back to Paris in disgrace as soon as the French capital had been liberated.

THE SEDUCTIVE SERB
Tricycle (Dusan "Dusko" Popov) was another Abwehr recruit who

secretly changed sides. Next to Garbo and Brutus, he was probably the most successful of all MI5's double agents. A flamboyant womanizer, he was persuaded by his friend Johnny Jebsen — who himself was to be "turned" successfully later during the war — to join him in spying for the Abwehr in early 1940. Popov secretly contacted MI6 in Belgrade and offered to work for the British instead. On December 20, having journeyed first to Lisbon to contact Ludovico von Karsthof, his designated Abwehr controller, he landed at Whitchurch, and was immediately chauffeured to London to meet Robertson. His career as a double agent had begun.

Tricycle soon started living up to his code name, shuttling back and forth between Britain and Portugal in the guise of a Yugoslav businessman. The Germans were so pleased with what he told them that, in August 1941, they sent him to the U.S. to spy on the Americans. MI5 thought this was the perfect opportunity for Popov to create an American equivalent of

Double Cross. Unfortunately, J. Edgar Hoover and the FBI loathed him. The Germans, too, began to doubt his bona fides.

On October 4, 1942, Popov arrived back in Lisbon, primed with fresh information by MI5 to help him rehabilitate himself in German eyes. Von Karsthof put it to him that, although his work in Britain had been "very good" and in the U.S. initially "excellent," it had then become "medium" and, for the last three months, "terribly bad." The self-assured Serb had an immediate answer. It was all the Abwehr's fault, he said, for sending him to the U.S. "with no help whatsoever, no contacts," and "a few miserable dollars." Von Karsthof was more than willing to accept the story, especially since he had been creaming off dollars from the money he had been supposed to despatch.

Popov was in the clear. He was sent back to London to resume his spying and was soon being hailed as "the best man the Abwehr has." In early 1944, he returned to Lisbon for one last time to pass "a mass of detailed information" to von Karsthof. The Abwehr man swallowed the deception whole. He told Berlin that "the landing in Western Europe will not take place until next spring."

Above: *A Waco CG-4 glider is examined by German troops. The airborne landings caused considerable confusion amongst Normandy's defenders.*

A COMPLETE SUCCESS

As D-Day neared, the volume of false information pouring into German hands reached a crescendo. On the ground, too, major deception schemes were being mounted. An entire phantom U.S. Army Group, supposedly commanded by the redoubtable General George Patton, was reported as being readied for an assault on the Pas de Calais. Any invasion in Normandy would be a ruse, specifically designed to draw off German troops before the main assault. An attack on Norway by the equally fictitious British 4th Army was also a "strong possibility," according to German Intelligence, and an attack on Denmark was rated a "certainty."

It was little wonder that the Germans were painfully slow to react when D-Day dawned. Even after the landings, the crack German 15th Army stayed in position in the Pas de Calais waiting for an assault which never came. The decision to impose a stand-still order was largely the result of Garbo's analysis of supposed Allied intentions — the Germans were so convinced by it that it ended up in the hands of Hitler himself. The stand-still lasted for seven weeks. By the time it was finally lifted, the Allied armies had broken out of their bridgeheads and were penetrating farther deep into German-occupied territory. It was a fitting conclusion to what one military historian later called "the most successful strategic deception of all time."

The Mysterious Death of Glenn Miller

TOP SECRET
CLASSIFIED
TOP SECRET

On the night of December 15, 1944, the legendary U.S. bandleader Glenn Miller — now a 40-year-old major in the U.S. Army Air Force — boarded a light aircraft to fly the English Channel to Supreme Headquarters Allied Expeditionary Force (SHAEF) outside Paris to prepare for his band's visit to the French capital to give a Christmas concert. The aircraft never reached its destination. No trace of it or its passengers was ever found. The episode remains one of the greatest riddles of the entire war.

Above: *Glenn Miller sacrificed his civilian stardom to enlist in 1942. The new band he founded for the U.S. Army Air Force became world-famous.*

Opposite: *Miller hitched a ride in a Norseman like this to fly to Paris in December 1944. He never arrived. The plane vanished somewhere over the English Channel.*

Glenn Miller became an all-American musical legend. His celebrated orchestra, formed in 1938, rose out of initial obscurity to achieve speedy greatness. In just four years, 70 of the disks Miller and his musicians cut became Top Ten hits; Time magazine noted that "of the 12 to 24 disks in each of today's 300,000 U.S. jukeboxes, from two to six are usually Glenn Miller's."

The band, Miller leading as principal trombone, became a household name. Its first hit was the 1939 *Wishing (Will Make It So)*, closely followed by *Moonlight Serenade*. The following year, *In The Mood, Tuxedo Junction*, and *Pennsylvania 6-5000* all climbed to the top of the charts. The orchestra was now universally recognized to be the U.S.'s top dance band. It was not for nothing that Miller was dubbed the "King of Swing."

A MUSICAL VOLUNTEER

In 1942, with his orchestra at the height of its popularity, Miller amazed Tin Pan Alley by disbanding it. Like hundreds of thousands of his fellow Americans following Pearl Harbor, he abandoned civilian life. He tried to get into the U.S. Navy, but was turned down as being too old to fight. By pulling every string in Washington he could, he managed to get into the Army Specialist Corps in August 1942. He was transferred to the U.S. Army Air Force that October.

Miller, however, did not leave music behind him. What he wanted to deliver to the troops was "real, live American music." His aim, so he said, was to "put a little more spring into the feet of our marching men and a little more

sought him out to compliment him: "Next to a letter from home," he said, "your orchestra is the greatest morale booster in the European Theater of Operations."

TWO BRUSHES WITH DEATH

Miller had been agitating to be allowed to take his band overseas for some time, but the air force had been reluctant to give its consent. It took an appeal from General Dwight D. Eisenhower, the Allied supreme commander in Europe, to General Arnold to get Miller and his musicians shipped across the Atlantic.

Miller and his band were feted everywhere they went. They played on airfields, in aircraft hangars, for the wounded, and performed on the American Forces Radio Network and the BBC weekly. Among their most enthusiastic fans were Princesses Elizabeth and Margaret — George VI's young daughters. Their oddest appearance was probably on a program called *The Wehrmacht*

joy into their hearts." To do this, he needed to create a new band. On March 20, 1943, the 50-strong 418th Army Air Force Band made its debut playing to an audience of cadets undergoing their military training at Yale University.

Initially, Miller's efforts to introduce swing into marches met with some resistance within the military hierarchy. One senior officer reminded him coldly that John Philip Sousa had been good enough for the American armed forces during World War I. "Are you still flying the same planes you flew in the last war?" Miller reposted. Luckily, General Henry "Hap" Arnold, commander-in-chief of the U.S. Army Air Force, liked Miller and his music. So, too, did Lieutenant-General James "Jimmy" Doolittle, now commanding the U.S. 8th Army Air Force. After a concert Miller gave at Wycombe Abbey on July 31, 1944, Doolittle

Hour, broadcasting a potent blend of swing — and propaganda — to the troops battling the Allies. Miller himself spoke to his enemy listeners, although, according to reports, he had something of a struggle with his German.

Right at the start of the tour, however, Miller and his band had a close encounter with death. Initially, they were housed at 25 Sloane Court, London. This was situated in the heart of what was nicknamed "Buzz Bomb Valley" — so-called because it lay immediately beneath the flight path of the deadly VI pilotless missiles with which Hitler was now pitilessly bombarding the capital. Miller immediately decided to move his musicians out of London to Bedford. They left for their new quarters on July 2. The next day, a VI crashed directly in front of their Sloane Court billet, demolishing the building and killing more than 100 people. When he heard the news, Miller commented laconically to Lieutenant Don Haynes, the band's manager: "As long as the Miller luck stays with us, we have nothing to worry about."

Miller and his band had another, even closer brush with a VI. They were playing at an open-air concert in Kent when the characteristic puttering of the missile's ram jet was heard overhead. It suddenly cut out — a sure signal that the missile was about to crash and explode. The audience dived for cover. Miller and his musicians played on regardless even through the

Above: *When he heard a VI had destroyed his London billet, Miller joked that his legendary luck was still holding good.*

explosion. They were given a standing ovation.

THE FATEFUL FLIGHT

The strain of constant performance began to tell as fall gave way to winter. In one month alone, according to a letter Miller wrote to a friend, "we played at 35 different bases and, in our 'spare time,' did 46 broadcasts."

On average, he and the band were spending 18 hours a day performing or recording.

Miller was becoming somewhat homesick, but nevertheless he was determined to continue with the tour. In particular, he wanted to visit France to perform for the front-line troops. This was deemed impracticable, but a compromise

was agreed. Miller and his musicians would move to Paris, where they could entertain Allied soldiers on leave. The plan was to start with a gala concert on Christmas Day.

On November 15, Miller's planned visit finally got the official go-ahead. At first, the idea was for Don Haynes to fly to Paris ahead of the musicians to make all the necessary preparations, but, at the last minute, Miller decided to go himself. The problem was the weather. Foggy flying conditions had grounded the SHAEF shuttle on which Miller had been ordered to fly and even when flights resumed, the passenger backlog meant that he was likely to be bumped off the plane. Then, he had what looked like a stroke of luck. The day before he was due to fly, he ran into Lieutenant-Colonel Norman F. Baesell, a friend of Haynes, who was flying to Paris the following day in a general's private plane. There was room for another passenger. Baesell invited Miller along.

As take-off time neared, the C-46 Norseman sat waiting on the tarmac. Its pilot, Flight Officer John Morgan, told his two passengers that, though it was raining heavily and visibility was poor, the word was that the weather was clearing over the Continent. Miller apparently was somewhat dubious. First, he raised doubts about the aircraft — the Norseman was a single-engined light plane. Baesell countered by reminding him that one engine had been enough for Charles Lindbergh, the first man to fly solo across the Atlantic in 1927. Then, as Miller took his seat, he asked "Hey, where

Left: *An Avro Lancaster bomber in flight. It is possible that a bomb dropped by a Lancaster could have fatally damaged the plane carrying Glenn Miller on his final flight.*

the hell are the parachutes?" Baesell jocularly retorted: "What's the matter, Miller? Do you want to live forever?"

The Norseman slowly taxied into its take-off position. As Morgan started to accelerate down the runway, Haynes stood waving Miller goodbye. He was the last person to see Miller alive. The Norseman never reached France. No trace of it, its pilot, or its two passengers was ever found.

ACCIDENT OR HEART ATTACK?

What exactly happened to the Norseman and its passengers has never been fully explained. Indeed, it was not until Haynes himself arrived at SHAEF in search of Miller on December 18 that it was even realized he had been on board the missing aircraft. A search was hurriedly mounted, but it found nothing. The 8th Air Force set up

a Board of Enquiry. It said that Miller had boarded the wrong plane on the wrong day without the knowledge or approval of his military superiors.

The Norseman, in the Board's opinion, had either crashed in the English Channel as a result of pilot disorientation, or suffered a disastrous engine failure, possibly due to fuel icing inside the carburetor. Poor weather, the Board added, had certainly been a contributing factor. Flying conditions were marginal at best and were deteriorating rapidly. The unspoken conclusion was that the Norseman should not have been in the air at all.

Even before the Board of Enquiry reported, however, rumors about the true nature of the accident — if there was one — were mounting. As late as the 1980s and 1990s, new theories

IN MEMORY
Major A. Glenn Miller
0505273
U.S. Army Air Force- W. W. II
Born- Clarinda, Iowa-
March 1, 1904
Missing in Action-
Europe, Dec. 15, 1944
1943 - 1944
418th A.A.F.T.T.C. Band-
Yale University- New Haven, CT.
I SUSTAIN THE WINGS

Sustineo Alas

Above: *Glenn Miller's memorial in Grove Street Cemetery, New Haven, Connecticut. His music lived on even after his death.*

Opposite: *General Henry "Hap" Arnold was commander-in-chief of the U.S. Army Air Force. He personally broke the news of Miller's disappearance to the great bandleader's wife.*

were emerging to expose the real reasons for Miller's untimely death. Some of these theories are plausible, at least on the surface. Some are ridiculous. At one time or another, all have come under heavy critical fire.

One of the strangest theories was put forward by German journalist Udo Ulfkotte in 1997. According to *Bild* magazine, Ulfkotte had come across hitherto secret evidence while researching a book he was writing on German intelligence agencies. The evidence stated, so *Bild* claimed, that Miller had never been on board the Norseman at all. In fact, he had arrived safely the day before on December 14, only to die of a heart attack in the arms of a prostitute in a Paris brothel. The official story was a cover-up.

Later, however, Ulfkotte claimed that *Bild* had misquoted him. He had never told the magazine that he had found evidence to support his claim. The story, he said, had been told to him by wartime German intelligence specialists in an off-the-record conversation.

UNDERCOVER SPY

An even more far-fetched theory was put forward by journalist and retired U.S. Colonel Hunton Downs in his 2007 book *The Glenn Miller Conspiracy*. In it, Downs stated that Miller was an undercover OSS superspy, who died while on a secret mission for General Eisenhower. The mission, so Downs claimed, involved Miller getting into Germany to make contact with a group of dissident German generals and persuading them to turn against Hitler. He was also to get in touch with the Reich's leading rocket and nuclear scientists, including Wernher von Braun, and offer them sanctuary should they come over to the Allies.

Miller, said Downs, was betrayed, captured, tortured, and finally beaten to death by Nazi extremists. They smuggled his battered corpse back to Paris, where it was unceremoniously dumped on the doorstep of a brothel in Rue Pigalle. Miller's body, Downs claimed, was flown back to the U.S. and buried in Ohio in a secret location. The theory convinced some, but many considered it unbelievable.

FATAL ILLNESS OR FRIENDLY FIRE?

Two other theories also gained wide currency. One came from no less a person than Herb Miller, the bandleader's younger brother. He broke a nearly 40-year silence in 1983 to say that "Glenn Miller did not die in a plane crash over the Channel, but from lung cancer in a hospital."

Miller, his brother explained, had indeed boarded the Norseman that December afternoon, but only half an hour into the flight he had been taken so ill that the aircraft was forced to make an emergency landing. He was rushed by ambulance to a military hospital where he died the following day. It was Herb Miller who concocted the story of a mid-Channel air crash as a last service to his brother, who had wanted to die a hero and not "in a lousy bed."

Herb produced supporting evidence to back up his claim. To substantiate the story, he cited a letter that the chain-smoking musician had written earlier that summer. "I am totally emaciated, although I am eating enough," it read. "I have trouble breathing. I think I am very ill."

Other testimony indeed seemed to confirm the fact that Miller was suffering from an undiagnosed illness. He often appeared exhausted and suffered from what he described as repeated sinus attacks. According to Don Haynes, the bandleader had lost a lot of weight. His tailor-made uniforms, Haynes noted, "didn't fit him well at all. They merely hung on him." He had lost much of his customary optimism and bounce. George Voutsas, the director of Miller's radio broadcasts, recalled a late-night discussion of postwar plans. "I don't know why I spend time making plans like this," Miller apparently sighed: "You know, George, I have an awful feeling you guys are going home without me."

It all sounded convincing, but it ran up against a specific fact. Herb Miller's account of his brother's death was never confirmed by the U.S. military authorities. Why, after so long, should it still be kept secret? And why was Miller's body apparently buried anonymously in a military cemetery?

Another equally plausible explanation for Miller's disappearance emerged the following year, when Fred Shaw, a former RAF Bomber Command navigator now living in South

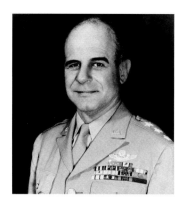

Above: *Lieutenant General Jimmy Doolittle congratulated Miller on his band's morale boosting-performances.*

Africa, succeeded in getting his story about the vanishing Norseman published after years of trying. On the day Miller's plane vanished, Shaw was on board a Lancaster bomber returning from an aborted raid on the railway yards at Steigen. Approaching Britain's south coast, the bomb-aimer dropped the aircraft's bomb-load as it entered the officially designated South Jettison Zone. The bomb-load included a 4,000-pound (1,800 kg) "cookie" which apparently exploded just before the bomb hit the sea. As Shaw looked out from the cockpit to catch a glimpse of the explosion, he spotted a small plane, which he identified as a Norseman, flying below him. A moment later, the rear gunner called out over the intercom "Did you see that kite (RAF slang

for plane) go in?" Shaw believed that the shock waves from the explosion had literally knocked the Norseman out of the sky.

Back in Britain, Alan Ross, a member of the Glenn Miller Appreciation Society, contacted the Air Historical Branch of the Ministry of Defence and asked them to investigate Shaw's allegation. The reply was noncommittal. The Norseman and the bomber stream, the investigators said, could have crossed in flight. Equally, they could have been miles apart.

Ross had more luck with an advertisement he had placed, asking anyone who could confirm Shaw's story to come forward. Victor Gregory, the Lancaster's pilot, responded. Although he personally had seen nothing, he confirmed that Shaw and the rear gunner, who was now dead, had spotted the Norseman and said what they had said.

Gregory never mentioned the incident on his return to base. "Don't think me unsympathetic or callous," he said, "but when I heard of the plane going down, I would have said he shouldn't have been there — forget him." Forgetting Glenn Miller, however, was something that anyone who had ever heard his band play could never do.

32 USA

GLENN MILLER

Above: *A Glenn Miller commemorative stamp, issued in 1996. Even today, speculation continues about where and how he disappeared and what possibly caused his death.*

The *Cap Arcona* Tragedy

On May 3, 1945 — four days after Hitler's suicide in his Berlin bunker — the German passenger liner Cap Arcona was sunk in the Baltic by RAF fighter-bombers. The pilots who attacked the ship believed it was carrying fleeing SS troops, but, in fact, it was packed with prisoners from the Neuengamme concentration camp near Hamburg. Out of the 4,500 passengers, only 500 managed to survive. It was one of the greatest disasters in maritime history.

Above: *In the closing weeks of the war, Allied aircraft wrought havoc on German shipping.*

On the morning of May 3, 1945, the skies over northern Germany and the Baltic Sea were bleak, misty, and overcast. The Germans welcomed the bad visibility, because it gave them some respite from attacks by the Allied fighter-bombers, which, for days now, had been mercilessly pounding the shipping crammed into the north German ports or clustered around them offshore. The ships were packed with military personnel and equipment of all kinds. Most of them were bound for Norway, where the German High Command was planning to make a desperate last stand.

Most of the shipping attacks were carried out by the RAF's Second Tactical Air Force, although Coastal Command and the U.S. 9th Army Air Force also took part in them. It was the RAF's deadly Hawker Typhoon fighter-bombers that the Germans feared the most. Ever since the Allied landings in Normandy in June 1944, the Typhoons had harried the Germans remorselessly from the air as they fell back into their homeland. Now they were star players in the last act before the curtain finally fell on Hitler's vaunted thousand-year Third Reich.

Armed with four 20 mm cannon, the Typhoon could also

Right: *A RAF Mosquito strafes an enemy transport ship. There is a complete absence of enemy anti-aircraft fire, allowing the pilot a clean shot at his target.*

carry up to 1,000 pounds (450 kg) of bombs or eight rockets, each with a 60-pound (27 kg) high-explosive warhead. A full salvo of rockets had the destructive force of a broadside fired from a cruiser. It was more than enough to tear any merchant ship apart.

SHIP-BUSTING IN LUBECK BAY

The weather soon turned in the Allies' favor. On the afternoon of May 3, the skies cleared. The Second Tactical Air Force could now unleash its Typhoon squadrons against the enemy shipping in Lubeck Bay, where several large vessels already had been spotted by aerial reconnaissance. Four squadrons from 123 Wing were briefed to carry out the mission. The planes from 184, 263, and 198 Squadrons were armed with rockets, whereas the aircraft from 197 Squadron carried bombs. The pilots were certainly keyed up for the attack.

"No quarter was asked for or given in the air today," that evening's Air Intelligence Survey reported, "and operations proceeded at full blast."

It was four Typhoons from 197 Squadron that carried out the first attack on what the pilots described as a "two-funnel cargo liner of 10,000 tons with steam up in Lubeck Bay." She was, in fact, the 21,046-ton passenger liner *Deutschland*, which was in the process of being converted into a hospital ship. The Typhoon pilots had no means of knowing this, however. Only a single small Red Cross had been painted on the side of one of her funnels, both of which had been painted white.

When the Typhoons struck, *Deutschland* had only an 80-strong skeleton crew on board, plus a 26-strong medical team. The ship was hit by four bombs, one of which failed to explode. Another started a small fire, which was quickly extinguished. No one was

hurt in the attack. After it, the medical team went ashore, while the vessel's captain ordered white sheets to be draped over the *Deutschland* and all her lifeboats to be swung out in their davits, ready for a speedy launch if or when the RAF returned.

STRIKE TWO, STRIKE THREE

The second attack, some three hours later, was delivered by nine Typhoons from 198 Squadron. They were led by Group Captain Johnny Baldwin, who also commanded 123 Wing. This time, the Typhoons attacked two vessels — a large three-funnel liner and a smaller ship moored nearby. It was devastatingly successful. Forty rockets out of the 62 that were fired struck the bigger vessel, their warheads smashing through her hull to explode deep inside her. She was soon ablaze from stem to stern. Thirty more rockets ships hit the smaller ship. She began to list heavily and then to sink, continuously belching thick black smoke into the sky.

There were few survivors from the second vessel. Bogdan Suchowiak, a 38-year-old Polish prisoner from Posen, was one of them. "It was clear to me that if we did not jump overboard immediately," he recalled, "we would all be drawn down into the deep by the suction of the sinking ship. I undressed to my shorts and let myself down slowly by a rope. The water was damned cold. I clung to a wooden plank. It must have been around 3:30 p.m. in the afternoon, the sun was shining, but then there were passing clouds and rain showers. The sea was relatively calm with small waves. It was about five kilometres to the shore."

Somehow, Suchowiak managed to stay afloat for a couple of hours. Then he spotted a minesweeper looking for survivors and swam as fast as he could toward it. When he got close, he could hear a young officer shouting at the crew through a loudhailer. "Don't pick up any prisoners," he was directing them, "only SS personnel and sailors." Luckily for Suchowiak, he spoke fluent German and so was able to talk his way on board.

The third attack, made by 263 Squadron, was again directed against the *Deutschland*. As the Typhoons darted in, her crew scrambled into the lifeboats and made for the shore unharmed. The *Deutschland*, though, was set on fire and was sunk a few minutes later by bombs dropped by 197 Squadron's Typhoons.

Top: *RAF armorers load a Typhoon with air-to ground rockets — a totally lethal combination.*

Middle: *A Hawker Typhoon fighter-bomber ready for take-off on yet another mission.*

Bottom: *The* Cap Arcona *in happier peacetime days sailing from Hamburg for South America.*

Opposite: *Lubeck Bay looks tranquil enough here. In 1945 it was a different story.*

Left: *Bomb damage in Hamburg. The city never really recovered from the great fire storm raised by Allied bombers in 1943.*

Right: *Wesel in northern Germany — or what was left of it — photographed in May 1945 after the Germans surrendered.*

THE GRIM REALITY

The Typhoon pilots headed back to their bases along the River Elbe. The next day, British ground forces entered the port of Lubeck — and the full horror of what had happened was revealed. The second two ships indeed had been packed to capacity, but not with German troops being evacuated to Norway. They had been filled with thousands of concentration camp inmates.

As the war in Europe approached its inevitable conclusion, Reichsführer Heinrich Himmler, the head of the SS, had ordered that no concentration camp inmates should be allowed to fall into Allied hands. Those who could still walk were to be force-marched back, away from the Allied line of advance. The remainder were to be killed.

At Neuengamme, near Hamburg, where half the prisoners were either Russians or Poles, 1,000 of the camp's inmates were murdered immediately. Many of the 20,000 others were quickly dispersed across northern Germany, but, during the last days of April, several thousand more were herded into Lubeck. Around 2,300 of them were forced to board the 1,936-ton freighter *Athen*, which ferried them to the three-funnel liner. This was the 27,561-ton *Cap Arcona*. Before the war, this luxury liner had been known as "the Queen of the South Atlantic," plying the seas between Hamburg and Rio de Janeiro. Now, she was to become a prison ship.

Heinrich Bertram, the liner's captain who had only taken over command on February 27, did not like the idea. After the war, he reported to the ship's owners, telling them at first he had refused to allow the prisoners on board. The SS, however, were not taking no for an answer.

Betram continued: "On Thursday April 26, 1945, SS Sturmbanführer Gehrig, who was in charge of transport, appeared, accompanied by an advisory merchant marine captain and an executive Kommando, consisting of soldiers armed with machine-guns. Gehrig had brought a written order for my attention. It called for me to be shot at once if I further refused to take the prisoners on board. At this point, it became clear to me that even my death would not prevent the boarding of the prisoners and so I informed the SS officer that I categorically renounced any responsibility for my ship."

The captain concluded: "Gehrig proceeded to order the transfer of the prisoners from the *Athen* to *Cap Arcona*. Additional transports arrived from Lubeck, so that on April 28 I had a total of about 6,500 prisoners on board in spite of the statement of the merchant marine officer that the ship was capable of holding a limit of 2,500." The luckless Bertram had to find room to accommodate 500 SS guards into the bargain.

Below: *Despite being designed as a high-altitude interceptor, the Hawker Typhoon really excelled in low-level ground attacks.*

Left: *Shellfire damage in an unknown German town. As the war drew to a close, many towns were quick to capitulate.*

Right: *Luftwaffe Field Marshal Erhard Milch (center) together with Arms Minister Albert Speer to his left. Both men struggled to keep weapons production going in the face of Allied bombing.*

Meanwhile, 3,000 more prisoners had been loaded onto another vessel, the 2,815 ton freighter *Thielbeck*. On both vessels the prisoners were battened down below for days in darkness and stinking squalor, many half-dead already from starvation. In addition, two large barges were filled with several hundred men, women, and children from another concentration camp at Stutthof.

DISASTER IN THE BAY

Events proceeded inexorably to their tragic conclusion. On May 2, a transfer of prisoners took place between *Cap Arcona*, *Thielbeck*, and *Athen*. This left 4,150 prisoners on the liner and 2,750 on the freighter. Another 2,000 were

on board *Athen*, whose captain decided to put back to port. The SS guards on board protested, but, according to some accounts, were disarmed by the crew.

The vessel put into Neustadt. Mikelis Mezmalietis, one of the prisoners on board, recalled what happened. "On the morning of May 3," he wrote, "there was a terrible explosion. After a short time, one of the stronger prisoners who had been aloft ran down to tell us that the Americans (sic) had bombed *Cap Arcona* and sunk it. Everyone who could move got very excited and tried to get to the one exit. In a moment, we felt the ship starting to move fast. Then it stopped."

"Nobody spoke for an hour," Mezmalietis went on. "Then all those who could, got up and ran out, especially the German crew: we had arrived at Neustadt. I was unable to move and was left for dead. After perhaps another hour, I crawled on all fours up to the top deck ... "

"That afternoon two strong young prisoners boarded the ship to see what they could take. They were not from my ship; they turned out to be French students. They were very surprised to see me; they went searching for other prisoners but found none. Then they carried me from the ship and took me to the barracks at Neustadt, where they washed me and put me to bed in a spare bed in their room."

SWIMMING FOR SURVIVAL

Meanwhile, on board the stricken, blazing *Cap Arcona*, more than 4,000 prisoners were burning to death or suffocating in the smoke. A few managed to jump into the sea, where they were picked up by some fishermen. Berek Bronek (later Benjamin Jacobs) was one of their number. In his memoirs,

The Dentist of Auschwitz, he recalled the moments leading up to his rescue.

"I heard people begging to be picked up," he wrote. "As a man was pulled from the water, I waved and yelled to get their attention. 'We can't take anyone! We have no more room! We are full!' they shouted back to me. But

that did not deter me. In a final effort, I lurched, throwing my arms forward to get a bit closer to them. Then I saw how low their boat was in the water, just barely above the waterline. I begged and pleaded with them until I could shout no more. 'It's Bronek, the dentist. Let's try to take him,' someone yelled. The motor slowed and the boat turned and headed in my direction. A minute later, a few hands pulled me into the boat. I slumped down, barely conscious. My naked comrades and the sunburned fisherman were my archangels. As the little boat slowly plowed through the water toward the shore, many people were begging to be picked up. 'If we take one more, we'll all go down,' the fisherman cautioned."

"The small engine pulled the heavily laden boat as the waves rolled it up and down. The fisherman skillfully maneuvered it to avoid capsizing. I sat still with my head between my pulled-up knees and thought of my brother. I had cheated death once more, but he could not. All hope that Cap Arcona would stay afloat was fading."

More survivors — about 350 in all, many suffering from burns — managed to escape before the liner capsized and swim unaided to the shore, only to be shot and clubbed to death by SS troops and fanatical members of the Hitler Youth. Of the 2,750 prisoners on Thielbeck, only around 50 managed to escape. Most of them met the same fate as the survivors of Cap Arcona.

As for the hundreds of prisoners on the two barges, there were no survivors. When British troops arrived on the scene, they found the barges stranded on the shore and the beaches littered with corpses. The adults had been shot, the children clubbed to death with rifle butts. Max Pauly, the commandant of Neuengamme concentration camp and the man responsible for the massacre, was later tried as a war criminal in Hamburg and hanged, together with several of his subordinates.

AFTERMATH

That should have been the end of the Cap Arcona affair — but it was not. Nearly 40 years later a series of sensational articles in the West German press claimed that the true facts behind the attacks had been kept secret for decades. One of the claims was that British Intelligence had known that the vessels were packed with concentration camp inmates, but had not warned he RAF this was the case. Another was that the RAF, knowing whom the ships carried, nevertheless had deliberately allowed them to be attacked to give new pilots fresh from Britain some operational experience before the war ended.

Such claims are nonsense. In fact, the British had issued clear warnings that all shipping in the Baltic would be open to air attack, unless the vessels concerned were displaying prominent Red Cross markings. This was not the case. The RAF had no reason to believe that they were carrying anything other than troops — and perhaps even members of the Nazi leadership — to sanctuary in Norway. To turn the argument on its head, it is not impossible that the ships were used as a convenient dumping ground for the unwanted prisoners by the Nazis in the hope that they would be sunk, so completing the Nazis' dirty work for them.

Whatever the truth, one mystery still remains unsolved. Mikelis Mezmalietis recalled how the decks of the Athen were crammed with tons of sugar, rice, flour, and macaroni. The Athen was to have remained in company with the other two ships, so who were the supplies intended for? The quantities were far greater than would have been needed to meet the needs of the ships' crews and the SS guards. It is just possible that they were intended to keep the prisoners alive while the SS attempted to use them as a bargaining counter with the Allies in order to save themselves — tragic pawns in a last desperate gamble by murderers who had nothing to lose but their lives.

KOM OOK
IN DEN GERMAANSCHEN
LANDDIENST
IN HET OOSTEN

Above: *A colorful recruiting poster calls on Dutch civilians to volunteer for the German Land Army.*
The grim alternative was to be deported for forced labor.

Drugs, Doctors and the Führer

In 1941, Adolf Hitler was a relatively healthy man who looked younger than his years. By April 1945, he was "a shell of a man no longer able to lead Germany," according to an army doctor summoned to attend him in his Berlin bunker just days before he killed himself. What turned the Führer into a physical and mental wreck? Was his decline caused by an illness his physicians failed to diagnose or could not treat? Or was there another, more sinister reason?

From a relatively young age, Hitler was a hypochondriac — a man obsessed with his health. But, as a future Führer he knew that he could never afford to be seen to be ill. This was why he kept it quiet when the early symptoms of what was to become his first significant illness appeared in the late 1920s. Doctors today hold that what he was suffering from was almost certainly gallstones, associated with intermittent obstruction of his bile ducts, but, at the time, the condition remained undiagnosed.

MYSTERY PAINS

The first symptoms Hitler suffered from were episodes of sharp cramping pain in the upper right of his abdomen. The pain usually occurred after meals and, when it did, Hitler left the room. Sometimes he came back after the spasm had passed. Sometimes, he did not return at all. According to Albert Speer, Hitler later told him that things became so bad that he was suffering pain after every meal. He also complained of abdominal distension accompanied by duller pain and frequent belching.

From the start, the underlying cause of the pain remained a mystery. It occurred for no obvious reason and usually

Opposite: *Hitler's doctor was already worried about his health when he addressed the Reichstag in December 1941.*

Right: *Hitler was fit and well when he became Chancellor in 1933.*

disappeared after an hour or so. Some attacks were severe enough to incapacitate the Führer, whereas others were milder — more like a nagging soreness. Sometimes, Hitler was free of pain for several months, but it always came back to haunt him. The condition was chronic. Attacks continued to recur for the rest of the Führer's life.

HITLER TREATS HIMSELF

Any normal person would have consulted a doctor, but Hitler, always reluctant to take the advice of experts, refused to undergo a comprehensive medical examination. Whether this could have helped him much is open to doubt; as what causes abdominal pain is often difficult to diagnose precisely. What he did decide to do was to treat himself.

Sensibly enough, Hitler started by reassessing what he ate and

drank. He noted which foods led to the worst pains and cut them out of his diet. He eschewed rich pastries and meat in favor of vegetables and cereals, although some of the former — notably cabbage and beans — still proved troublesome. Zwieback, honey, mushrooms, curds, and yogurt all became dietary staples with oatmeal soup. Mashed linseed, potatoes baked in linseed oil, and muesli were added for variety. Cakes and sweets, which Hitler had greatly enjoyed, were eliminated completely, as was bacon, which, up to 1932, had been a breakfast favorite. Even bread and butter no longer found a place on the Führer's table.

Hitler turned to patent medicines for relief as well. He started by dosing himself liberally with a medicinal oil called Neo-Balestol. Originally, Balestol was a gun-cleaning oil

Above: *Theodore Morell became Hitler's personal physician in 1937. The Führer trusted him, but many thought he was a charlatan.*

Opposite: *Hitler is beginning to show the signs of age on this 1944 postage stamp.*

used by soldiers in World War I. Word got around in the trenches that it was also an effective cure for stomach pains. After the war, an enterprising businessman had concocted a similar oil, which was marketed under the trade-name of Neo-Balestol.

The problem was that one of Neo-Balestol's constituents was fusel oil. This was poisonous. Hitler, however, retained his faith in it, even though he suffered from headaches, double vision, dizziness, and ringing in his ears immediately after taking a dose of it. The oil's potential toxicity was such that, according to Professor Ernst-Gunther Schenck, Neo-Balestol was eventually banned by the Reich Health Agency.

The Führer finally settled on a different over-the-counter remedy — Dr. Koester's Antigas Pills. The pills' ingredients included strychnine, belladonna or deadly nightshade, and gentian. The gentian was harmless enough, but, taken in sufficient amounts, the strychnine and the atrophine contained in belladonna would prove poisonous. The pills were safe enough provided Hitler stuck to the recommended dose of no more than two to four pills before each meal. In fact, he was probably swallowing as many as 20 of them on a daily basis.

Hitler also dosed himself with laxatives regularly, wrongly believing that they would help to relieve his stomach pains and also would stop him gaining weight. His standby was a laxative called Mitilax, although later he experimented with other laxatives and enemas. He was terrified of becoming portly. He once commented to one of his aides: "Imagine the Führer of the Germans with a pot belly!"

HITLER'S PERSONAL DOCTOR

Diet and self-medication did nothing to relieve the underlying condition from which Hitler was suffering. The various doctors he reluctantly consulted could do nothing to help him. The Führer became convinced that he was going to die in the not-too-distant future — probably of cancer like his mother.

Hitler confided his fears to Speer. "I shall not live much longer," he told him. "I always counted on having time to realize my plans. I must carry out my aims as long as I can hold up, for my health is getting worse all the time." Back in 1935, Hitler had anxiously asked Professor Carl von Eicken, a noted ear, nose, and throat specialist called in to excise a tiny polyp on his vocal cords which was

affecting his voice, whether the growth was malignant. Von Eicken reassured him. The polyp turned out to be benign.

The abdominal pains continued to recur. Hitler grew weaker and thinner. Then he developed eczema. "I had it on both legs," he recalled. "It was so bad that I was covered in bandages and couldn't even get my boots on." Then, during Christmas 1936, he was introduced to a new doctor.

Theodor Morell was a fashionable Berlin general practitioner who had successfully treated Heinrich Hoffman, Hitler's close friend and personal photographer. It was Hoffman who introduced Morell to the Führer. Most of Hitler's entourage disliked the obese, balding, venal, and sycophantic Morell intensely. The Führer's other doctors — the young surgeon Karl Brandt and the physicians Werner Haase and Hanskarl von Hasselbach — were united in dismissing him as a charlatan.

Hitler, however, took to Morell immediately. When he promised to cure him "inside one year," the Führer was delighted. He praised him to the skies. "Nobody has ever told me so clearly and precisely what is wrong with me," he said. "His method of cure is so logical that I have the greatest confidence in him. I shall follow his prescriptions to the letter." From then on until the Führer finally turned against him, Morell was Hitler's Doktorchen ("little doctor") — his resident court physician.

MUTAFLOR AND OTHER MEDICINES

First, though, Morell had to fulfill his promise. He suspected that abnormal bacteria in the intestinal tract were responsible for Hitler's stomach pains. Fortunately, so he thought, he had a suitable remedy to hand. This was Mutaflor, the trade name for a strain of living bacteria first cultivated by Professor Alfred Nissle in 1917. The healthy bacteria in Mutaflor overgrew the abnormal types and so restored a normal bacterial balance in the gut.

Above: *Hitler gloried in public acclaim until the war went against him. Then he shunned public appearances.*

Hitler liked the sound of Mutaflor. He had an inbuilt sympathy with all doctors who had broken away from standard medical practices, turning to naturalistic treatment with herbs, massage, or other unconventional methods instead. He gave Morell the green light to start his Mutaflor course. The Führer's new doctor accordingly began dosing him with Mutaflor capsules — a yellow capsule on the first day, a red one from the second to the fourth days, and then two red capsules a day for as long as the treatment lasted.

Nissle advised carrying on with Mutaflor even when the samples of faeces Morell submitted to

him for analysis showed that the bacterial balance had returned to normal. He said it would help "Patient A" as Morell code named Hitler, to cope with his heavy workload since "one's nervous energy is increased." Perhaps both men's enthusiasm was not that surprising since Nissle owned the rights to Mutaflor and Morell was a director of the company that manufactured it.

Morell kept administering Mutaflor to Hitler until 1943, though, as time passed, it became less and less effective. To take its place, he started giving the Führer Glyconorm, which had to be injected intramuscularly. So, too, did Euflat, the next gastrointestinal drug he tried. When this, too, failed, he turned to a cocktail of Eukodal, a synthetic narcotic, and Eupaverinum, an anticonvulsant made from poppies. Morell mixed the two together in the same syringe and injected them intravenously.

It was the thin end of the wedge. As time passed the number of medicines Morell injected into the Führer multiplied. By mid-1943, Hitler was averaging three to five different shots daily. His arms were punctured so often that Morell sometimes could not find anywhere to insert a

Above: *Edward Bloch was the Hitler's family doctor when the Führer was a boy. He was also a Jew.*

needle into the scarred veins. It was not for nothing that Goering sardonically christened Morell the "Reich Injection Master."

No one knew precisely what Morell was injecting into Hitler. Dr. Erwin Giesing, an ear, nose, and throat specialist who, much to Morell's displeasure, was called in to treat Hitler's head traumas after he was wounded in the July 1944 bomb plot, was particularly scathing. "Morell," he later wrote, "converted the largely healthy man that Hitler had earlier been into one constantly plied with injections and fed with tablets which made Hitler more or less dependent on him. He played on Hitler's neuropathic nature by spouting utter rubbish about how Hitler's heavy workload meant that he was burning energy at the same rate as people in the tropics, and that the lost energy had to be replaced by all manner of injections like iodine, vitamins, calcium, heart-and-liver extract, and hormones."

DRUG DEPENDENCE

The doctors were not the only ones to start asking questions. In June 1943, Foreign Minister Joachim von Ribbentrop cross-examined Morell personally about his treatment of the Führer. Was it a good idea for Hitler to be given so many injections, Ribbentrop wanted to know? Was he getting anything other than glucose (Morell injected this regularly to provide the Führer with extra calories)? Was Morell giving him anything else? All Ribbentrop could get out of Morell by way of a reply was the laconic sentence: "I give him what he needs."

Many of the drugs Morell employed — most were the product of his own Hamma factory — were harmless.

Above: Just before his death, Hitler sacked Morell. He suspected the doctor of trying to poison him.

Opposite: Hitler as he would have wished to be remembered — a poster produced for the 1939 Party Day.

Some, like Ultraseptyl, which he liberally dispensed to treat colds, coughs, and catarrh, were not. In particular, the Hamma-produced Vitamultin-CA, with which, from late 1941 onward, Morell injected Hitler nearly every morning before he had even got out of bed, was suspect. It was Morell's practice to add a dose of Strophantin, a digitalis preparation, to the same syringe.

Was anything else added?

Certainly, the injections produced remarkable results. Heinz Linge, Hitler's valet, personally testified to its dramatic effects. Hitler, he said, immediately became "fresh" — alert, active and ready for the day — even while the needle was still in his arm and before the injection had been completed. Other members of the Führer's

headquarters staff concurred, especially when, as the news from the battlefronts worsened, Morell stepped up the number of injections. Walter Hewell, a Foreign Ministry official, recalled how Hitler became cheerful, talkative, and tended to stay awake long into the night. Traudl Junge, one of Hitler's secretaries, said that, after an injection, he became extremely alert and garrulous. Even outsiders noticed the difference.

It is more than probable that Morell was injecting Hitler with some type of stimulant. The likelihood is that it was Pervitin, the trade name for methamphetamine, the German form of amphetamine. Methamphetamine was also present in the Vitamultin-F pills Hitler took to combat tiredness — a major problem for one whose sleeping habits were erratic to say the least. It seems Vitamultin-F was a one-off, prepared personally by Dr. Kurt Mulli, Hamma's chief chemist, in his own home laboratory solely for the Führer's use.

Hitler took up to 10 Vitamultin-F pills daily. According to Linge, they enabled him "to work long after his secretaries became too fatigued to work." In addition to vitamins and methamphetamine, the pills contained caffeine, another stimulant that significantly increased the methamphetamine's effects.

HEART DISEASE AND PARKINSONIANISM

Constant dosing with methamphetamine — although, at times, Morell tried to wean Hitler off the drug — probably contributed to the Führer's developing heart disease. Morell took his first electrocardiogram of Hitler's heart in August 1941; according to Dr. Karl Weber, a well-known cardiologist Morell consulted, the tracing showed clear evidence of incipient coronary sclerosis. Subsequent cardiograms showed the condition slowly worsening.

Morell, however, did not reveal Weber's diagnosis to Hitler until December 1942, at the time of the siege of Stalingrad. Then he told the Führer that he was the victim of progressive heart disease, adding that, as the blood vessels of the coronary artery narrowed, he might suffer attacks of angina pectoris as well. It was confirmation of a gradual, but constant physical decline that was to continue until Hitler's suicide at the end of the war.

There were other new symptoms as well. Early in 1943, Morell noticed that Hitler had developed a slight tremor in his left arm and saw that he was perceptibly dragging his left leg. He had dealt with the Führer's previous illnesses — notably dysentery and jaundice — effectively, but these symptoms were new to him. He initially thought they were hysterical in origin, but, to be on the safe side, he stepped up his intravenous glucose and iodine injections, combing them with intramuscular injections of a male sex hormone called Testoviron. Exactly what he thought this would accomplish is unclear, but it had little or no effect.

Paradoxically, the tremors stopped after Hitler was caught in the July 1944 bomb blast. However, they returned and grew steadily worse. Professor Maximilian de Crinis, a leading neurologist, put them down to Parkinson's disease, although he never personally examined the Führer. Morell disagreed. Nevertheless, starting on April 16, 1945, he began injecting Hitler with Homburg 680, a well-known belladonna-type drug specific for the condition. It was the last addition to the exhaustive catalog

of drugs he had prescribed for the Führer. On April 21, Hitler turned on him and sacked him. Morell fled beleaguered Berlin for the comparative safety of Munich.

The tremors probably indicated that Hitler was suffering from Parkinsonian syndrome, rather than the disease itself. He may also have suffered a minor stroke. Whatever their cause, Hitler was a physical wreck. Traudl Junge described him as being "hardly able to walk" and "needing help to sit down or stand upright." Heinrich Hoffman concurred. His old friend, he said, was "mentally stunted to the point of derangement and physically exhausted beyond redemption." He was, Hoffman concluded, "but a shivering shadow of his former self." On April 30, the Führer took the only course of action left open to him. He committed suicide.

The Race for the A Bomb

Despite the commanding lead the Germans had established in nuclear physics before World War II, their efforts to build an atomic bomb failed. Was this because of Hitler's rabid anti-Semitism, which meant that their best nuclear physicists, who were Jewish, fled abroad? Was it due to basic flaws in their research? Or was it because their foremost scientists did not want to build a bomb for Hitler at all and sabotaged the process?

Left: *King Haakon VII of Norway congratulates the men who took part in Operation Gunnerside, destroying all the heavy water the Norsk Hydro plant had produced for the Germans.*

Opposite: *German nuclear physicist Carl-Friedrich von Weizsacker claimed he had never wanted to build an A bomb for the Nazis.*

The story began in October 1938, when Otto Hahn and Fritz Strassman, two leading German scientists working at the Kaiser Wilhelm Institute in Berlin, discovered that when they bombarded uranium with neutrons they could split the uranium atoms' nuclei into two. Lise Meitner, a brilliant Jewish physicist whom Hahn had helped to flee to safety in Sweden, and Otto Robert Frisch, her young nephew, used the Berlin results to work out the basic mathematics of nuclear fission — the term coined by Frisch to describe what happened as energy and neutrons were released. The following March, French physicist Frederick Joliot, the son-in-law of Marie Curie, the discoverer of radium, took the next step forward, when he demonstrated that the liberation of extra neutrons during the fission process was the result of a chain reaction. A whole new science had been born.

It was obvious to many physicists around the world that, at least in theory, it was now possible to create a self-perpetuating chain reaction, which would be triggered by the neutrons from one split atom bombarding the atoms surrounding it, splitting them in their turn. If controllable, such a chain reaction could be employed for constructive peaceful purposes. If, on the other hand, it was uncontrolled, the result would be an explosion of incalculable power. The great fear was that the German physicists would use this newfound knowledge to build a Nazi nuclear bomb.

THE ALLIED PHYSICISTS

It was in Britain, though, that the possibility of creating an atomic bomb was first debated. Rudolf Peirls, a young physicist who, like many of his Jewish contemporaries, had fled Germany to escape Nazi persecution, was one of the key figures in the process.

Peirls was the first physicist to address in practical terms the question of how much uranium would be needed in order to make an atomic bomb work. His initial conclusion was that the amount would be so massive that it could not possibly be carried by any airplane of the day. Soon, however, he changed his mind. In early 1940, he and his friend Otto Frisch began to try to calculate the proportion of U235 — the uranium isotope 235 — to uranium that would be needed to produce the explosive force required in an atomic bomb. As the two men worked on the problem, Peirls realized that his previous assumption had been incorrect. It now seemed as if the critical mass necessary to sustain a chain reaction might well weigh less than a pound.

Through an intermediary, Peirls and his associates communicated their findings to Sir Henry Tizard, the inventor of radar and one of the government's most respected scientific advisers. His backing led to the setting up of a scientific committee to investigate the feasibility of producing an atomic bomb. The conclusion, which the committee reached in December 1940, was short and stark. An atomic bomb, it opined was "not just feasible; it was inevitable." The committee's recommendation was that Britain should launch a full-scale effort to make such a bomb.

Progress was being made on the other side of the Atlantic as well. Long before the U.S. entered the war, physicists there

Above: *Walter Gerlach was another German physicist deeply involved in nuclear research.*

were determined to alert the U.S. government to the risk of the Nazis becoming the first to build an atomic bomb. Many of these physicists — notably Leo Szilard, Enrico Fermi, and Edward Teller — were themselves political refugees. Eventually, through Albert Einstein, they managed to alert President Roosevelt to their fears. The President grasped the significance of what he was being told immediately. "Alex," he said to Dr. Alexander Sachs, who had been tasked with getting Einstein's fateful letter to the White House, "what you're after is to see that the Nazis don't blow us up."

What quickly became clear to the Americans and the British was

that, in nuclear physics, there were no shortcuts to success. Creating an atomic bomb inevitably was going to be incredibly costly. Nearly bankrupted by the cost of the war, Britain made a deal with the U.S. to hand over its latest technology — including the results of its nuclear research — as a quid pro quo for the arms, foodstuffs, and other supplies the Americans were providing under the terms of lend-lease. Most of the scientists who had been involved in the project also moved across the Atlantic, where the U.S. program to develop an atomic bomb — code named the Manhattan Project — was getting underway with Robert Oppenheimer, Professor of Physics at Berkeley, California, as its scientific director.

NUCLEAR NAZIS

Almost up to the moment of the German capitulation, Oppenheimer and his fellow physicists lived in fear that the Nazis might pull the cat out of the bag and be the first to produce an atomic bomb. They had a healthy respect for German nuclear physics and its prewar achievements. They also knew what an effort it had been — at least initially — to persuade the

Right: *Werner Heisenberg, deviser of the theory of quantum mechanics, headed the German nuclear effort.*

Below: *Lieutenant-General Leslie R. Groves, a brilliant organizer, was put in charge of the Manhattan Project in September 1942.*

a nuclear reactor — these chain reactions would generate energy. If uncontrolled, the result would be a "nuclear explosive" many times more powerful than any conventional one.

Whereas only natural uranium was suitable for use in a "uranium machine," Heisenberg concluded that U235 could be employed as an explosive. In summer 1940, Carl Friedrich von Weizsacker, one of his colleagues, took the speculation further. If, he said, a "uranium machine" could be made to sustain a chain reaction, some of the more common isotope U238 in the uranium fueling it would be transmuted into what he called "Element 94" — in other words, plutonium. This, von Weizsacker postulated, would be far easier to obtain than U235 and would be just as powerful an explosive.

Heisenberg himself summed up what von Weizsacker was hoping to accomplish. In a lecture he gave to high-ranking Nazi bigwigs in early 1942, he said: "As soon as such a machine is in operation, the question of the production of a new explosive takes a new turn, according to an idea of von Weizsacker. The transformation of uranium in the machine produces, in fact, a new substance, which is most probably,

Western democracies to act to get the nuclear program up and running. Things must have been so much easier for their German counterparts, they reckoned. In a dictatorship like Hitler's, what the Führer decreed automatically became law.

The physicists were worrying unduly. They were convinced that the Nazi economy was geared up for total war, whereas the opposite, in fact, was the case. Hitler and his fellow Nazis had little time for strategic thinking and long-term planning. Their diplomatic, military, and economic efforts revolved around the notion of waging short, sharp wars. Thus, potentially war-winning weapons that would take time to develop

were mostly put on the back burner or simply ignored.

With this kind of attitude it was hardly surprising that the Nazi nuclear effort was slow to get off the ground. What was christened the "uranium project" started shortly after the outbreak of war in 1939, when an army research team, headed by physicist Kurt Diebner, began investigating possible military applications of nuclear fission. By the end of the year, Werner Heisenberg, the leading German physicist of the day, had calculated that, in theory, fission chain reactions were achievable. If slowed down and controlled in a so-called "uranium machine" — what otherwise would be termed just like U235, an explosive of the same unimaginable effect. This substance can be obtained much more easily from uranium than U235 because it may be separated chemically from the uranium."

The German physicists were already aware that they could create significant amounts of U235 only by isotope separation. First they tried a chemical process known as thermal diffusion and then, when this proved a failure, turned to building massive centrifuges to literally spin the various uranium isotopes apart. Plutonium looked like an easier bet, but, of course, it required a nuclear reactor capable of achieving a self-sustaining chain reaction to make it. The Germans never accomplished this; the reactor they started to build toward the end of the war never went critical.

Left: *The Norsk Hydro plant was the Germans' sole source of the heavy water they needed as a moderator for their atomic pile. They mistakenly believed graphite would not work.*

Below: *Members of the Allied Alsos team, tasked after the war with ferreting out Nazi Germany's closely guarded nuclear secrets.*

THE NAZIS MISCALCULATE

Two crucial miscalculations contributed to the delay. To produce a controlled reaction, a "uranium machine" needs what is technically termed a moderator — a substance that slows down the fast neutrons liberated by the chain reaction. The Americans chose graphite, which was relatively easy to obtain. In Germany, however, because the industrial granite he used in his experiments was not pure enough, Professor Walther Rothe mistakenly convinced his colleagues that what is technically termed heavy water would have to be used instead.

The only plant producing heavy water in any quantity was located in Norway. After the Nazi occupation of the country in 1940, production was ordered to be stepped up, although it still fell short of what was needed to satisfy German demands. Then, in 1942 and 1943, British commandos, aided by the Norwegian Resistance, tried to sabotage the plant. The second attempt was successful.

The Germans decided to abandon production in Norway and move all the existing stocks of heavy water to Germany. The ferry carrying the stocks across Lake

Left: *Examining the German nuclear pile after the war. It never went critical.*

Below: *Samples of the deuterium oxide, or heavy water, produced by the Norsk Hydro plant.*

Tinnsjo was sabotaged and sank in deep water. The Nazi nuclear program never recovered from the loss. The other miscalculation was made by Heisenberg himself. He grossly overestimated the amount of fissile material that would be needed to make an atomic bomb.

What is also clear from the historical record is that, unlike the Manhattan Project, there was no single driving force behind

the Nazi nuclear effort. Certainly, Heisenberg's role was ambivalent to say the least. When it came to organizing the attempt to develop an atomic bomb, he seems to have left the competing research teams to squabble among themselves. For whatever reason, too, when Heisenberg met with Albert Speer, Hitler's armaments minister, in June 1942, he downplayed what his colleagues had accomplished and was pessimistic about

Above: *The RAF and USAAF tried to bomb the Norsk Hydro plant unsuccessfully several times. The failure forced the Allies to resort to sabotage.*

whether or not a bomb could be produced at all.

When Speer enquired what financial support would be needed in order to speed the program up — the armaments minister had it in mind to give Heisenberg several hundred million marks immediately — all Heisenberg asked for was a million or so marks to fund further research. Speer immediately concluded that there was no possibility of producing a German atomic bomb in the foreseeable future. He poured the money he had been thinking of allocating to the nuclear program into rocket research instead.

After the war, Heisenberg recalled how he and his colleagues "felt already in the beginning that, if it were possible at all to actually make explosives, it would take such a long time and require such an enormous effort that there was a very good chance that the war would be over before that could be accomplished ... we thought that the probability that this would lead to atomic bombs during the war was nearly zero." Rudolf Meutzel, the head of German weapons research, not only concurred with Heisenberg, but went further. In July 1943, he reported to Goering. "Though the work will not lead in a short time toward the practical use of engines (nuclear reactors) or explosives, it gives on the other hand certainty that in this field the enemy cannot have any surprises in store for us."

WHY THE GERMANS FAILED

Such over-confidence, as much as anything else, was one of the major reasons for the German failure. If they, the best nuclear physicists in the world, could not produce an atomic bomb, then no one else could possibly achieve the breakthrough. Their self-confidence was demonstrated by the reactions of 10 of their number — Heisenberg and Otto Hahn among them — to the news that the Americans had dropped the first atomic bomb on Hiroshima. At the time, they were interned at Farm Hall, a house near Cambridge, following their capture at the end of the war. The house was bugged so that their captors could listen in on their conversations.

Shortly before dinner on August 6, 1945, Otto Hahn was the first of the Germans to be told that an atomic bomb had been dropped successfully on Hiroshima. He promptly broke the news to his fellow internees. The Farm Hall transcripts clearly demonstrate how stunned the German physicists were by the news. They simply could not believe that the Americans had succeeded where they had failed. Heisenberg's immediate reaction was to dismiss the news as nothing more than a gigantic bluff.

After dinner, the Germans crowded around a radio to listen to a full report of the bombing for themselves. They spent the next two days trying to establish

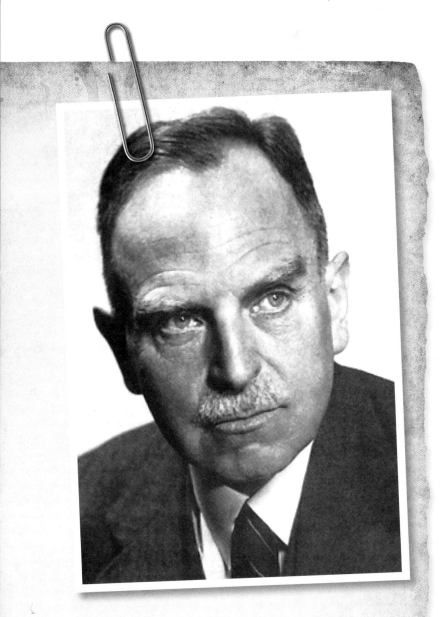

Above: *When Norwegian saboteurs sank this ferry in February 1944, the loss of the heavy water it carried finally put an end to Germany's nuclear research program.*

Opposite: *Otto Hahn was one of the first to recognize that a uranium atom would split when bombarded by neutrons.*

how the Allies had succeeded in building the atomic bomb and the reasons why they had failed to do so. It was apparent from their conversations that they still did not understand the complex workings of the bomb completely — or, indeed, those of a nuclear reactor — but gradually they began to piece the picture together.

Otto Hahn, who himself was relieved that the Nazis had not succeeded in building a bomb and had had nothing to do with the nuclear research program, taunted his fellow-scientists with their failure. "If the Americans have a uranium bomb," he said, "then you are all second-rate." Horst Korsching commented that the news showed "at any rate that the Americans are capable of real cooperation on a tremendous scale," adding that this "would have been impossible in Germany." Von Weizsacker admitted that "even if we had got everything we wanted, it is by no means certain whether we would have got as far as the Americans and English have now." Heisenberg said that he "was absolutely convinced by the possibility of our making a 'uranium engine,' but I never thought we would make a bomb." For his part, he continued, "at the bottom of my heart, I was really glad that it was to be an engine and not a bomb. I must admit that."

THE BOMB THAT WASN'T

Up until 2005, the accepted consensus was that the Nazi attempt to build nuclear weapons had been a total failure. Then, in 2005, German historian Rainer Karlsch came forward with a highly controversial claim. He said he had hard evidence that a second German nuclear research team, led by Kurt Diebner, had managed to develop a primitive fission-fusion bomb. This was tested, Karlsch alleged, three times — first on the Baltic island of Ruegen in fall 1944 and then in Thuringia in March 1945.

Karlsch's assertions, though, have been dismissed by practically every other serious historian. Germany, they say, never possessed the U235 and plutonium necessary to build any sort of true nuclear device. The most the Germans could possibly have achieved was the construction of a so-called "dirty bomb" — a conventional weapon laced with enough radioactive material to pollute everything in the area surrounding the explosion — but this, too, is considered highly unlikely.

Above: *The Allies won the race when they dropped two atomic bombs on Hiroshima and Nagasaki in August 1945. Had the German nuclear effort succeeded, mushroom clouds could well have shrouded New York and London.*

Index

Picture Credits

Bundesarchiv, pp.54, 59b, 60, 68, 69, 115, 211, 233, 232, 236, 238

Getty Images, pp.65, 148

Catwalker, Shutterstock.com, p.221

Golovniov, Igor, Shutterstock, p.136

Johnbraid, Shutterstock.com, p.22

Kingsley, Gregory J, p.25

Klebsattel, Rolf, Shutterstock.com, p.224

MrHanson, Shutterstock.com, p.239b

Neftali, Shutterstock.com, p.235

Penfield, Daniel, p.131

Robert Jackson Collection, pp.12, 13, 14, 15, 17, 18, 19, 21, 22, 24, 29, 30, 32, 33, 36, 38, 39, 40, 41, 42, 43, 44t/b, 45, 46, 47, 49, 50, 52, 53, 55, 57t/b, 58, 59t, 62, 66, 67, 72, 73, 74, 75, 77, 80, 82, 83, 84, 85t/b, 88, 89, 90, 92, 96, 98, 99, 100, 101, 102, 104, 105, 106, 107, 108, 109, 110, 111, 118b, 120b, 122, 124, 125, 126, 127, 129, 130, 132, 134, 135, 137, 138, 139, 141, 142, 143, 144t/b, 145, 146, 147, 149, 150t/b, 152, 153, 155, 156, 157, 158, 161t, 162, 164, 165t/b, 169, 170t/b, 171, 172, 173, 174, 175, 176, 177, 179, 180, 181, 182, 183, 184, 185, 186, 187t/b, 188, 189, 190, 191, 192, 193, 194, 195t/b, 196, 197, 198t/b, 199, 202, 203, 204, 208, 212, 213, 214, 219, 220, 222, 223, 225t/c/b, 226tl/tr, 227, 228, 229, 231, 234, 237, 240, 242, 243t/b, 244, 245, 246t/b, 247, 248, 249, 250, 251

Wikipedia, pp.27, 28, 35, 64, 71t/c, 78, 79, 81, 86, 95, 97, 112, 114, 117, 118t, 120t, 133, 161b, 205t/c/b, 206, 207, 209, 210, 215, 216, 218